Practical
Opening
Tips

CADOGAN CHESS SERIES

Chief Advisor: Garry Kasparov
Editor: Murray Chandler
Russian Series Editor: Ken Neat

Other titles for the improving player include:

For a complete catalogue of EVERYMAN CHESS and CADOGAN CHESS books please write to:
Everyman Publishers plc, Gloucester Mansions, 140 Shaftesbury Avenue, London, WC2H 8HD
Tel: (0171) 539 7600 Fax: (0171) 379 4060

Practical
Opening
Tips

Everyman Chess, formerly Cadogan Chess, is published by Everyman Publishers, London

First published 1997 by Cadogan Books plc, now Everyman Publishers plc, Gloucester Mansions, 140 Shaftesbury Avenue, London, WC2H 8HD

Reprinted 1999

British Library Cataloguing in Publication Data
A CIP catalogue record for this book is available from the British Library

ISBN 1 85744 186 9

Distributed in North America by The Globe Pequot Press, PO Box 833, Old Saybrook, Connecticut 06475 Tel: 800-2430495 Fax 800-820-2329

All other sales enquiries should be directed to Everyman Publishers plc, Gloucester Mansions, 140 Shaftesbury Avenue, London, WC2H 8HD

Typeset by ChessSetter

Proofreading: Tim Wall and Alexander Meynell

Printed and bound in Great Britain by The Cromwell Press Ltd

Contents

Preface

We are living in the technology era. What technology can do well is readily available to us. Among the most obvious successes of technology is the whole field of data storage, processing and distribution. Of direct applicability to the chess player is the processing and availability of information about openings. This has spawned a never-ending industry of data compilation and publication on opening theory. There is so much information and it is so easy for the computer to process it into a reasonable form that a book titled *The Complete Sicilian Defence* would run to well over two thousand pages. Such a book will not be published because it would cost too much and would therefore lack buyers. But various monographs on the Sicilian are coming out. For example, there is a well-regarded book on the Soltis variation within the Yugoslav Attack against the Dragon Variation. The book has 333 pages! Yet the question remains unasked: how many players in the world can absorb the information available in such books? After all, any reasonable opening repertoire will need to have knowledge of at least some twenty variations. Multiplying 333 pages by twenty gives 6660 pages to understand and remember!

Quite obviously such an approach is beyond the practical ability of more than 99% of all players. *What players do need is to learn what strategies the GMs use in making their decisions regarding opening play.* The purpose of this book is to provide this information in a readily accessible form to the person who is not a GM but is keenly interested in improving his opening play. In the first part, I present how the GM looks at the aims of opening play, followed by a discussion of "how to master a new opening".

In the second part the most important themes are considered. The importance of capturing towards the centre and how to tell when the position is "equal" are two of the subjects covered. In Part Three, "The Modern Thinking" and Part Four, "The Modern Approach in the Selection of Your Opening Repertoire", much specific information is presented within the important broad strategies.

The book is largely based on my extremely well received "Opening Forum" series as published in *Chess Life* magazine. To make the book as useful as the title implies, additional subject matter has been included. Of course, all material has been checked, updated and enhanced to reflect the current status of opening theory.

In general the following standard sources have been utilised in the preparation of this book: personal knowledge, personal contacts, leading chess periodicals and chess books. When appropriate, direct credit is given in the text.

To ensure that the reader and the author are on the same wavelength regarding the meaning of the question and exclamation marks as they are used in the characterisation of moves, these are the presently accepted meanings:

!   = a strong move
!! = a very strong move; a fantastic move
?   = a bad move; a weak move
?? = a horrible move; a blunder
!? = an enterprising move; a move worthy of consideration
?! = a dubious move, for theoretical or practical reasons

In an undertaking of such scope, some errors are almost inevitable. The author accepts responsibility for all of these. Your assistance in bringing them to my attention will be appreciated.

As always, my deepest gratitude goes to my wonderful blonde wife, Baiba, not only for typing the entire manuscript bur also for never-ending physical and moral support.

Edmar Mednis
New York, 1997

Part One: Basics

1 Opening aims: the modern view

The game of chess starts with the opening. This phase is considered to last 10-15 moves until the middlegame is reached. The general goal of the opening phase is to get ready for middlegame action. Therefore what is important in the middlegame – king safety, the centre, purposeful piece deployment – is what good opening play should try to achieve. The three specific principles of correct opening play are:

(1) Bring your king into safety by castling.

(2) Develop your pieces towards the centre so that they are ready for later middlegame action.

(3) Control the centre, either by actual possession, or by short-range or long-range action of pieces or pawns.

Of course, you want to achieve the above in the most efficient way possible. Try to choose your moves in accordance with the following guidelines:
- Use each move to develop a new piece.
- Develop knights before bishops; develop your minor pieces before your rooks or queen.
- Make sure your centre is in good order before looking at other parts of the board.

Rather than a philosophical exercise, a game is a fight between two sides. Each side wants to achieve its aim while hindering the opponent from realising his objectives. An important aim of early opening play is to ensure that you reach the particular variation or sub-variation that you are interested in playing. Conversely, if possible, you want to prevent the opponent from playing the variation that he favours and will aim for. The science of move-orders is used for this purpose. For instance, assume that you are facing a 1 d4 player but dislike playing against the main lines of the Slav Defence, something your opponent loves to do and is good at. After 1 d4 d5 2 c4 c6, a good practical approach is, instead of the more common 3 ♘f3, to play 3 ♘c3 ♘f6 4 e3. Now 4...♗f5?! allows White a strong initiative after 5 cxd5 cxd5 6 ♕b3. Thus Black's correct responses are 4...e6 or 4...g6 – perfectly reasonable variations, but Black has been prevented from using his beloved Slav.

It has long been recognised in grandmaster play that White starts off with a small, yet clear, advantage. This is because he can impose his will on the opponent. If your opponent plays the Sicilian Defence, already on the second move you can choose the approach that suits you best. You may prefer the centre-building 2 c3, go for a more closed variation with 2 ♘c3, or keep your options open with 2 ♘f3, only deciding on the next move whether to open the position with 3 d4. *Black's* options regarding high-quality choices are always more limited than White's.

What the above means is that White generally should select those openings where, according to current knowledge, he can reach the early middlegame with at least a slight advantage. Whatever White chooses, it is foolhardy to select a variation where he knows that if Black plays correctly, *Black* winds up with the advantage. On the other hand, Black must recognise that if White chooses a high quality opening, the best that Black can expect even after correct play is a slight inferiority in the early middlegame. Therefore, Black should not expect miracles in early play. The important decision for Black is whether to select a defence which aims for dynamic equality or safe equality. Robert J. Fischer's selections were always of the dynamic kind, as are Garry Kasparov's. Conversely, Tigran Petrosian and Anatoly Karpov have preferred going first for solid equality.

2 Mastering a new opening

Suppose that your defence to 1 d4 has always been the Orthodox Defence of the Queen's Gambit Declined (1 d4 d5 2 c4 e6 3 ♘c3 ♘f6 4 ♘f3 ♗e7). Overall it has been a satisfactory opening, but you have had difficulties in beating "weaker" opponents. Therefore, you would like to add something "sharper" to your opening repertoire. You have decided that, based on your chess interests, playing style and work habits, the "Nimzo-Indian/Queen's Indian complex" is for you. Diagram 1 shows the basic position of the Nimzo-Indian Defence (after 1 d4 ♘f6 2 c4 e6 3 ♘c3 ♗b4); Diagram 2 shows the basic position of the Queen's Indian Defence (after 1 d4 ♘f6 2 c4 e6 3 ♘f3 b6). In the discussions to follow, I shall use examples from these two openings.

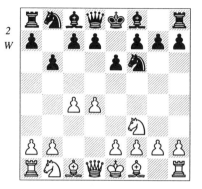

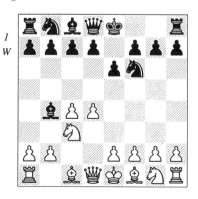

I have already noted in the previous chapter the importance of move-orders in early opening play. A number of additional move-orders are often employed to reach a particular "normal" position. For instance, the Nimzo-Indian is also frequently reached via 1 c4 ♘f6 2 ♘c3 e6 3 d4 ♗b4; the Queen's Indian can arise after 1 d4 ♘f6 2 ♘f3 e6 3 c4 b6 and 1 ♘f3 ♘f6 2 c4 e6 3 d4 b6.

In this chapter I will describe what the key steps are in mastering an opening and remaining a "master" of it. It is an eight-step operation:

(1) Obtain a clear and complete *verbal description of the main characteristics of the opening.*

Absolutely the worst way to start learning an opening is to immediately begin memorising "important" variations. Such a rote method never works, because as soon as the memorised line ends the player is at a loss regarding what to do next. It is imperative to first obtain a full *understanding* of what an opening is about. An excellent discussion of this for the Nimzo-Indian appears in *How To Play The Nimzo-Indian Defence* by Raymond Keene and Shaun Taulbut; for the Queen's Indian, *The Complete Queen's Indian* by Efim Geller may be highly recommended.

(2) *As far as possible, obtain a clear verbal description of the main characteristics of each of the variations that you are considering selecting.*

Of course, if you have no idea what you want to play against a particular White variation, e.g. Rubinstein's 4 e3 against the Nimzo-Indian, then learn about all highly-rated Black options. In the 4 e3 Nimzo-Indian, consider 4...b6, 4...c5 and 4...0-0; these may lead to systems involving only ...c5, only ...d5 or both ...c5 and ...d5. If you already "know" that you want to play Nimzowitsch's 4...b6, then it is enough to just obtain a clear verbal description of that. The following sources are suggested for obtaining a high-quality verbal description:

(a) High-quality books by experts in that field. (The two books mentioned earlier fit the bill.)

(b) Articles on the variations by GMs or strong IMs in chess magazines.

(c) Your personal trainer if he or she is an expert in the specific variation.

It is just so important to grasp as deeply and in as sophisticated a way as possible the true essence of a variation. Wherever possible, go to the "source". If that is not possible, only trust true experts of that variation. For instance, I do not consider myself qualified to instruct anyone in the fine points of the Benko gambit. I don't play it for Black; I don't allow it as White – and it is a fantastically sophisticated opening.

Lev Polugayevsky has a wonderful section on *his* variation in the Najdorf Sicilian (1 e4 c5 2 ♘f3 d6 3 d4 cxd4 4 ♘xd4 ♘f6 5 ♘c3 a6 6 ♗g5 e6 7 f4 b5) in his excellent book *Grandmaster Achievement*. He emphasises the importance of "understanding" his variation in the following way (p.49): "First and foremost it is essential to understand the essence, the overall idea of any fashionable variation and only then include it in one's opening repertoire. Otherwise the tactical trees will conceal from the player the strategic picture of the woods, in which his orientation will most likely be lost." Eloquently said – and equally true for all variations.

(3) *Select the opening variation you will play.*

After you have become familiar with the essence of the potential variations, select that one which best agrees with your chess interests, playing style and work habits. When learning a new opening only learn one variation to counter each of your opponent's lines. *Learn one but learn it well*. It is much better to learn one variation well than two variations not so well. Once you have mastered one variation and still have additional time "free", only then consider learning a second one.

Current opening theory in both the Nimzo-Indian and Queen's Indian defences is broad and well-developed. This means that reliable information is available to enable you to make your specific selections with a high degree of confidence. Indeed, you *must* make selections. Unless you are able to narrow the amount of theory that must be mastered, you will not have the time to do so. For instance, in the Queen's Indian a very important variation for White is the kingside fianchetto with 4 g3. According to current theory, Black has two high level responses: 4...♗a6 and 4...♗b7. Which one should you choose? The specific variations after each are quite different. The choice is strictly up to you. What I can add, however, is that at the moment the theory of 4...♗a6 is developing considerably faster than that of 4...♗b7 and therefore there is much more to keep up with.

A much more difficult question is what should Black choose in

the Nimzo-Indian if White plays (from Diagram 1) 4 ♕c2. The current problem is that after the previously "time-tested" 4...c5 5 dxc5 0-0, which had been considered to be an equalising line for well over 30 years, White is achieving a clear and pleasant advantage with 6 a3 ♗xc5 7 ♘f3.

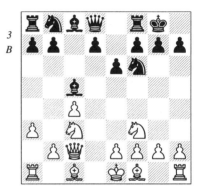

3 B

Therefore Black players have been exploring the newer 4...0-0 or returning to the old 4...d5, where many interesting improvements for Black are being discovered.

(4) *Learn the key lines thoroughly.*

The preparations have been completed and now it is time for the actual work of learning the key lines. Your basic text should be a recent opening monograph by expert(s) on that opening or one of the revised editions of the *Encyclopedia of Chess Openings*. Encyclopedias "B", "C", "D" and "E" have been revised and are excellent. However, in order to reach a universal audience, the "Encyclopedias" avoid words and use only symbols. Therefore, you must obtain the preliminary "understanding" knowledge from other sources.

When I speak of "learning key lines", I do not mean just blind memorising. In particular, when the openings are inherently strategic, such as the Nimzo-Indian and the Queen's Indian, the approach should be to learn the first 10-16 moves of key lines sufficiently well so that you can recall them as needed during tournament games. I would not worry if you cannot recall everything during a 5-minute blitz game.

As basic texts, I recommend, in addition to the two books mentioned in section (1), *Winning with the Queen's Indian* by Zoltan Ribli. The revised edition of *Encyclopedia E* (covering among other openings the Nimzo-Indian and Queen's Indian) was published in 1991. It is chockfull of reliable information and excellent value for the money spent.

It must be stressed that it is not enough to just learn the key variations. You must also become knowledgeable regarding the thematic developments in the middlegame and, if applicable, the endgame.

Therefore study complete games – at least as far as their course is "thematic" from the opening variation.

(5) *Check your lines against their current theoretical status.*

Because the science of opening theory is advancing so rapidly, books on openings can be considered to be "obsolete" the instant they are published. As much as a year can pass from the moment a manuscript is completed to the date the book reaches the store. Much can happen in a fashionable variation during this period. Don't panic – just check the reference-type literature that has come out since the book's publication. Currently the two most useful references are *Chess Informant* which comes out every four months and the quarterly *New in Chess Yearbook*. Since you will be using these sources as your ultimate "arbiter", always check them for the following three possible problems:

(a) *Typographical errors* – most typos are inconsequential or sufficiently grotesque as to be immediately noticeable. Others are more dangerous. A particular problem is the use in notation of "c" in place of "e" or vice versa. A typical example is from a 1976 issue of *The Chess Player* (an excellent publication of the 1970s). In annotating the game J.Timman-S.Garcia, Orense 1976, after 1 d4 ♘f6 2 c4 e6 3 ♘c3 ♗b4 4 ♗g5 h6 5 ♗h4 c5 6 d5 d6 7 e3 g5 8 ♗g3 ♘e4 9 ♕c2 ♕f6, Timman gives the following variation: 10 ♕xe4 ♗xc3+ 11 ♔d1 ♗xb2 12 ♖b1 ♗d7! 13

♗d3 ♘a6 with a slight edge for Black.

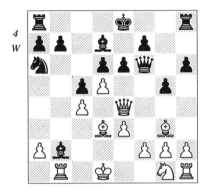

He then continues with 14 dxe6? ♗xe6. You should be curious enough to ask yourself the following question: what does Black do after 15 ♕xb7 when three of his pieces are *en prise*? The answer is that Timman *never suggested* *14...♗xe6?*. That is simply a typo in place of the correct and winning 14...♗c6.

(b) *Tactical errors in analysis* – The chances are excellent that an obvious tactical shot in the game itself has not been overlooked by the analyst. However, the odds are much higher that variations in the analysis contain tactical errors. In complicated lines use "natural vigilance" as you check over the tactics.

(c) *Strategic misjudgements* – You should make sure that evaluations and suggestions make sense based on your understanding of the strategic essence of the variation. Consider the following

situation. As Black in the Queen's Indian, you have selected 4...♗a6 as your variation against 4 g3. It is the autumn of 1980 and the latest (No 29) *Chess Informant* has come out. You look up "your variation" and notice the game S.Tatai-Y.Seirawan, Torremolinos 1980, annotated by Tatai as follows: 1 d4 ♘f6 2 c4 e6 3 ♘f3 b6 4 g3 ♗a6 5 b3 ♗b4+ 6 ♗d2 ♗e7 7 ♗g2 c6 8 0-0 d5 9 ♕c2 ♘bd7 (9...♘e4!?) 10 ♖c1!N 0-0 11 a4

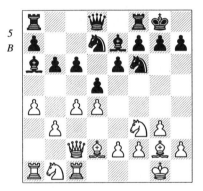

11...♖c8 12 ♘a3 ♘e4 13 ♗e1 f5 14 b4 ♗b7 15 ♕b2 a6 16 c5 b5 17 ♘e5 ♗f6 18 f3 ♘g5 19 ♗d2 ♘f7 20 ♗f4 ♘fxe5 and now if White had played 21 ♗xe5! he would retain a clear advantage. You should be making the following observations:

• Black was handling the position more like a Dutch Defence, rather than a "closed Catalan" which is the characteristic set-up for the variations after 5 b3 ♗b4+ 6 ♗d2 ♗e7.

• Tatai's plan seemed to "refute" the above variation. But why should moves such as 10 ♖c1, 11 a4 and 12 ♘a3 be so strong?

I asked myself the above questions when preparing for my game against FM Gonzales-Mesters of Spain at Barcelona 1980. My conclusion was that all that Black needs to do is to play "thematically" from Diagram 5. This position arose in my game and I played, consistent with the Catalan Opening, 11...c5! 12 ♘a3 ♗b7! 13 ♕b2 ♘e4. Black already has full equality and White's queen now looks rather stupid on b2, with ...♗f6 coming up.

(6) *Test your new opening before playing it in tournaments.*

Book knowledge is all very well, of course, but the practical player wants this knowledge to help him score points in tournaments. Therefore, you should get in some practice with your new opening. Skittles games probably will not be very effective, because you will not be concentrating sufficiently to get the most out of your knowledge. Blitz games are just too fast to "learn openings" except perhaps for those with exceptional discipline and work habits. A practice clock game with a tournament-type time limit is nice if you have a friend of approximately equal strength who is unselfish enough to act as your "trainer" over a number of games.

I believe that on the current chess scene the best approach is to try out your new opening in 30 minute games. If you don't want to risk your rating while "practising", try to find an unrated tournament or one with a "quarter K" condition (K is the factor used to determine the degree of a rating change). Thirty minutes does allow time for thinking. And be sure to carefully go over the game after it is finished, or at least the opening phase of it.

(7) *Play your new opening with confidence in tournaments; analyse the games carefully at home.*

Since you are now well-prepared for playing your new opening , start playing it. There is no reason why you should not be confident about your chances for success. Nothing is gained by delaying the acid test until you are "better prepared". Playing in tournaments is the single best way of enhancing your mastery of an opening. Because your mind is in full gear, the likelihood is excellent that you will start grasping possibilities and concepts that would have remained unknown to you in the relaxed comfort of your home.

However, playing without a critical review of the game is insufficient. The major problem is that there is a tendency to be overly influenced by the result of the game. For instance, if you do not like your position after the opening and go on to lose the game, you conclusion can become: "The Nimzo-Indian Defence is no good; let me learn the King's Indian". What you need to do is to review the game carefully within a week or so to find out where the actual problem arose so that you can work to fix it before the next game. If you get a good opening and go on to win the game, this too should be reviewed. Maybe your opponent just played a horrible move when the correct one would have caused you trouble? It is also valuable to learn that both sides played well. That discovery will give you confidence for your future games.

(8) *Keep up with the latest developments in your opening.*

Sad to say, "once learned, always learned" does not apply to opening theory. There are too many discoveries being made, because there are so many players and so many tournaments. Therefore you must keep up with the latest developments. How can this be done?

I feel that every serious tournament player should get the *Chess Informant* when it appears (three times a year). If you have lots of time to spend on opening theory, you should also get the quarterly *New in Chess Yearbook*. However, since they are reference works their appearance is relatively infrequent. Moreover, because they are meant for world-wide distribution, they are languageless and use symbols rather than words. This makes it difficult to understand new concepts.

Surely every USCF member should take advantage of his/her free monthly *Chess Life* to look for the latest games employing the openings of interest to him/her. Other highly recommended chess magazines in the English language include: *Inside Chess, New in Chess Magazine, Chess Monthly* and *British Chess Magazine*. Subscribe to one of them so that you can keep up with developments in your opening(s) in the four-month interval between the appearance of the *Chess Informant*.

Part Two: Important Themes

3 The magic of rapid development

The strong player admires Paul Morphy as the first modern master – one who understood the whole of the game, whether it be pawn structures, endgames, strategy, tactics or anything else. The general chess public, however, cherishes him more for his beautiful combinations. Yes, Morphy did play brilliant moves, but this was just the dessert of a gourmet meal. In the 1920s and 1930s Alexander Alekhine was justly celebrated for his combinations. At one such "celebration", Rudolf Spielmann is reputed to have exclaimed: "I can play combinations just as well, but only Alekhine can create the positions from which these combinations are possible!"

So also for Paul Morphy. His deep understanding of opening principles allowed him to quickly create the positions where a tactical shot is possible. One of the most important aims of good opening play is *to develop your pieces toward the centre so that they are ready for middlegame action*. As was the custom in the middle of the 19th century, Morphy preferred to play open games with either colour. He quickly became unsurpassed in achieving rapid, purposeful, centrally oriented development. He can teach us much about this aspect of opening play. Therefore I have selected four quick wins – two from each side.

With White

Perhaps his most famous combination occurs in the following game:

Philidor's Defence (C41)
Paul Morphy – Duke of
Brunswick and Count Isouard
Paris 1858

1 e4 e5 2 ♘f3 d6 3 d4 ♗g4?!
A type of move which is still found in simultaneous exhibitions. It is faulty because after White's response Black cannot keep the pin in place. The theoretical moves are 3...♘d7, 3...♘f6 and 3...exd4.
4 dxe5! ♗xf3 5 ♕xf3 dxe5 6 ♗c4
Developing the f1-bishop to an excellent square while threatening mate in one.
6...♘f6?

Black does see the threat, but not White's response which carries a lethal double attack. Black would "only" be clearly worse after 6...♕f6 7 ♕b3 ♗c5! 8 0-0 ♗b6 9 a4 a5 10 ♘c3 ♘e7 11 ♗e3 ♘d7 12 ♖ad1. The reason for White's advantage is his much superior development in an open position.

7 ♕b3! ♕e7

Because White threatens to capture on f7 with mate to follow (7...♘xe4 8 ♗xf7+ ♔d7 9 ♕e6#), Black has to guard that weakness. He hopes to escape into a pawn down ending after 8 ♕xb7 ♕b4+. Understandably Morphy is looking for bigger things because of his significant lead in development.

8 ♘c3!? c6 9 ♗g5

White develops the c1-bishop to an active square, while immobilising the f6-knight. Black's position is close to critical, e.g. 9...♕c7 10 0-0-0 ♗c5 loses to 11 ♗xf7+! ♕xf7 12 ♖d8+. Black *must* work on his development with 9...♘a6!

when the best I see for White is to ruin Black's queenside pawn formation with 10 ♗xa6. Instead ...

9...b5?

Being unfamiliar with the importance of rapid development, the Black players think that the annoying c4-bishop can just be chased away. But ...

10 ♘xb5! cxb5 11 ♗xb5+ ♘bd7 12 0-0-0

White already has two pawns for the piece. Moreover, look at the development side of the equation: White's king is safely castled, both of White's bishops, the d1-rook and queen are actively developed, whereas Black's king is stuck in the centre and his kingside pieces are undeveloped. White already threatens to win the d7-knight by playing 13 ♗xf6, 13 ♗xd7+ or 13 ♖xd7. Castling queenside is suicidal (12...0-0-0 13 ♗a6+ ♔c7 14 ♕b7#) and the forced reply only holds for a few moments.

12...♖d8 13 ♖xd7! ♖xd7 14 ♖d1

Now *all* of White's pieces are developed and attacking Black. A bean counter may say that Black is a rook up, yet in real life Black is a bishop down, because his kingside is not participating in the fight. After 14...♕b4 Black loses prosaically: 15 ♗xf6! gxf6 16 ♗xd7+ etc. We can be grateful to the counts for playing ...

14...♕e6

and allowing ...

**15 ♗xd7+! ♘xd7 16 ♕b8+
♘xb8 17 ♖d8#**

Paul Morphy does deserve credit for his brilliant play. Yet please do note the developmental characteristics of the final position: Black is still playing without his h8-rook and f8-bishop, while the king's knight has become undeveloped on b8, whereas all of White's pieces – thanks to rapid development – have participated in the fray.

King's Gambit Accepted (C34)
Paul Morphy – Amateur
New Orleans 1858

1 e4 e5 2 f4 exf4 3 ♘f3 c6?! 4 ♘c3 ♗b4?!

A continuing characteristic of amateurs is that they rush to exchange off enemy knights so that the risk of a nasty knight fork is eliminated. However, in the kind of open position seen both in the previous game and this one, it is the bishop which is the more dangerous minor piece. Of course, the logical follow-up to Black's previous move is 4...d5.

5 ♗c4 ♗xc3?

Absolutely horrible: Black furthers White's development and seriously weakens the dark squares. Either 5...d6 or the ambitious 5...d5 6 exd5 ♘f6!? make sense.

6 dxc3! ♘e7 7 ♕d6! 0-0 8 ♗xf4 ♘g6 9 ♗g5 ♕e8 10 0-0! ♔h8

Taking the pawn by 10...♕xe4 gives White open lines and full

development, for example 11 ♗b3 followed by 12 ♖ae1 or 11 ♘d4 ♕e5 12 ♘f5. In either case, Black's end is near.

11 ♖ae1!

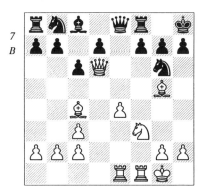

Again, admire Morphy's development: it is only move 11 and *all* of his pieces have been actively and purposefully developed; moreover, his king is safely castled. On the other hand Black is playing without his queenside. Under such conditions, combinations appear as if "from the sky".

11...f6 12 e5!

To take maximum advantage of superior development, lines should be opened. After 12...fxg5 13 ♘xg5 Black has no hope of defending, e.g. 13...♘a6 14 ♖xf8+ ♕xf8 15 ♖e4! ♘c5 16 ♕xg6! hxg6 17 ♖h4#.

12...f5 13 ♘d4 f4 14 e6

Again with the principle of opening lines. Some fifty years later, Maroczy pointed out that 14 h4! h6 15 h5 hxg5 16 hxg6 g4 17 ♔f2 followed by 18 ♖h1# would have been even faster.

14...dxe6 15 ♘xe6 ♗xe6 15 ♖xe6 ♕c8 17 ♖xg6!

Sacrificing an exchange for a pawn to denude Black's king is hardly risky since Black's queenside is not participating.

17...hxg6 18 ♕xg6 ♕f5 19 ♖xf4!

Beautiful, but only possible because Black's pieces on a8 and b8 are undeveloped, while (again!) all of White's pieces are participating.

19...♕xg6 20 ♖xf8+ ♔h7 21 ♗g8+ ♔h8 22 ♗f7+ ♔h7 23 ♗xg6+ ♔xg6 24 ♗f4 1-0

The pinned knight is lost, leaving White a piece and two pawns up.

With Black

Two Knights' Defence (C55)
Theodor Lichtenhein –
Paul Morphy
First American Chess Congress,
New York 1857

1 e4 e5

Morphy's favourite response because now Black's pieces also have the maximum potential for rapid development. If White tarries with his development, then Black has excellent prospects for quickly seizing the initiative.

2 ♘f3 ♘c6 3 d4 exd4 4 ♗c4 ♘f6 5 e5

By transposition the game has gone from the Scotch Opening into a line of the Two Knights'

still popular today. (The usual move-order is 1 e4 e5 2 ♘f3 ♘c6 3 ♗c4 ♘f6 4 d4 exd4 5 e5.) Morphy responds with a counter-thrust quite common in modern times, but at the cutting edge in his time.

5...d5! 6 ♗b5 ♘e4 7 ♘xd4 ♗d7 8 ♘xc6?!

The text loses an important tempo. After the correct 8 ♗xc6 bxc6 9 0-0 White probably has a tiny edge.

8...bxc6! 9 ♗d3 ♗c5

Rapid and active development! With his next move White hopes to decrease Black's pressure, but Black has a zwischenzug to keep the initiative.

10 ♗xe4 ♕h4! 11 ♕e2

A perfectly reasonable approach: White wants Black to capture on e4 with his pawn and thus be left with a broken pawn structure on the queenside. After the routine 11 0-0 ♕xe4 Black has, at no cost, the advantage of the bishop pair in an open position and therefore a pleasant advantage.

11...dxe4 *(D)*

The *Encyclopedia of Chess Openings*, Volume C now recommends 12 0-0, judging the position as slightly superior for Black due to the potential of the bishop pair. Instead White wants to immediately neutralise Black's c5-bishop, but has not noticed the precarious position of his king and undeveloped queenside.

12 ♗e3? ♗g4!! 13 ♕c4

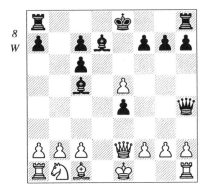

White must counterattack since the safe 13 ♕d2 loses routinely to 13...♖d8, with mate on d1 coming up.

13...♗xe3!

The attack continues. The main line as given by Soltis and Reinfeld is 14 ♕xc6+ ♗d7 15 ♕xa8+ ♔e7 16 g3 ♗xf2+ 17 ♔xf2 e3+ 18 ♔e1 (18 ♔g1 e2!) 18...♕b4+ 19 c3 ♕xb2 20 ♕xh8 (20 ♕e4 ♕c1+ 21 ♔e2 ♗b5 22 ♔f3 ♕xh1+) 20...♗g4 followed by mate on e2 or f2. Note that here too White's queenside is not developed, whereas Black's two remaining pieces have very active positions.

14 g3 ♕d8

Equally strong is 14...♕h6 15 ♕xe4 ♗c1.

15 fxe3 ♕d1+ 16 ♔f2 ♕f3+! 17 ♔g1 ♗h3 18 ♕xc6+ ♔f8 19 ♕xa8+ ♔e7 0-1

After 20 ♕xh8 Black mates on g2 or f1. Can White be considered to be two rooks up in the final position? I don't think so because neither the rook nor the knight is participating. When there is no

development there is no available force. Therefore a numerically inferior enemy "army" can readily be the decisive one.

Evans Gambit (C52)
N. Marache – Paul Morphy
New York 1857

1 e4 e5 2 ♘f3 ♘c6 3 ♗c4 ♗c5 4 b4 ♗xb4 5 c3 ♗a5 6 d4 exd4

The modern defensive approach is 6...d6. Even as Black, Morphy did not hesitate to go for a more open position, as long as his judgement told him that the risk accepted is tolerable.

7 e5?

White must look for rapid development as compensation for the sacrificed material. The text does not further development and meets a clear refutation. The developing 7 0-0 is in order when 7...♘ge7 is considered by theory to be the only correct response; eventual equality is the most likely outcome.

7...d5! 8 exd6 ♕xd6 9 0-0 ♘ge7!

Development of the kingside is in order.

10 ♘g5?

White is insufficiently developed to expect anything from such a knight sally. 10 ♗a3 ♕f6 11 cxd4 is logical, with some compensation for the pawn.

10...0-0 11 ♗d3

Notice how White is attempting to attack by moving the same

pieces repeatedly, rather than bringing new soldiers into play. Morphy, therefore, decides that he can both complete his development and gain a safe material advantage by an exchange sacrifice. In return he will get two or three pawns and a clear initiative.

11...♗f5! 12 ♗xf5 ♘xf5 13 ♗a3 ♕g6 14 ♗xf8 ♕xg5!

Gaining additional time as compared to 14...♖xf8.

15 ♗a3 dxc3

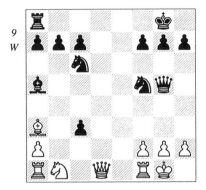

9
W

Black has three pawns in return for the exchange, excellently placed knights, active queen and has ...♖d8 coming up. White's queenside is undeveloped (again!) and he has no chance of coping with Black's initiative. The attempt to bring over the bishop to help out on the kingside will be insufficient, but there is nothing satisfactory.

16 ♗c1 ♕g6 17 ♗f4 ♖d8 18 ♕c2 ♘cd4

Black just walks in on the fifth-rank central squares, which have been left unattended because of lack of development on White's part.

19 ♕e4

The queen feels safe enough here, yet is surprised by an electrifying knight jump.

19...♘g3!! 0-1

White's queen is attacked twice while the normal 20 ♕xg6 allows the picturesque 20...♘de2#!

In summary, Paul Morphy fully deserved to win all of the above games. Yet his brilliant combinations were made possible by his opponents' failure to appreciate the need for rapid purposeful development in open positions. In all four games, his opponent left one half of his pieces completely undeveloped (once this was on the kingside and the other three times it was on the queenside).

4 The importance of capturing towards the centre

Quite frequently either you or your opponent has to make the decision as to whether to make a capture with one pawn in the direction of the centre or with another pawn away from the centre. The decision may have to be made early in the opening (as early as move 3!), during the course of the middlegame or even late into the endgame. Which is the correct capture? Because control of the centre is such an important goal during the opening phase and much of the middlegame, the following general principle applies: *always recapture towards the centre, unless there is a very good reason to do otherwise.*

In later stages of some middlegames as well as endgames with severely reduced material, the importance of central control decreases and the decision must be made based on the very specific demands of the position. However, in the early part of the game – the first 25 moves or so – the capture towards the centre will be the better choice more than 75% of the time.

The following is the general rule of thumb: *when in doubt, capture towards the centre.*

Decisions For Black

Still, the choice is often not so easy for *Black* in the early stages. The problem is simply that White starts off with the initiative and Black isn't only concerned with the centre, but has also to worry about speed of development, king safety and other important matters. In this section I will look at the three most common recapture decisions that Black has to make in the opening phase. The next section will consider White's needs and prospects.

(A) ...dxc6 vs. ...bxc6
(1) The classical example here is the Exchange Variation of the Ruy Lopez: **1 e4 e5 2 ♘f3 ♘c6 3 ♗b5 a6 4 ♗xc6**

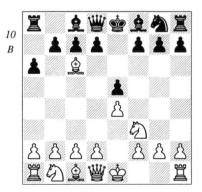

10
B

(a) **4...bxc6** is the thematic "towards the centre" recapture, but does not further Black's development. The important consequence is that Black finds it difficult to smoothly protect the vulnerable e-pawn. The main line then develops **5 ♘c3 d6 6 d4.**

What has happened is that White is now a whole tempo ahead of the following variation from the Steinitz Deferred Defence: 3...a6 4 ♗a4 d6 5 ♗xc6+ bxc6 6 d4. An extra tempo in an open game is usually a very significant advantage.

Black's defensive chores are unpleasant after both 6...exd4 7 ♕xd4 and 6...f6 7 ♗e3 ♘e7 8 ♕d3 ♗e6 9 0-0-0 ♘g6 10 h4 h5 11 ♘d2 a5 12 g3 exd4 13 ♗xd4 ♘e5 14 ♕f1 ♕b8 15 f4, N.Padevsky-Daskalov, Bulgarian Championship 1972. White's substantial lead in development and superior centre gives him a clear advantage.

(b) **4...dxc6**

Because of the problems with 4...bxc6, master-level play over the past twenty years has employed the text rather exclusively. Black risks being left with the permanently inferior pawn formation if his e-pawn gets exchanged for White's d-pawn, because then White's 4 vs. 3 pawn advantage on the kingside ensures him a passed pawn on that side, whereas Black's queenside majority is devalued by having doubled pawns. As compensation,

Black must look to his bishop pair and, as can already be seen, both bishops are on open diagonals. Moreover, the mobility of Black's queen along the d-file (5 ♘xe5? ♕d4 recovers the pawn with even a slight advantage to Black) makes it easier to defend the e-pawn. As a result, Black can restrict White's opening advantage to just the normal size. An important recent example is R.Fischer-B.Spassky, Sveti Stefan 1992, Match Game 9:

5 0-0 f6 6 d4 exd4 7 ♘xd4 c5 8 ♘b3 ♕xd1 9 ♖xd1 ♗g4 10 f3 ♗e6 11 ♘c3 ♗d6 12 ♗e3 b6 13 a4 0-0-0 (13...♔f7 is considered to be sounder) **14 a5 ♔b7 15 e5! ♗e7 16 ♖xd8 ♗xd8 17 ♘e4 ♔c6??** (necessary is 17...♗d5, with a slight pull for White after 18 ♖d1) **18 axb6 cxb6 19 ♘bxc5! ♗c8 20 ♘xa6 fxe5 21 ♘b4+ 1-0**

(2) Black has to make a similar decision in the Rossolimo Variation against the Sicilian Defence after the moves **1 e4 c5 2 ♘f3 ♘c6 3 ♗b5 g6 4 ♗xc6**

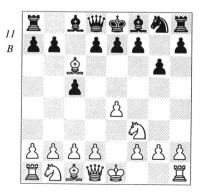

11
B

The early ♗xc6 has been successfully employed by both Garry Kasparov and Robert J. Fischer. Its idea is to combine quick kingside development with opportunities to exploit Black's doubled pawns. Yet in comparison to the situation in the Exchange Variation of the Ruy Lopez, Black is better off in three ways: the position is not as open, he has not expended a tempo with ...a6 and he doesn't have to lose time defending a central pawn. In my opinion, either recapture by Black is equally satisfactory.

(a) **4...bxc6**

Because it is thematic, this recapture is the more popular one in GM play. Its only disadvantage – development of the c8-bishop is delayed by one move – is mitigated by the relatively closed nature of the position.

After the normal **5 0-0 ♗g7 6 ♖e1**, two important variations are:

(1) **6...♘f6 7 e5 ♘d5 8 c4 ♘c7 9 d4 cxd4 10 ♕xd4**, when instead of 10...0-0?! 11 ♕h4 d6 12 ♗h6, with a clear advantage to White in the game G.Kasparov-V.Salov, Dortmund 1992, the World Champion recommends 10...d5!? 11 ♘c3 ♘e6 as keeping White's advantage to a minimum.

(2) **6...f6!? 7 c3 ♘h6 8 d4 cxd4 9 cxd4 0-0 10 ♘c3 d6 11 ♕a4 ♕b6 12 ♘d2 ♘f7 13 ♘c4 ♕a6**, with approximate equality, R.Fischer-B.Spassky, Sveti Stefan 1992, Match Game 13.

(b) **4...dxc6**

After this recapture Black's pawns have less central influence than after 4...bxc6, yet it is also satisfactory since a potential d4 advance by White will dissolve Black's doubled pawn, rather than give White a kingside pawn majority. A logical sequence then is 5 h3 ♗g7 6 d3 e5 7 ♗g5 f6 8 ♗e3 b6 9 ♕c1 ♗e6 10 a4 ♘e7 11 ♘a3 ♘c8 12 b3 ♘d6 13 ♘c4 with a slight advantage to White, according to L.Psakhis.

(B) *...exf6 vs. ...gxf6*

Unlike the situation under A), the recapture towards the centre, i.e. ...gxf6, causes a serious weakening of the king position. In the opening Black must be careful to ensure that this weakening can be tolerated. I will briefly discuss one situation from 1 e4 and one from 1 d4 where this capture is feasible.

(1) In the main line of the Caro-Kann Defence staring with **1 e4 c6 2 d4 d5 3 ♘c3 dxe4 4 ♘xe4**, Black has two solid continuations: 4...♘d7 and 4...♗f5. These are in fact Black's most popular choices. Yet there is also the much more unbalancing and ambitious **4...♘f6**, leading after **5 ♘xf6+** *(D)* to two quite different situations:

(a) **5...gxf6**

In selecting the Bronstein-Larsen variation, Black appears to "forget" that the Caro-Kann is

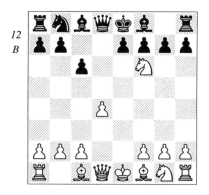

12
B

usually used as a sound way of striving for equality. Here Black intends to use the open g-file to exert pressure on White's kingside. His own king will look for safety on the queenside. Currently the variation is losing some popularity because White's attack is often the more dangerous. Yet the theoretical situation is far from clear. In J.Fedorowicz-D.Roos, France 1990, after 6 c3 ♗f5 7 ♘f3 ♘d7 8 g3 ♘b6 9 ♗g2 ♕d7 10 0-0 ♗h3 11 ♗xh3 ♕xh3 12 a4 ♕f5! 13 a5 ♘d5 14 c4 ♘c7 15 ♗f4 0-0-0 Black had good prospects for counterplay.

(b) **5...exf6**

This non-thematic recapture is "safe" in the sense that the king will have an extra (doubled) pawn to protect him and both bishops are already on open diagonals. Of course, there is also a cost to having these assets: White has a sound 4 vs. 3 pawn majority on the queenside. I would not suggest that you risk the black side against someone like Anatoly

Karpov, yet "mortal" GMs can be fair game. A good illustration of Black's prospects is shown by the game W.Watson-J.Hodgson, Malaysia 1992 (B16):

6 c3 ♗d6 7 ♗d3 ♗e6 8 ♘e2 ♕c7 9 ♕c2 ♘d7 10 c4 c5

Black is willing to allow a protected passed pawn, so as to immobilise White's queenside pawn configuration and gain control of some dark squares.

11 d5 ♗g4 12 h3 ♗xe2 13 ♕xe2+ ♔f8 14 0-0 ♖e8 15 ♕c2 h5 16 f4?!

White overvalues his prospects. Correct is 16 ♗f5! in order to exchange off his "bad" bishop for Black's knight.

16...g6 17 ♕f2 f5 18 b3 ♗e7! 19 ♗b2 ♗f6 20 ♗xf6 ♘xf6 21 ♕b2 ♔g7 22 ♖f3

Black now erred with 22...h4?, seriously weakening the kingside and losing in 42 moves. Instead Hodgson recommends 22...♕d6! followed by 23...♖e7 and 24...♖he8. White is then without active play and Black's grip on the open e-file gives him the advantage.

(2) Against the Trompovsky Attack – 1 d4 ♘f6 2 ♗g5 – one of Black's highly regarded responses is the solid 2...d5 when White players invariably go for 3 ♗xf6 *(D)*

White saddles Black permanently with doubled pawns and, should the position remain closed, hopes to prove that the nimble knights can be more effective

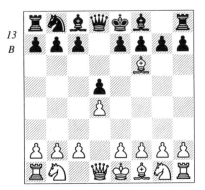

than Black's bishop pair. In tournament practice a majority of GMs prefer to recapture with the e-pawn, whereas the *Encyclopedia of Chess Openings D* (Revised) gives higher marks to the recapture with the g-pawn.

(a) **3...gxf6**

The closed nature of the position means that Black's king is safe enough, yet the doubled pawns are somewhat unwieldy and the isolated h-pawn can turn out to be a weakness later on. A thematic continuation now is 4 e3 c5 5 c3 ♕b6 6 ♕b3 e6 7 ♘d2 ♘c6 8 ♘gf3 ♗d7 9 ♗e2 ♘a5 10 ♕c2 cxd4 11 exd4 ♗b5 12 ♗xb5+ ♕xb5 13 a4 ♕c6 14 0-0 ♗d6, Fernandes-S.Tatai, Barcelona 1985. *ECO D* rates the position as equal.

(b) **3...exf6**

Just as in the corresponding Caro-Kann situation, Black prefers sound efficient development over having the more centrally dynamic doubled pawns. In L.Alburt-E.Mednis, New York (Heraldica) International 1980 White

retained a slight advantage after 4 e3 ♗d6 5 c4 dxc4 6 ♗xc4 0-0 7 ♘c3 ♘d7 9 0-0 ♘f6 10 ♕c2 a6 11 ♖fe1 ♖b8 12 ♖ad1 due to his space advantage. I believe that Black can improve with the active 7...c5! and thereby gain sufficient counterchances for eventual full equality.

(C) *...hxg6 vs. ...fxg6*

The most frequent occurrences of a recapture on g6 come from Caro-Kann or Slav Defence positions where Black's light-squared bishop has wound up on g6 and is captured either by White's king's knight or king's bishop. In the overwhelming majority of cases, the recapture should be with the h-pawn. Only if the recapture with the f-pawn offers special opportunities or recapture with the h-pawn is downright bad (e.g. White's attack along the h-file will be decisive as the h7-square can't be protected), should Black stray from the thematic "towards the centre" response.

(1) *...hxg6 is better*

An obvious example is the game B.Spassky-A.Karpov, Candidates Match 1974, Game 2, Caro-Kann Defence: **1 e4 c6 2 d4 d5 3 ♘c3 dxe4 4 ♘xe4 ♗f5 5 ♘g3 ♗g6 6 ♘f3 ♘d7 7 ♗d3 e6 8 0-0 ♘gf6 9 c4 ♗d6 10 b3 0-0 11 ♗b2 c5 12 ♗xg6 hxg6!**

The thematic recapture enhances Black's central influence and has no real flaw. Instead, the unmotivated 12...fxg6? achieves nothing positive and turns the e-pawn into a weakness. The players agreed on a draw after **13 ♖e1 ♕c7 14 dxc5 ♗xc5 15 ♕c2 ♖fd8 16 ♘e4 ♘xe4 17 ♕xe4.**

Even the strongest of players should resist the urge to capture non-thematically. V.Hort-D.Bronstein, Petropolis Interzonal 1973, Slav Defence, opened as follows: **1 d4 d5 2 c4 c6 3 ♘c3 ♘f6 4 ♘f3 dxc4 5 a4 ♗g4 6 e3 e6 7 ♗xc4 ♘bd7 8 h3 ♗h5 9 ♕e2 ♗b4 10 0-0 ♕e7 11 e4 e5 12 d5 a5?! 13 ♖d1! 0-0?! 14 g4 ♗g6 15 ♘h4! cxd5 16 ♘xg6**

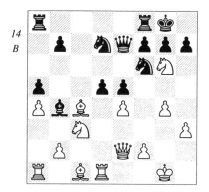

Black has played inexactly and after the normal 16...hxg6 17 ♘xd5 ♘xd5 18 ♗xd5 White has a small yet safe advantage due to having more space and more active pieces. This didn't seem attractive to the famous GM and he tried to mix things up by opening the f-file:
16...fxg6? 17 ♗xd5+! ♔h8
After 17...♘xd5 18 ♘xd5 White has a fantastic knight on d5.

18 ♗xb7 ♖ab8 19 ♗d5 ♘c5 20 ♗g5! Black's compensation for the pawn is meagre and White went on to win in 44 moves.

(2) ...fxg6 is better
Because this recapture is non-thematic, Black must be very hard-nosed when considering it. Only very good specific reasons will justify it! The kind of position where the decision is correct is shown in Diagram 15 from the game P.van der Sterren-E.Torre, Adelaide 1986/87, after White's 18th move in a main line of the Slav defence (1 d4 d5 2 c4 c6 3 ♘f3 ♘f6 4 ♘c3 dxc4 5 a4 ♗f5 6 e3 e6 7 ♗xc4 ♗b4 8 0-0 0-0 9 ♕e2 ♘bd7 10 e4 ♗g6 11 ♗d3 ♗h5 12 ♗f4 ♖e8 13 e5 ♘d5 14 ♘xd5 cxd5 15 h3 a6 16 ♖fc1 ♗g6 17 ♕e3 ♘b8 18 ♗xg6).

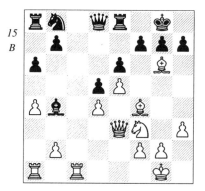

The normal recapture would now be 18...hxg6, yet that leaves Black with a lifeless and cramped situation on the kingside. Moreover, White can exploit the inherent weakness of the doubled pawns

by aiming for a kingside attack via ♘g5, placing the queen on h4 and/or advancing the h-pawn to h5 at the proper moment. Therefore, Torre selects the much more perceptive as well as better:
18...fxg6!
Black finds it now much easier to co-ordinate the defence of the kingside and, moreover, the opening of the f-file offers him attacking prospects along it.
19 ♕b3 a5 20 ♗g5 ♕b6 21 ♗e7?! ♘c6 22 ♗xg4 axb4 23 ♕d3 ♖f8! 24 ♖d1 ♖f4! 25 g3 ♖f5 26 ♘h4 ♖f7 27 ♖d2 ♖af8 28 ♖e1 ♘a5 29 f4 ♖c7!
The pressure along the f-file has caused White to weaken his kingside pawn formation and now Black swings over to the queenside to try to infiltrate behind White's back.
30 ♘f3 ♖c4 31 ♖c2?
Short of time, White tries to lessen his problems by exchanging off a pair of rooks, but the effect is the opposite. Torre suggests that the best defence is holding tight with 31 ♔g2 ♖fc8 21 h4.
31...♖fc8 32 ♖ec1 ♕c6! 33 ♖xc4 dxc4 34 ♕e3 ♖d8 35 ♘g5 ♘b3 36 ♖d1 c3 37 bxc3 bxc3 38 d5 c2 39 ♖c1 ♕xd5 0-1

Decisions For White

In the previous section I discussed the important situations where Black had to decide in the opening or early middlegame

whether to recapture towards the centre or away from it. Often this is a very sensitive decision for Black. Even though he would like to recapture in the thematic "towards the centre" manner, this may lead to problems with, for example, delay of development or king safety.

White has no such worries. Since he starts off with the advantage, chances are good that no matter how he recaptures he will still be at least equal. Even if, for instance, a recapture may be rated by opening theory as allowing Black to equalise with perfect play, if you like the resultant positions and are good at them, there is no reason to avoid playing them. In any case, the overall principle remains intact: *always recapture towards the centre unless there is a very good reason to do otherwise*. It turns out that there are far more openings in which White has to make a recapture decision; these differ significantly between open and closed games. In this section I will consider the important choices for open games; the next section will discuss closed game situations.

Open Games

(A) *axb3 v. cxb3*
By far the most frequent examples occur in the main lines of the Sicilian Defence. The piece captured on b3 is the king's bishop or

king's knight (after ♘d4-b3). The capturer is either Black's queen's bishop or queen's knight. It is easy to see that, both for central control purposes and long-term pawn formation quality, the recapture should be with the a-pawn. In addition, because the a-file has been opened for White's a1-rook, White has early pressure against Black's a-pawn, thereby delaying the thematic mobilisation of Black's a8-rook along the c-file. If White captures with the c-pawn, the following pawn formation results: on the queenside Black's a- and b-pawns hold White's a-pawn plus doubled b-pawns while on the other side Black has a healthy five-pawn chain as against White's four-pawn chain. The kind of considerations that go into making the correct decision are very well illustrated by looking at some of the lines of the Yugoslav Attack against the Dragon Variation.

(1) *axb3 is better*

White should recapture thematically, unless there are reasons to do otherwise. During the first ten or so years of the Yugoslav Attack (1954-1964) Black strove to exchange off White's light-squared bishop pretty soon after it arrived on c4. Let's look at the sequence **1 e4 c5 2 ♘f3 d6 3 d4 cxd4 4 ♘xd4 ♘f6 5 ♘c3 g6 6 ♗e3 ♗g7 7 f3 0-0 8 ♕d2 ♘c6 9 ♗c4 ♘a5 10 ♗b3 ♘xb3** *(D)*

White has three ways of recapturing:

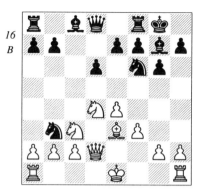

(1) **11 cxb3?!** is purposeless and after 11...d5! 12 e5 ♘e8 13 f4 (13 ♘db5 a6!) 13...f6! Black already has promising counterplay and a slight advantage.

(2) **11 ♘xb3** retreats a centralised knight while leaving c4 unguarded. After 11...♗e6 12 0-0-0 a5 13 ♘d4 ♗c4 14 ♗h6 ♗xh6 15 ♕xh6 e5 Black had equalised in A.Gipslis-B.Gurgenidze, USSR Championship 1961.

(3) **11 axb3**

After this normal recapture White retains a clear advantage. Two example from tournament practice:

(a) **11...d5** 12 e5 ♘d7 13 f4 ♘c5 14 ♘db5, Henkin-Cherepkov, USSR 1954.

(b) **11...a6** 12 h4 ♗d7 13 h5 ♖c8 14 ♗h6 e5 15 ♘de2 ♗e6 16 g4 ♕c7 17 ♘g3 b5 18 b4, B.Spassky-E.Geller, Semi-Final Candidates Match 1965, Game 8. White's attack is in full swing while Black's is nowhere. White castled queenside on move 25 and won decisively on move 39.

(2) *cxb3 is better*

As already mentioned, in the overwhelming majority of cases, recapturing with the a-pawn will be better. There are, however, two situations where the capture with the c-pawn should be preferred.

(a) *For defensive reasons*

With White castled queenside, the open a-file may give Black a dangerous attack if he can effectively mobilise his heavy artillery. This is illustrated in the following variation: **1 e4 c5 2 ♘f3 d6 3 d4 cxd4 4 ♘xd4 ♘f6 5 ♘c3 g6 6 ♗e3 ♗g7 7 f3 0-0 8 ♕d2 ♘c6 9 ♗c4 ♘xd4 10 ♗xd4 ♗e6 11 ♗b3 ♕a5 12 0-0-0 ♖fc8 13 ♔b1 ♖c6 14 h4 ♗xb3**

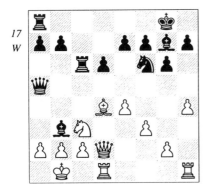

17
W

As is characteristic in the Yugoslav Attack, each side is going for the enemy king. Often the difference between success and failure is a single tempo. Therefore 15 axb3?! is simply foolhardy because after the immediate 15...♖a6 or the preparatory 15...b5 Black's attack along the a-file will be too

strong and White will have to rush to exchange queens and acquiesce to an equal endgame (15...♖a6 16 ♘a4; 15...b5 16 ♘d5). Therefore, White should play:

15 cxb3

Black's attack can now be defanged and White retains his prospects on the kingside. In the game A.Gipslis-I.Nei, USSR 1961, White retained a continuing advantage after 15...b5 16 a3! ♖ac8 (16...b4? is met by 17 ♘a2) 17 b4 ♕a6 18 e5 dxe5 19 ♗xe5 ♘e4! 20 ♘xe4 ♗xe5 21 h5 ♕b6 22 hxg6 hxg6 23 ♕g5. In the ending Black's superior pawn formation would give him the advantage, yet in this middlegame position it is White who has the better attacking chances.

(b) *For offensive reasons*

Just as the axb3 recapture opens the a-file for the uncastled a1-rook, so the cxb3 recapture opens the c-file for a potential incursion by White's rook(s) and/or queen. Of course, the prospects for this had better be clear as otherwise White will be saddled with the inferior pawn structure with nothing to show for it. An instructive exploitation of the potential is shown in Diagram 18, E.Mednis-R.Weinstein, US Championship 1963/64, after Black's 18th move (1 e4 c5 2 ♘f3 d6 3 d4 cxd4 4 ♘xd4 ♘f6 5 ♘c3 g6 6 ♗e3 ♗g7 7 f3 ♘c6 8 ♕d2 ♗e6 9 0-0-0 ♖c8 10 ♔b1 0-0 11 ♘xe6 fxe6 12 ♗c4 ♕d7 13 ♗b3 ♔h8 14 h4 ♘a5 15 ♕d3

♘h5 16 ♘e2 b5 17 ♗d4 e5 18 ♗c3 ♘xb3)

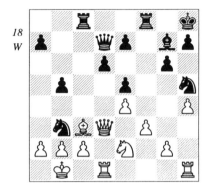

At the cost of absorbing some serious long-term and short-term liabilities (doubled e-pawns, deadened g7-bishop and h5-knight on the edge of the board) Black has minimised White's prospects for a breakthrough on the kingside. For instance, after the thematic 19 axb3 recapture, Black plays 19...h6 when 20 g4?! ♘f4 21 ♘xf4 ♖xf4 leaves White vulnerable along the f-file and with nothing to show for it since 22 g5 is met by 22...h5 and 22 h5 is foiled by 22...g5. Yet because of Black's concentration of effort on the kingside, White can turn to the other side for promising opportunities. Therefore in order is:

19 cxb3! h6 20 ♖c1! ♕b7 21 ♗d2!

Because White can quickly mobilise his forces to point in the direction of the queenside, Black's defensive job there is most unpleasant. He never comes up with

a satisfactory plan. Perhaps best is to get the knight into the game starting with 21...♘f6.

21...♖cd8 22 ♗a5 ♖d7 23 ♖hd1! ♗f6 24 ♗e1 e6 25 ♕c2 ♗e7 26 ♕c6! ♘g7 27 ♕xb7 ♖xb7 28 a3! ♔g8 29 ♖c6

The exchange of queens has not lightened Black's load. In particular, the a-pawn becomes quite vulnerable.

29...♔f7 30 ♖a6 ♖a8 31 f4!

To take advantage of Black's various pawn weaknesses, White should strive to open lines.

31...exf4 32 ♘xf4 ♖c8 33 g3 g5 34 hxg5 hxg5 35 ♘d3 ♖h8 36 g4 ♖h3?! 37 ♗f2 ♖h2 38 ♖xa7 ♖xa7 39 ♗xa7 ♖g2 40 ♘f2 ♘e8 41 a4 bxa4 42 bxa4 ♗d8 43 e5 ♗c7 44 exd6 ♗xd6 45 a5 ♗e7 46 ♗b6 ♘d6 47 a6 1-0

(B) bxc3 vs. dxc3

In early play this choice will be based on the same parameters as in the Exchange Variation of the Ruy Lopez (1 e4 e5 2 ♘f3 ♘c6 3 ♗b5 a6 4 ♗xc6) discussed in the previous section for Black. One result is again the creation of double pawns. The big difference is that White can be rather sure that either way he will have good chances for retaining the initiative. In other words, it will be Black who will have to strive hard to equalise. A good discussion point is the following "simple" variation against Alekhine's defence (B02):

1 e4 ♘f6 2 e5 ♘d5 3 ♘c3 ♘xc3

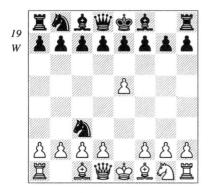

19
W

(1) *4 bxc3*

By turning the b-pawn into a c-pawn, White enhances his prospects in the centre, though at the cost of delayed development of the c1-bishop and some shakiness of the pawn structure. The following thematic sequence illustrates the trade-offs: **4...d6** (in Alekhine's Defence, White's e5-pawn must be challenged; thus 4...d5?! is inferior) **5 f4 g6** (because Black can't afford as much as White, attempting to play aggressively with 5...dxe5?! 6 fxe5 ♕d5 boomerangs: 7 ♘f3 ♘c6 8 d4 ♗g4 9 ♗e2 e6 10 0-0 ♗e7 11 ♖b1 b6 12 c4 ♕d7 13 c3 with a nice spatial superiority for White – Bagirov) **6 ♘f3 ♗g7 7 d4 0-0 8 ♗d3 c5 9 0-0 dxe5 10 dxe5** (The "towards the centre recapture" 10 fxe5?! leaves White's centre too shaky: 10...♘c6 11 ♗e3 ♗g4 12 ♗e4 ♕a5 13 ♕e1 ♖ad8, N.Padevsky-Vuković, Smederevska Palanka 1971, where Black's

pressure on d4 gives him the superior chances. The text does leave White with ugly doubled pawns, but with more space and attacking chances on the kingside as compensation.) **10...♘c6 11 ♗e3 ♕c7 12 ♕e1** with a slight advantage for White, A.Dückstein-H.Westerinen, Bamberg 1968.

(2) *4 dxc3*

White ensures smooth development and a secure pawn structure. The negative side is that he may wind up with a 3 vs. 4 pawn disadvantage on the kingside and nothing to show for it. I believe that Black's best approach is to aim for simplification with **4...d6** (again 4...d5?! is clearly inferior, with White gaining an edge after either 5 f4 or 5 c4) **5 ♘f3 dxe5!** (though theoretically playable, 5...♘c6 6 ♗b5 ♗d7 7 ♕e2! forces Black to be extra careful because of White's substantial lead in development) **6 ♕xd8+ ♔xd8 7 ♘xe5 ♔e8 8 ♗e3 ♘d7 9 ♘f3 e5 10 0-0-0 f6 11 ♘d2 ♗c5 12 ♗xc5 ♘xc5 13 ♗c4** and now instead of 13...c6?! 14 f4! b5 15 ♗e2! exf4 when White could have gained a significant advantage in Listengarten-V.Bagirov, USSR 1974 with 16 ♗h5+ g6 17 ♗f3, Bagirov recommends 13...♗g4! 14 f3 ♗h5 (15 g4 ♗f7) as leading to eventual equality for Black.

(C) *dxe5 vs. fxe5*

In open games this choice usually occurs as a result of White playing an early e4-e5 and Black responding with ...dxe5. Therefore White does not wind up with doubled pawns. It should also be stressed that dxe5 is not an "away from the centre" recapture, since the primary central e-pawn is replaced by the primary central d-pawn. Nevertheless, neither is White's centre enhanced. For this to be achieved, the "towards the centre" fxe5 recapture is necessary. Moreover, this often gives White attacking chances along the f-file. In general, we can say that dxe5 provides White with comfortable solidity and a slight space advantage, while fxe5 is an ambitious way of going for more.

The following variation of the Austrian Attack against the Pirc Defence will allow us to take a modern-day look at the recapture choices:

1 e4 d6 2 d4 ♘f6 3 ♘c3 g6 4 f4 ♗g7 5 ♘f3 0-0 6 ♗d3 ♘c6 7 e5 dxe5 (B09)

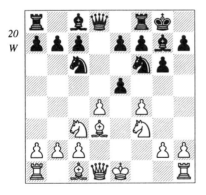

20
W

(1) **8 dxe5 ♘d5 9 ♗d2** With a secure centre and an edge in space,

White looks forward to building on these advantages. Black's task is not at all easy, as can be seen from the following variations:

(a) **9...♘xc3 10 ♗xc3 ♗f5 11 ♗xf5 ♕xd1+ 12 ♖xd1** gave White a clearly superior endgame in the game L.Szabo-J.H.Donner, Amsterdam 1972.

(b) **9...♗g4 10 ♗e4 e6 11 h3 ♗xf3 12 ♕xf3 ♘d4 13 ♕f2 c5** and now **14 ♘a4!** with the idea 14...f6 15 c3! is better for White (Suetin).

(c) **9...♘db4 10 ♗e4 f5 11 ♗xc6 ♘xc6 12 ♕e2** followed by 13 0-0-0 gives White a clear advantage.

In my opinion, Black must quickly regroup his forces and come up with sufficient counterplay. I am now following the game N.Weinstein-E.Mednis, Los Angeles International 1974:

9...♘cb4! 10 ♗e4 ♘b6 11 a3 ♘a6 12 ♕e2 ♘c5 13 0-0-0 ♘xe4 14 ♘xe4 ♕e8!

Black gets ready to activate the queen, e.g. 15 ♘d4 ♕a4! 16 ♗e3 ♕c4 with equality.

15 ♖he1 ♗e6 16 ♘d4 ♗d5! 17 ♕f2 ♕c8!

Black side-steps the threatened 18 ♘f6+ and prepares the thrust 18...c5. White should now be satisfied with approximate equality after 18 ♘c3. His attempt at playing for the attack allows Black to start taking over the queenside.

18 ♕h4? c5 19 ♘f3 f6 20 ♗c3 ♕c6 21 ♘f2 ♘a4! 22 ♖e3 b5 23 ♘g4 ♘xc3 24 ♖xc3 ♖ad8! 25 exf6 exf6 26 f5 ♗e4 27 ♖xd8

♖xd8 28 b4?! ♗xf5 29 ♘e3 ♗e6 30 ♘d4 ♕d7! 31 ♘xe6 ♕xe6 32 bxc5 ♕a2 33 ♖d3 ♖xd3 34 cxd3 ♕xa3+ 35 ♔d2 ♕xc5 36 ♕e4 f5 37 ♕e6+ ♔f8 38 ♘d5 b4 39 ♕d7 ♗h6+ 40 ♔e2 ♕c2 41 ♔e1 ♕d2+ 0-1

(2) *8 fxe5*

If White can get away with it, this is the perfect recapture. By, in effect, exchanging his f-pawn for Black's d-pawn, White has significantly increased his central superiority. Moreover, White's two primary central pawns are actively placed: the d-pawn on the fourth rank and the e-pawn on the fifth (even in Black's part of the board!). On the other hand, Black's only primary central pawn – the e-pawn – is back at home on e7. White's aim should be to first consolidate his central and spatial superiority and then to use it to further pressure Black. Black must try to challenge White's centre, as otherwise he may be suffocated alive. Therefore, although Black's f6-knight has five reasonable squares to head to, two of these are inherently too passive to offer sufficient prospects for counterplay: 8...♘e8?! and 8...♘d7. The other three possibilities lead to these thematic sequences:

(a) **8...♘d5** gets a good evaluation in *Encyclopedia of Chess Openings B* (Revised), but I don't trust it. After 9 ♘xd5 ♕xd5 10 c3 ♗e6 11 0-0 ♖ad8 12 ♗f4! ♕d7 13

♕e1 White has safeguarded his centre and retains promising kingside attacking prospects. In J.Ehlvest-V.Anand, Reggio Emilia 1988/89, White went on to win as follows: 13...♗f5 14 ♗xf5 ♕xf5 15 ♕g3 h6 16 ♖ae1 ♕e6 17 a3 ♘a5 18 ♗g5! ♖d7 19 ♕h4! h5 20 b4 ♘c4 21 ♗c1 ♘b6 22 ♘g5 ♕c6 23 e6 fxe6 24 ♖xf8+ ♗xf8 25 ♕f2! 1-0.

(b) **8...♘g4** has been played a lot, but does not work out well. The knight just can't get smoothly back into the game, e.g. 9 ♗e4 f6 10 h3 ♘h6 11 exf6 exf6 12 ♗d5+! ♔h8 13 0-0 ♘f5 14 ♖e1. Here White's pieces are more active than Black's and the d-pawn covers key central squares. In Golovey-Borisenko, USSR 1971 Black tried tactics to break the bind, yet after 14...♘cxd4 15 ♘xd4 ♘xd4 16 ♕xd4 c6 17 ♗f4 cxd5 18 ♘xd5 ♗f5 19 ♖e7 White's pieces continued to rule the board.

(c) **8...♘h5** turns out to be the best square, a discovery made by "trial and error". After 9 ♗e2 ♗g4 10 ♗e3 f6! 11 exf6 ♗xf6 12 ♘e4 ♕d5 13 ♘xf6+ exf6 14 0-0 ♖ae8 15 ♗h6 ♘g7, Katalymov-Kuzmin, USSR 1980, Black has smoothly completed his development. White retains a tiny edge with 16 c3 because he is the only one with a primary central pawn.

Closed Games

The majority of grandmasters currently prefer closed openings when playing White. The main reason for this is their confidence that they will be able to obtain some characteristic advantage from the opening (e.g. more space, superior central influence, faster piece development), while running less risk of tactical surprises than if opening 1 e4. More control and more comfort at less risk are the reasons for the popularity of 1 d4, 1 c4 and 1 ⬥f3.

The comfort of playing White in a closed opening also means that there is more leeway in applying the principle "recapture towards the centre". If in doubt, do so, yet much more often than is true for the situations when you are Black or White in 1 e4 openings, either recapture will be equally good. A person's playing style often becomes the determining factor. In this section I will discuss the three most important recapture situations.

(A) *cxd4 vs. exd4*
This important choice occurs frequently when Black challenges White's d-pawn via ...c5 and White decides to support d4 by playing both c3 and e3. This motif is a familiar guest in the Colle Opening (1 d4 ⬥f6 2 ⬥f3 e6 3 e3 c5), the Torre attack (1 d4 ⬥f6 2 ⬥f3 e6 3 ⬥g5 c5) as well as several variations against the King's Indian.

It should be stressed that whereas cxd4 is truly a "toward

the centre" recapture, exd4 is a neutral one because the e-pawn replaces the d-pawn. Still, it will also have its positive points. Let us consider the following line of the London system against the King's Indian Defence (A48): **1 d4 ⬥f6 2 ⬥f3 g6 3 ⬤f4 ⬤g7 4 ⬥bd2 0-0 5 e3 d6 6 h3 c5 7 c3 cxd4**

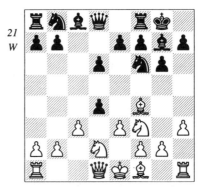

21 W

(1) *8 cxd4*
White hereby enhances his central influence since – despite the otherwise symmetrical central configuration – his d-pawn is on the fourth rank while Black's is on the third rank. Yet the most important question is: will White be able to control the open c-file? Because of the time lost in safeguarding the dark-squared bishop (6 h3), the prospects for this are poor and therefore so are his chances for an opening advantage. In P.Keres-F.Gheorghiou, Varna Olympiad 1962, Black achieved ready equality in a quasi-symmetrical position after 8...⬥c6 9 ⬤c4

♗f5 10 0-0 ♖c8 11 ♕e2 ♘a5 12 ♗d3 ♗xd3 13 ♕xd3 ♕b6 14 ♖ab1 ♘d5 15 ♗g5 h6.

(2) 8 exd4

White unbalances the position at the risk of leaving Black with the only e-pawn. If Black can safely get in ...e5, White can find himself with the inferior centre. White's strategy should be to aim for some pressure along the half-open e-file while preventing ...e5 and trying to enjoy the spatial advantage from the d4-pawn. Black should not play ...d5 as that will seriously weaken e5 and open up the diagonal of White's dark-squared bishop. At present, whenever White is playing seriously for the win, the asymmetrical 8 exd4 recapture is chosen. A thematic sequence then is: 8...♘c6 9 ♗e2 ♖e8 10 ♘c4! ♗e6 11 0-0 ♖c8 (11...♘d5?! 12 ♗d2 ♖c8?! just misplaces Black's pieces, leading to an initiative for White after 13 ♘g5 ♗d7 14 ♕b3 h6 15 ♗f3, D.Janowski-F.Marshall, New York 1924) 12 ♗h2 (12 ♘e3! is better) 12...♗h6 13 ♖e1 ♘a5 with probably equal chances in an unbalanced position, R.Holmov-E.Gufeld, USSR 1959.

If White knows how he wants to recapture, then, of course, he should respond to ...c5 with the "desired" pawn. In the Torre Attack, after **1 d4 ♘f6 2 ♘f3 e6 3 ♗g5 c5** (A46) – see Diagram 22 – Black threatens to destroy White's control of d4.

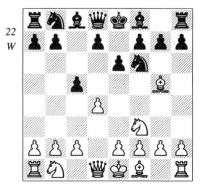

22
W

To prevent this, White must choose either 4 c3 or 4 e3. Moreover, after either move , Black can attack White's queenside with 4...♕b6. Therefore White must also have confidence in having a comfortable response to that. The consequences are as follows:

(1) 4 c3 ♕b6! 5 ♕c2 cxd4! 6 cxd4

White has safeguarded b2 and retained control of d4. However, Black gets first jump on the c-file with comfortable equality:

6...♘c6 7 e3 d5 8 ♘c3 ♗d7! 9 ♗b5 (9 ♗e2 ♖c8) 9...♘e4 10 0-0 ♘xc3 11 ♗xc6 ♕xc6 12 ♘e5! ♕a4 13 ♕xc3 ♖c8 14 ♕d2 f6, F.Marshall-S.Tartakower, Berlin 1928.

(2) 4 e3

Just as in Diagram 21, so here it has become established by GM practice that the exd4 recapture is required to retain hopes for some advantage. The two thematic responses now are:

(a) **4...cxd4 5 exd4 ♗e7 6 ♘bd2 d6 7 c3 ♘bd7 8 ♗d3 b6 9 ♘c4 ♗b7 10 ♕e2 ♕c7 11 0-0 0-0 12 ♖fe1**

♖fe8 13 ♖ad1 ♘f8, C.Torre-Emanuel Lasker, Moscow 1925. White's spatial superiority should give him a small edge, but Black's position remains very solid.
(b) **4...♕b6 5 ♘bd2! ♕xb2 6 ♗d3 ♕c3 7 0-0,** G.Kamsky-N.de Firmian, Reykjavik 1990. White's substantial development advantage compensates fully for the missing pawn.

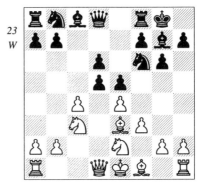

(B) *cxd5 vs. exd5*
This has become the most important "choice" question for White in closed games. It occurs in Benoni or King's Indian systems where Black has challenged White's d4 either by playing ...c5 or ...e5, White has advanced his pawn to d5 and Black again confronts the d-pawn via ...e6 or ...c6. The over-all recapture principles are as follows:

- Where the sequence has been: "1"...e5 2 d5 c6 and 3...cxd5, White should usually recapture towards the centre with cxd5.
- Where the sequence has been: "1"...c5 2 d5 e6 and 3...exd5, both 4 cxd5 and 4 exd5 are usually of equal value.

(1) The first situation can be well illustrated by the following important line in the Sämisch Variation against the King's Indian Defence:
1 d4 ♘f6 2 c4 g6 3 ♘c3 ♗g7 4 e4 d6 5 f3 0-0 6 ♗e3 e5 7 d5 c6 8 ♘ge2 cxd5 (E89)

White has three ways of recapturing:
(a) **9 ♘xd5,** though "playable", is not played because the exchange of two sets of minor pieces after 9...♘xd5 10 cxd5 ♗h6! (11 ♗xh6 ♕h4+) decreases the importance of White's spatial superiority while 10 ♕xd5?! ♘c6 11 ♕d2 f5 12 ♘c3 ♘d4, K.Robatsch-L.Barden, Hastings 1961/62, already yields the initiative to Black.
(b) **9 exd5?!** is inferior because Black remains with the only e-pawn which is already well placed on the fourth rank and with the potential, after ...f5, to advance further to e4, thereby opening the a1-h8 diagonal for Black's dark-squared bishop.
(c) **9 cxd5** is thematic and best. White enhances his central and spatial superiority, opens the c-file for possible infiltration, keeps Black's dark-squared bishop closeted – and has no deficiencies whatever.
(2) Depending on how White recaptures, the following sequence

can lead to either the Benoni Defence or the King's Indian Defence:

1 d4 ♘f6 2 c4 g6 3 ♘c3 ♗g7 4 e4 d6 5 f4 0-0 6 ♗e2 c5 7 d5 e6 8 ♘f3 exd5

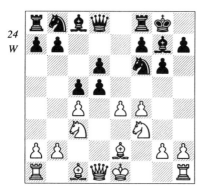

24
W

Here also there are three moves to consider:

(a) **9 e5?!** is overambitious and Black gains the advantage after 9...♘e4! 10 cxd5 ♘xc3 11 bxc3 ♘d7 12 e6 fxe6 13 dxe6 ♘b6.

(b) **9 cxd5** is thematic and ambitious, transposing to the Benoni (the Benoni move-order is 1 d4 ♘f6 2 c4 c5 3 d5 e6 4 ♘c3 exd5 5 cxd5 d6 6 e4 g6 7 f4 ♗g7 8 ♘f3 0-0 9 ♗e2). White has built a ferocious-looking centre: the d-pawn is into Black's territory, the sole e-pawn on the board has advanced to the fourth rank and the secondary f-pawn is also on the fourth rank, already in a position to support the e5 advance. The danger of course is that the centre may explode, leaving White's position in a shambles. A typical continuation

is 9...♗g4 10 h3 ♗xf3 11 ♗xf3 ♖e8 12 0-0 a6 13 a4 ♘bd7 14 ♕c2 ♕c7 15 a5 c4 16 ♗e3 and now instead of 16...♘c5?! allowing 17 e5!, M.Franett-R.Gutman, Portland 1991, with a clear advantage to White, Ftačnik and Franett suggest 16...♖ac8 as correct.

(c) **9 exd5** eliminates all danger to White's centre by voluntarily "removing" the e-pawn from the board. White counts on the space advantage formed by having the d-pawn on d5 as the building block for some initiative. Recent experience has shown that Black needs to respond radically with 9...♘h5! 10 0-0 ♗xc3! 11 bxc3 f5 to prevent White from exploiting his central and spatial superiority.

It is instructive to note that "good", quiet play does not offer equality, e.g. 9...♖e8 10 0-0 ♘g4 11 h3 ♘e3 12 ♗xe3 ♖xe3 13 ♕d2 ♖e8 14 ♗d3 ♘d7 15 ♖ae1 ♖xe1 16 ♖xe1 ♘f8 17 g4 with a comfortable advantage to White. He has the more active pieces and more space in the centre and queenside. Black has no compensation for his strategic inferiority.

(3) The prospects that White gains from the "neutral" exd5 recapture were well illustrated by B.Spassky-R.Fischer, Belgrade 1992, Match Game 26, which opened: **1 d4 ♘f6 2 c4 c5 3 d5 d6 4 ♘c3 g6 5 e4 ♗g7 6 ♗d3 0-0 7 ♘f3 ♗g4 8 h3 ♗xf3 9 ♕xf3 ♘bd7 10 ♕d1 e6 11 0-0 exd5**

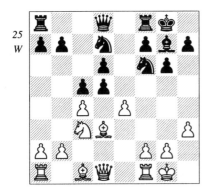

The centrally thematic recapture is, of course, 12 cxd5, leading to Benoni-type clashes where the implication is that White must aim to get in the e5-break to hope to exploit his central superiority. Since Black is well placed to prevent that advance (the d-pawn, and the pieces on d7, g7, f8 and d8 can be mobilised for this), success will require much effort and some risk-taking; even then the result is far from guaranteed. Thus the experienced GM prefers a much more modest approach:

12 exd5

White satisfies himself with the space advantage derived from the d5-pawn and the potential of the bishop pair. Moreover, Black's chances for counterplay are negligible.

12...♘e8 13 ♗d2! ♘e5 14 ♗e2 f5 15 f4 ♘f7 16 g4! ♘h6 17 ♔g2 ♘c7 18 g5 ♘f7 19 ♖b1 ♖e8 20 ♗d3 ♖b8 21 h4 a6 22 ♕c2 b5 23 b3 ♖b7?!

Here and in the future Black should close off the queenside

with 23...b4. Then he would only have to worry about coping with White's kingside initiative.

24 ♖be1 ♖xe1 25 ♖xe1 ♕b8 26 ♗c1 ♕d8 27 ♘e2 bxc4?

The losing move: Black voluntarily opens the queenside so that White's pieces, including the king and both bishops, can infiltrate there. Black should play 27...b4 and come up with a viable plan for defending his kingside. Not that it's easy – and Black's "swimming" with 23...♖b7?!, 25...♕b8 and 26...♕d8 shows it.

28 bxc4! ♘e8 29 h5 ♖e7 30 h6 ♗h8 31 ♗d2 ♖b7 32 ♖b1 ♕b8 33 ♘g3 ♖xb1 34 ♕xb1 ♕xb1 35 ♗xb1 ♗b2 36 ♔f3 ♔f8 37 ♔e2 ♘h8 38 ♔d1 ♔e7 39 ♔c2 ♗d4 40 ♔b3 ♗f2 41 ♘h1 ♗h4?!

With White's king ready to move towards Black's queenside, Fischer's chances are bleak. Yet that is hardly a reason to stalemate the bishop on the edge on of the board! Black should have tried 41...♗d4.

42 ♔a4 ♘c7 43 ♔a5 ♔d7 44 ♔b6 ♔c8 45 ♗c2 ♘f7 46 ♗a4 ♔b8 47 ♗d7 ♘d8 48 ♗c3 ♘a8+ 49 ♔xa6 ♘c7+ 50 ♔b6 ♘a8+ 51 ♔a5 ♔b7 52 ♔b5 ♘c7+ 53 ♔a4 ♘a8 54 ♔b3 ♔c7 55 ♗e8 ♔c8 56 ♗f6 ♘c7 57 ♗xg6! hxg6 58 ♗xd8 1-0

A detailed analysis of this strategic masterpiece by Spassky appears on p.81 in the January 1993 issue of *Chess Life*. See also *Chess Informant* 55, Game 608.

(C) *fxg3 vs. hxg3*
This important recapture question comes about when White's queen's bishop has wound up on g3 and is exchanged off by either Black's king's bishop or king's knight. I will present an example of each. On an over-all basis – compared to the situation where Black's light-squared bishop on g6 is exchanged off by White's king's knight or king's bishop – the decentralising fxg3 will turn out to be fully playable a considerable number of times. Yet it is important for White not to abuse this freedom!

(1) In the Exchange variation of the Slav Defence Black has the choice of whether to aim for early development of the c8-bishop or to emphasise kingside development first. If the latter approach is chosen, then the following line is important: **1 d4 d5 2 c4 c6 3 ♘f3 ♘f6 4 cxd5 cxd5 5 ♘c3 ♘c6 6 ♗f4 e6 7 e3 ♗d6 8 ♗g3** (D13). White does not exchange on d6 since that gains nothing, while helping to develop Black's queen. Instead, paradoxically, White is willing to allow doubled pawns and lose a tempo to induce Black to capture. After **8...♗xg3**, how should White recapture?

(a) **9 fxg3?!** is a ridiculous move: White is left with an ugly e-pawn and decreased central influence, whereas it is not to be seen how the only positive aspect – the half-open f-file – can be utilised.

(b) Correct is the thematic **9 hxg3**. White's central potential is somewhat enhanced, the pawn chain on the right-hand side remains complete and in case Black castles kingside, the half-open h-file will be an effective route along which to attack. White is sure to retain a comfortable opening advantage, e.g. 9...♕d6 10 ♗d3 ♗d7 11 ♖c1 ♖c8 12 ♗b1 h6 13 a3 0-0 14 ♖h4! e5 (otherwise 15 g4 followed by 16 g5 is strong) 15 dxe5 ♘xe5 16 ♘xe5 ♕xe5 17 ♕d4!, V.Chekhov-Kakageldyev, USSR 1979.

To minimise the danger of the attack along the h-file, current theory holds that Black should exchange on g3 *only after White has castled kingside*. Therefore 8...0-0 followed by 9...b6 and 10...♗b7 is considered to be more accurate.

(2) However, either recapture is correct in the following double-edged variation of the Queen's Indian Defence: – **1 d4 ♘f6 2 c4 e6 3 ♘f3 b6 4 ♘c3 ♗b4 5 ♗g5 h6 6 ♗h4 g5 7 ♗g3 ♘h5 8 e3 ♘xg3** (E12) *(D)*.

Black's ambitious pawn advance on the kingside has fundamentally weakened his position on that side of the board, offering White promising vistas along the f- or h-files. Also, in either case White's own king position remains safe enough.

(a) **9 fxg3!?**, though obviously anti-positional, offers potential along the f-file. This is well shown

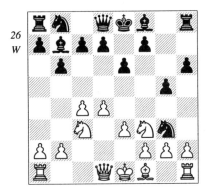

26
W

in O.Romanishin-Z.Ribli, Riga Interzonal 1979: 9...♗g7 10 ♗d3 d6 (safer is 10...♘c6) 11 0-0 ♘d7 12 ♗c2 ♕e7 13 ♕d3 a6?! (safer is 13...0-0-0) 14 ♘d2 c5 15 ♘de4 f5?! 16 dxc5!! ♘xc5 17 ♘xd6+ ♔f8 (17...♔d7 is met by 18 ♘xf5+!) 18 ♘xf5! with a large advantage and a quick White win: 18...exf5? (only the

ending after 18...♘xd3 19 ♘xe7+ offered some drawing chances) 19 ♕xf5+ ♔g8 20 ♘d5 ♕e8 21 ♖ad1 ♖c8 22 b4 ♘e6 23 ♘xb6 ♖c7 24 c5 h5 25 ♖d6 ♖h6 26 ♖xe6! 1-0

(b) **9 hxg3** is strategically correct and keeps Black's h-pawn under pressure, thus discouraging kingside castling. A fighting sequence is shown by M.Taimanov-L.Polugayevsky, USSR 1979: 9...♗g7 10 ♗d3 ♘c6 11 g4 ♕e7 12 ♕a4 a6 13 ♖c1 ♘b4 14 ♗b1 c5 15 a3 cxd4 16 ♘xd4 ♘c6 17 ♗e4 ♗xd4 18 exd4 f5 19 ♗f3 fxg4 20 ♗xg4 ♘xd4 21 ♗h5+ ♔f8 22 0-0, when Taimanov considers that Black's draughty king situation gives White full compensation for the pawn. The game was drawn on move 41.

5 How to tell when equality is reached

You look up a variation in the *Encyclopedia of Chess Openings* and at the end of it there is an = sign; you play over a game from the latest *Chess Informant* and at move 13 there again is the = notation; you open *Chess Life* and in discussing your favourite opening the GM calls the position "equal". Have you ever wondered about the reasoning behind this decision, how the decision was arrived at, and exactly why this position is presumed to be equal? I know that in my early chess-playing days I often wondered about these questions. Here I will try to answer them based on our present level of understanding chess theory. The following two observations are in order: (1) Black can feel satisfied if he/she gains equality in the opening phase; (2) Many re-evaluations of specific variations are continually occurring. Therefore, it is possible that what is currently considered "equal", may not be a year – or even a month – hence.

The "opening equalities" can be divided into the following four categories:

(1) *Symmetrical Equality*

Symmetrical equality means that the position is symmetrical and that *being on move brings no advantage*. For example, in the Symmetrical Variation of the English Opening (see also part Four):

1 c4 c5 2 ♘c3 ♘c6 3 g3 g6 4 ♗g2 ♗g7 5 e3 e6 6 ♘ge2 ♘ge7 7 0-0 0-0 8 d4 cxd4 9 ♘xd4 ♘xd4 10 exd4 d5 11 exd4 d5 11 cxd5 ♘xd5 12 ♘xd5 exd5

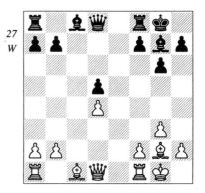

we see that White has no way of establishing permanent pressure. For instance, 13 ♕b3 ♗e6! 14 ♗e3 ♕d7 15 ♖fc1 ♖fc8 16 a4 h5 17 h4 ♖c6 ½-½ I.Bilek-F.Gheorghiu, Palma de Mallorca 1972. Therefore, it is quite in order to call the diagram position "equal".

The following innocuous way of handling the Exchange Variation of the Slav Defence also leads to symmetrical equality: **1 d4 d5 2 c4 c6 3 ♘f3 ♘f6 4 cxd5 cxd5 5 ♘c3 ♘c6 6 ♗f4 ♗f5 7 e3 e6 8 ♗d3 ♗xd3 9 ♕xd3 ♗d6 10 ♗xd6 ♕xd6 11 0-0 0-0 12 ♖ac1**

½-½ A.Wojtkiewicz-E.Torre, Manila 1991. After 12...♖ac8 the symmetrical equality continues.

As can be seen from these two examples, if there is no central tension, nor the chance of introducing this tension, then the likelihood of a symmetrical position leading to symmetrical equality is great. However, if White can initiate central action from a symmetrical build-up, then his chances of keeping an advantage are great. In the Réti Opening's Double Fianchetto Variation: **1 c4 c5 2 ♘f3 ♘f6 3 g3 b6 4 ♗g2 ♗b7 5 0-0 g6 6 b3 ♗g7 7 ♗b2 0-0 8 ♘c3**, continuing the symmetry by means of **8...♘c6** does not guarantee equality because White can break in the centre with **9 d4!**. Then after **9...♘xd4 10 ♘xd4 ♗xg2 11 ♔xg2 cxd4 12 ♕xd4 d6**, White gains clear a spatial superiority with **13 e4** and thereby a normal opening advantage.

As we delve more deeply into some formerly "harmless" variations, we learn that there is more to them than thought earlier. The Exchange Variation of the French Defence, 1 e4 e6 2 d4 d5 3 exd5 exd5, has lately moved up markedly in reputation. After 4 ♘f3, White has a bit of an initiative after both 4...♘f6 5 ♗d3 c5 6 0-0, G.Kasparov-V.Korchnoi, Tilburg 1991 and 4...♗d6 5 c4 ♘f6 6 ♘c3, because in each case White has more options than Black. (See Chapter 14.)

(2) *Forced Equality*

Forced equality results when neither side can afford to deviate from a repetition of moves. A characteristic example is from the following variation of the Grünfeld Defence: **1 d4 ♘f6 2 c4 g6 3 ♘c3 d5 4 ♗f4 ♗g7 5 e3 c5 6 dxc5 ♕a5 7 cxd5** (7 ♖c1 keeps the game going, even though Black obtains approximate equality) **7...♘xd5 8 ♕xd5** (at this point alternatives already lead to an advantage for Black) **8...♗xc3+ 9 bxc3 ♕xc3+ 10 ♔e2 ♕xa1 11 ♗e5 ♕c1!** (11...♕b1? 12 ♗xh8 ♗e6 13 ♕d3! is good for White because Black lacks 13...♗c4) **12 ♗xh8 ♗e6! 13 ♕xb7** (13 ♕e4 ♗c4+ 14 ♔f3 ♕xf1 15 ♕xb7 ♕d1+ 16 ♔g3 ♕d5 also offers White nothing) **13...♕c2+**.

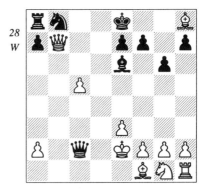

Perpetual check is unavoidable:
(a) **14 ♔f3 ♕f5+ 15 ♔e2** (15 ♔g3?? ♕g4#) **15...♕c2+ ½-½** Vaughan-Purdy, Correspondence 1945.
(b) **14 ♔e1 ♕c1+ ½-½** A.Lupian-A.Adorjan, Manila 1991.

Of course, forced equality does not only appear as a result of such violent clashes. Sophisticated repetitions are also possible. One very important example has robbed White of any chance for an opening advantage in a formerly well thought of variation of the Giuoco Piano: **1 e4 e5 2 ♘f3 ♘c6 3 ♗c4 ♗c5 4 c3 ♘f6 5 d4 exd4 6 cxd4 ♗b4+ 7 ♗d2 ♗xd2+ 8 ♘bxd2 d5 9 exd5 ♘xd5 10 ♕b3**. For over 60 years the normal response was 10...♘ce7, but after 11 0-0 0-0 12 ♖fe1 White's more active pieces and central superiority give him a slight, pleasant riskless initiative.

It was so until A.Miles-V.Korchnoi, South Africa 1979, when Black defanged White's plan with the paradoxical looking **10...♘a5!** 11 **♕a4+ ♘c6!!** (11...c6? 12 ♗xd5! ♕xd5 13 0-0 leaves Black's knight dangerously exposed on the edge, of the board, E.Mednis-B.Rozsa, US Open 1953) Suddenly it turns out that White's queen, bishop and d2-knight co-ordinate poorly and already Black threatens 12...♘b6 exchanging off White's bishop. Moreover, after 12 ♗b3 0-0 Black's active knights are well placed to start menacing White's isolated d-pawn. White also has no way of exploiting the immediate pin on Black's c6-knight, e.g. 12 ♘e5?! 0-0! 13 ♘xc6 ♕e8+ and the initiative is already with Black.

Therefore, White has nothing better than 12 ♕b3 and after the

"forced" **12...♘a5 13 ♕a4+ ♘c6**, the players agreed on the draw.

(3) *Practical equality*

When in a given position factor(s) which in theory should offer an advantage lead to nothing usable, then practical equality exists. Perhaps the most common examples occur from many of the main line strategic lines of the Caro-Kann Defence (3 ♘c3 dxe4 4 ♘xe4 ♗f5 or 4...♘d7). Somewhere around moves 16-20 White still has a slight central advantage as a result of having the d-pawn on d4, but Black has smoothly completed his development, has no structural weaknesses and some minor pieces have been exchanged. Therefore, in a practical sense, the position is equal.

How can we tell that a position has practical equality? Of course, hindsight with the help of analysis and tournament play is a great teacher. However, good positional players with experience in a strategic opening will also make the correct evaluation in a large majority of situations. Let us see how we can learn to make the correct judgements from the following popular variation of the English Opening: **1 c4 c5 2 ♘f3 ♘f6 3 ♘c3 ♘c6 4 g3 g6 5 ♗g2 ♗g7 6 0-0 0-0 7 d4 cxd4 8 ♘xd4 ♘xd4 9 ♕xd4 d6 10 ♕d3 ♗f5 11 e4 ♗e6 12 ♗d2 a6 13 b3 ♖b8 14 ♖ac1 ♕d7** *(D)*

White's c- and e-pawns, being on the fourth rank, give White a

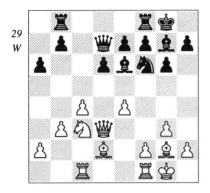

slight spatial advantage in the centre. This is White's only trump. Can something be done with it? Let's see:

(1) The game J.Ehlvest-U.Andersson, Reggio Emilia 1991 continued: **15 a4** (to stop counterplay by 15...b5) 15...♗h3! 16 f3 ♗xg2 17 ♔xg2 ♖fc8! 18 ♗e3 ♕d8. White still has his spatial advantage, but the exchange of light-squared bishops has lightened Black's load and Black's remaining pieces are well co-ordinated to repulse any White activity. Ehlvest rates this position "=", i.e. Black has *practical equality*. Obviously not satisfied with such a situation, Ehlvest improved from Diagram 29 the very next time he had the opportunity:

(2) J.Ehlvest-G.Kamsky, Reggio Emilia 1991: **15 ♘d5!** b5 16 ♖fe1! ♖b7 17 ♕f1!. White has activated his forces, while preventing the exchanging ...♗h3.

The dividing line between "practical equality " and "no equality" can be very narrow even when

queens have been exchanged off early. In the game B.Gulko-R.Cifuentes, Novi Sad Olympiad 1990, Black chose an unusual third move and White immediately entered the endgame: **1 d4 d6 2 e4 ♘f6 3 ♘c3 e5!? 4 dxe5 dxe5 5 ♕xd8+ ♔xd8 6 ♘f3 ♗d6 7 ♗c4.**

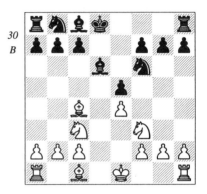

White has a bit of an initiative, Black has given up the castling privilege and his dark-squared bishop is tied down to defending the e-pawn. However, the queens are off and the pawn formation is symmetrical. The valid question therefore is: how close is Black to equality?

The game continued:

7...♔e7 8 ♗g5 ♗e6 9 ♘d5+

After 9 ♗xe6 ♔xe6 Black has practical equality because White is not able to do anything with his slight edge in development.

9...♗xd5 10 ♗xd5 c6 11 ♗b3 h6?!

This loss of time has serious consequences. Cifuentes instead suggests "11...♘bd7 =". What he is referring to is *practical equality*. After 12 0-0-0, the main line seems to be 12...♘c5 (12...h6?! 13 ♘h4! is unpleasant for Black, e.g. 13...g6 14 ♗xf6+ ♘xf6 15 ♗xf7!) 13 ♗xf6+ gxf6 14 ♘h4 ♘xb3+ 15 axb3 ♔e6 16 ♘f5 ♖ad8 17 ♖d3 ♗c7!. This is unclear to me and requires a considerable amount of additional work.

In any case, I think that Black has an easier route in going for practical equality with 11...♘a6 12 0-0-0 ♖ad8. Then in some variations neither the ♘d7 nor the ♗d6 hang. One example: 13 ♘h4 g6 14 ♖d3 ♘c5! 15 ♗xf6+ ♔xf6 16 ♖f3+ ♔g5 and Black is fine.

12 ♗xf6+! ♔xf6 13 0-0-0 ♖d8 14 ♖d3! with a clear advantage for White.

(4) *Dynamic equality*

Dynamic equality means that *the chances are equal*. In general, hard work – both at home and over the board – is required to ascertain that a position is in dynamic balance. Moreover, since the position is inherently unbalanced, there is always a substantial risk that a new discovery will change the evaluation from "equal". And even if the chances are in fact equal, the unbalanced nature of the position still means that whoever will play better will win.

I will illustrate this section with an example where the predominant considerations are strategic in nature and with another example where tactical features predominate.

(a) *Primarily strategic*

Return again to Diagram 30. Gulko, having been on the White side in the previous example, found himself Black some months later in W.Browne-B.Gulko, US Championship 1991, Match Game 1. Not wanting to labour towards practical equality he chose a more ambitious plan:

7...♗e6!? 8 ♗xe6 fxe6 9 ♗e3 ♘c6!

It is the text that is a genuine novelty and Gulko rates the position after it as "=", i.e. having dynamic equality. As compensation for his isolated doubled pawns, Black has control of d5 and f5, chances along the half-open f-file and control of the important d4-square.

Yet I want to caution the reader not to uncritically accept such doubled isolated pawns. In fact, in Antunes-L.Brunner, Haifa 1989, after the insipid move 9...♘bd7?! Black did not have sufficient compensation for his structural deficiency.

10 a3 a6 11 ♔e2 ♔e7 12 ♖hd1 h6 13 h3 ♖hf8 14 ♖d3 ♘h5

Now instead of the careless 15 ♘h4? ♘d4+! (16 ♗xd4? ♘f4+) and advantage to Black, Gulko suggests 15 g3 ♘f6!, with continued dynamic equality. Black's pressure on f4 and e4 compensates for the weakness of the doubled pawns.

(b) *Primarily tactical*

An important tactically balanced position arises from the following variation within the Richter-Rauzer Attack of the Sicilian Defence: **1 e4 c5 2 ♘f3 d6 3 d4 cxd4 4 ♘xd4 ♘f6 5 ♘c3 ♘c6 6 ♗g5 e6 7 ♕d2 a6 8 0-0-0 h6 9 ♗f4 ♗d7 10 ♘xc6 ♗xc6 11 f3 d5 12 ♕e1 ♗b4 13 a3 ♗a5 14 ♗d2**

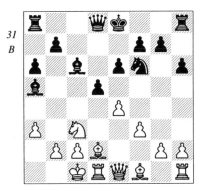

31
B

The has all the hallmarks of the Sicilian: White will attack in the centre and kingside; Black's chances remain on the queenside. Black's 8...h6 has made his kingside vulnerable to a pawn storm; White's 13 a3 has exposed the queenside to a pawn attack. This variation became very popular in 1990 and 1991, with Black running into difficulties after 14...d4, 14...dxe4 and 14...♕e7. Thus in I.Glek-G.Serper, USSR 1991 Black attempted to improve with

14...b5!?

Writing in *Chess Informant* 52, Serper called this position "=",

which obviously refers to dynamic equality. In hindsight the text appears obvious, i.e. since Black's chances are on the queenside, he proceeds directly with his attack. An important aspect of playing ...b5 immediately is that now closing the centre by 15 e5 ♘d7 16 f4 only helps Black because after 16...♗b6! the b-pawn is already mobilised so Black is ready to start storming White's queenside. According to analysis by Holmov, Black can even afford to undermine White's central support by 16...g5!.

However, in the later game R.Lau-Kovalev, Germany 1992, White improved with 15 ♔b1!, threatening 16 ♘xd5!. Therefore, currently Black prefers to go for dynamic equality with the developing 14...♖c8.

15 exd5 ♘xd5 16 ♗d3 ♖c8! 17 ♔b1

Serper points out that after 17 ♕g3 Black also plays 17...0-0, as 18 ♗xh6? ♗xc3 19 bxc3 ♕f6 leaves White's king the more exposed.

17...0-0 18 ♘xd5 ♗xd2

Now after 19 ♕xd2?! ♗xd5 Black had the superior attacking chances and went on to win in 49 moves. According to Serper, White can retain dynamic equality with 19 ♕e4! g6 20 ♖xd2 ♗xd5 21 ♕e3 since White's queen and d2-rook are then more actively placed and the pawn cover for Black's king is somewhat looser.

6 Minor piece or three pawns: which is better?

It is accepted knowledge that a bishop or knight is worth approximately three pawns. I fully agree that as part of calculating a material balance this relationship is sound and should be used. Therefore, for making an actual decision during a game, the relevant questions become:

(1) You are rather sure of getting three pawns in return for sacrificing a minor piece. Should you do it?

(2) You are planning a move which allows your opponent to sacrifice a minor piece for three pawns. Should you go ahead with it?

Of course, there are no cookbook answers available. Yet there are reliable principles to serve as guides. These are:

(1) The closer a position is to an endgame, the more likely it is that the pawns are better than the piece.

(2) If the side with the extra piece is behind in development, the chances are good that that side will not be able to exploit the advantage of the piece. Then the side with the pawns usually has the superior chances.

(3) The earlier the stage of the game, the more likely that the piece is important. Early play generally stresses development rather than pawns and an extra piece in the attack can easily be the decisive element.

(4) In open positions, the side with the piece usually has the advantage because it can make faster use of its forces. Mobilising pawns is an inherently slower process.

Open variations in the Sicilian Defence offer excellent opportunities for White to give up a minor piece for three pawns. The two most common sacrificial points are on b5 and e6. I shall take a look at four instructive examples.

(1) *Three good pawns in a stable position, bordering on an endgame, normally favour the pawns' side.*

Let us follow the course of developments in E.Mednis-D.Kerr, US Open 1956, Sicilian Defence, Najdorf Variation (B95):

1 e4 c5 2 ♘f3 d6 3 d4 cxd4 4 ♘xd4 ♘f6 5 ♘c3 a6 6 ♗g5 e6 7 ♕f3

In the early days of the sharp 6 ♗g5 variation (mid 1950s), the text was normal. Subsequently, 7 f4 became the main line.

7...♘bd7 8 0-0-0 ♕c7 9 ♕g3 b5?!

Too ambitious. The sound approach is 9...♗e7.

10 ♗xb5! axb5 11 ♘dxb5 ♕b8
The alternatives are worse:

(1) **11...♕a5?** 12 ♗xf6 ♘xf6 13 ♖xd6! ♘xe4 14 ♘c7+ ♕xc7 15 ♖xe6+ ♔d7 16 ♖d1+ ♘d6 17 ♘b5 ♕c5 18 ♘xd6 ♔xe6 19 ♕b3+ ♔e5 20 f4+! ♔xf4 21 ♕g3#, Grankin-Gutkin, USSR 1968.

(2) **11...♕c5?** 12 ♗e3! ♕c6 13 ♘xd6+ ♗xd6 14 ♖xd6 ♕b7 15 e5 ♘h5 16 ♕g4 g6 17 ♖xe6+! fxe6 18 ♕xe6+ ♔f8 19 ♗h6+ ♘g7 20 ♘d5, with a crushing attack, Verner-Belyavsky, USSR 1970.

12 ♘xd6+ ♗xd6 13 ♕xd6 ♕xd6 14 ♖xd6

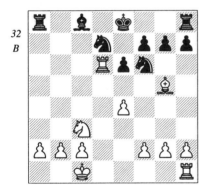

32
B

White has the advantage since he has three connected passed pawns, no vulnerable point and is even somewhat ahead in development.

14...♖a6?!
Exchanging off Black's rook simplifies the position, something which is generally good for the side with the pawns. Moreover

the absence of the queen's rook makes it easier for White to mobilise the queenside. No better is 14...♗b7?!, when White won rapidly in H.van Riemsdyk-Silva, Brazil 1978: 15 ♖hd1 0-0-0 16 f3 h6 17 ♗h4 ♘e5 18 ♘b5! ♘c6 19 ♗f2 ♔b8?! 20 ♗g3! ♔a8 21 ♖1d3! ♖xd6 22 ♖a3+ ♔b8 23 ♘xd6 e5 24 ♖b3 ♘a5 25 ♖b5 1-0.

I believe that Black does best by immediately "putting the question" to the bishop with 14...h6!, though after either 15 ♗d2 ♗b7 16 f3, Bronstein-Najdorf, USSR-Argentina 1954 or 15 ♗xf6 ♘xf6 16 ♖hd1 ♗b7 17 f3, Fichtl-Dolezal, CSSR Championship, 1954, White retains an advantage.

15 ♖xa6 ♗xa6 16 f3 ♔d8 17 ♖d1 ♔c7 18 ♗f4+ e5 19 ♗e3 ♖e8 20 a4! ♖e6 21 b4
The queenside pawns represent White's trump, and therefore energetic mobilisation is highly desirable.

21...♗c4 22 ♔b2 ♖d6 23 ♖a1!
In principle White would like to exchange rooks, but the moment isn't yet right since after 23 ♖xd6?! ♔xd6 Black gets counterplay on the kingside with 24...♗f1 and 25...♗g2.

23...♔b7 24 b5 ♘e8 25 ♔a3! f6 26 ♔b4 ♗f7 27 a5 ♘c7 28 a6+ ♔b8 29 ♖d1!
With White's king and queenside mobilised and Black's bishop deactivated, the exchange of rooks is bound to enhance White's "pawn power".

29...♖xd1 30 ♘xd1 ♘e6 31 c3 ♘f4 32 ♗xf4 exf4 33 ♘b2 ♔c7 34 c4 ♘e5 35 c5 ♗e8 36 c6 ♔b8 37 ♘c4! ♘xc4 38 ♔xc4 g5 39 ♔c5 1-0

The pawns win, e.g. **39...♔a7 40 ♔d6 ♔b6 41 c7.**

(2) *Some looseness in the pawns' structure give the side with the extra minor piece good chances for sufficient counterplay, even if the queens are off.*

The above principle is well illustrated by M.Tseitlin-L.Polugayevsky, USSR Championship 1971, Sicilian Defence, Najdorf Variation (B96):

1 e4 c5 2 ♘f3 d6 3 d4 cxd4 4 ♘xd4 ♘f6 5 ♘c3 a6 6 ♗g5 e6 7 f4 ♘bd7 8 ♗c4

The flexible 8 ♕f3 has largely superseded the text, yet Black should give it sufficient respect and respond with 8...♕b6.

8...b5?! 9 ♗xe6! fxe6 10 ♘xe6 ♕a5

White's attack is too strong after 10...♕b6? 11 ♘d5! ♘xd5 12 ♕xd5, e.g. 12...♗b7?! 13 ♘c7+! ♕xc7 14 ♕e6+ ♗e7 15 ♕xe7#.

11 ♘xf8 ♖xf8 12 ♕xd6

Here also White's attack is very strong (12...b4? 13 ♘d5!), forcing Black to head for the exchange of queens.

12...♕b6 13 0-0-0 ♕xd6 14 ♖xd6 *(D)*

White's piece deployment is exactly the same as in Diagram 32. However, the pawn configuration on the board is completely

33
B

different and this factor is favourable to Black. As a general principle, the player with the piece wants to have pawns on both sides of the board so as to deny the opponent the inherent power of three connected passed pawns.

Theory rates this position as unclear. I would not be surprised if *with perfect play*, Black can prove that the chances are equal. However, in practical play Black has the harder task – as shown by the fact that it is the much stronger player who loses.

14...b4 15 ♘a4

Subsequently, in M.Matulović-G.Tringov, Vrnjačka Banja 1973, White was successful with 15 ♘e2 h6?! (according to Krnić, the immediate 15...♘c5 is required) 16 ♗h4 ♘c5 17 ♘g3 ♗b7 18 ♖e1 when Black's king was very uncomfortable in the centre.

15...h6 16 ♗h4 a5 17 ♖hd1 ♖a6 18 ♖6d4! ♖c6 19 h3 ♘h5 20 f5 g5 21 ♗e1 ♘f4?

According to Polugayevsky, correct is the immediate 21...♖f7 with roughly equal chances. It turns out that on f4 the knight is more a spectator than a player.

22 ♖1d2 ♖f7 23 ♗g3 ♘e5 24 ♖d8+ ♔e7 25 b3 ♘d7?!

Chases the rook to a better location. Black should play the active 25...♗a6! (Polugayevsky).

26 ♖h8 ♗b7 27 ♔b2 ♖cf6 28 h4!

The start of the undermining of Black's position. He can't respond with 28...♗xe4?, as the bishop is lost after 29 ♗xf4 gxf4 30 ♖e2.

28...♖g7 29 hxg5 hxg5 30 ♗f2! ♖d6 31 ♗d4 ♗xe4 32 g3! ♖f7

The knight cannot be saved: 32...♘g2 33 f6+ ♘xf6 34 ♗c5.

33 gxf4 gxf4 34 ♘b6! ♖xf5

More poetic is the loss after 34...♘xb6 35 ♗c5 ♘d5 36 ♖h6.

35 ♘c8+ ♔e6 36 ♖e8+ 1-0

(3) *With queens on the board and no particular problems on either side, dynamic equilibrium is the most likely result. Whoever plays better will win.*

An excellent example of this course is G.Kamsky-I.Gurevich, US Championship 1991, Sicilian Defence, Najdorf Variation (B97):

1 e4 c5 2 ♘f3 d6 3 d4 cxd4 4 ♘xd4 ♘f6 5 ♘c3 a6 6 ♗g5 e6 7 f4 ♕b6 8 ♘b3 ♗e7 9 ♕f3 ♘bd7 10 0-0-0 ♕c7 11 ♕g3 b5! 12 ♗xf6

Because White's d4-knight has been "shunted" to the inactive b3 location, the sacrifice on b5 needs preparation. If now 12...♗xf6 13 ♗xb5! Black should reply 13...0-0, hoping for queenside counterplay as compensation for the pawn, because 13...axb5? is bad: 14 ♘xb5 ♕b8 15 ♘xd6+ ♔f8 16 e5 with three excellent pawns for the piece and a strong bind on the position (Gurevich).

12...♘xf6 13 e5!

White is not tempted by 13 ♕xg7?! ♖g8 14 ♕h6 ♘g4 15 ♕xh7 ♔f8 when Black has strong counterplay (Kamsky). Instead White starts his own sacrificing:

13...dxe5 14 fxe5 ♘d7 15 ♗xb5!? axb5 16 ♘xb5 ♕b6 17 ♕xg7 ♖f8 18 ♘d6+ ♗xd6 19 exd6

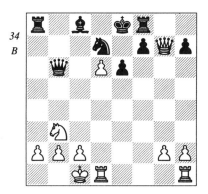

The smoke has cleared and White has his "three good pawns" for the piece and even has four connected passed pawns. Yet the pawns are where White's king is and with Black's queen and a8-rook ready to menace the king, the pawns are required as shelter. Moreover, Black's minor pieces are also "quite good": the knight effectively blockades the d-pawn and the bishop will find an open long diagonal. I think the position is in dynamic balance.

Black now avoids 19...♖xa2 because of 20 ♖he1, threatening 21 ♖xe6+. Moreover, White can then capture the h-pawn at his convenience. Instead Black improves the position of his queen while forcing back the enemy queen.

19...♕e3+! 20 ♔b1 ♕e5 21 ♕g4!

The exchange of queens favours Black: his bishop and f8-rook will have open lines, the e-pawn is passed and it will be difficult for White to mobilise his queenside. 21 ♕xh7?! allows Black to activate his forces: 21...♖h8 22 ♕d3 ♗a6 23 ♕d2 ♗b7! 24 ♖he1 ♕xh2 (Kamsky).

21...h5 22 ♕h4 ♕f6 23 ♕xh5 ♖h8 24 ♕g4 ♗b7 25 ♖he1 ♕h4

According to Gurevich Black also has good counterplay after 25...♔f8!? 26 ♖f1 ♕h6 27 ♕c4 ♖c8 28 ♕b5 ♗c6 29 ♕a6 ♔g7 30 ♖d4 ♘e5!.

26 ♕g7 ♕f6 27 ♕g3 ♕h4?

White now achieves excellent piece co-ordination and puts a stop to Black's queenside play. Correct is 27...♖a4! 28 ♕d3 ♖hh4 29 a3 ♗c6! which Gurevich considers "unclear".

28 ♕e3 ♕xh2 29 ♘d4! ♗d5 30 b3 ♕h6 31 ♕e2 ♔f8 32 ♘b5 ♗c6 33 ♘d4

Stronger is 33 ♘c7! ♖b8 34 ♕c4 ♗xg2 35 ♖g1! when the vulnerable Black king position will give

White a winning attack (Gurevich).

33...♗d5 34 ♖f1 ♕g6 35 g4! ♖e8?! 36 ♘b5 ♖d8 37 ♘c7 ♗e4 38 ♖f4! ♘f6 39 ♘xe6+! fxe6 40 ♖df1

As a result of having denuded Black's king, White wins back the material with interest. The resulting material balance of rook and passed pawns vs. two minor pieces is outside our theme so that I'll give the rest of the moves without comments. Kamsky realises his positional and material superiority convincingly.

40...♖h1 41 ♖xh1 ♔g7 42 ♖hf1 ♘d5 43 ♖f7+ ♔g8 44 ♕d2 ♕xg4 45 d7! ♕h4 46 ♕a5 ♗xc2+ 47 ♔b2! ♗f5 48 ♖7xf5! ♖xd7 49 ♕a8+ ♖d8 50 ♖g1+ ♔h7 51 ♕b7+ 1-0

(4) *When planning to sacrifice a minor piece for three pawns, make sure that in fact you get three pawns. The inexhaustibility of chess does periodically cause unpleasant surprises.*

It is very instructive to see what befalls White in L.Ljubojević-F.Gheorghiu, Petropolis Interzonal 1973, Sicilian Defence, Richter-Rauzer Attack (B67):

1 e4 c5 2 ♘f3 d6 3 d4 cxd4 4 ♘xd4 ♘f6 5 ♘c3 ♘c6 6 ♗g5 e6 7 ♕d2 a6 8 0-0-0 ♗d7 9 f4 b5!?

This variation is Black's most ambitious and risky way of facing the Richter-Rauzer Attack. Currently White's most popular method of retaining an opening advantage is 10 &xf6. However, in the 1970s repeated attempts were made to punish Black with the violent:

10 &xb5?! axb5 11 ②dxb5

White has three attackers menacing d6 and Black only has one defender. "Common sense" should tell us that the d-pawn must fall. Yet Black has a most surprising indirect defence/counterattack which turns the tables.

11...②b4!!

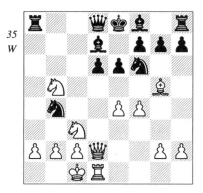

The difference from the earlier examples is that Black's queen's knight is more actively placed on c6 than on d7 and thus can be immediately used for a counterattack. White has no satisfactory continuation:

(1) **12 e5 ②xa2+ 13 ②xa2 ℤxa2 14 &b1 &xb5! 15 &xa2 ₩a8+ 16 &b1 ②e4**, with Black having the attack and a slight material advantage.

(2) **12 &b1 ②xa2! 13 ②xa2 &xb5**. White is a piece down and has the less safe king.

(3) **12 a3 ②a2+! 13 ②xa2 &xb5 14 ②c3 &c6 15 ₩e2 ₩b6**. White has no compensation for his material inferiority, Zukov-Zavyalov, USSR 1977.

12 &xf6

The published sources give the game continuation as 12 ②xd6+ &xd6 13 ₩xd6 ②xa2+ 14 ②xa2 ℤxa2 15 &b1 ℤa7 16 &xf6 gxf6. However, instead of 15...ℤa7, the immediate 15...₩a8! is so obviously decisive (16 b3 ℤa1+ 17 &b2 ₩a2+ 18 &c3 ②xe4+) that I find it inconceivable that Gheorghiu would have missed it. Therefore, I'm using the move-order which to me seems the more likely one.

12...gxf6 13 ②xd6+ &xd6 14 ₩xd6 ②xa2+ 15 ②xa2 ℤxa2 16 &b1 ℤa7!

Protecting the bishop and so threatening the potent 17...₩a8. White's problems are that having only two pawns for the piece, endgames are untenable and in the middlegame his insecure king doesn't allow the luxury of just concentrating on attacking the enemy king.

17 ℤd3 ₩a8 18 b3

The attempt at fleeing with 18 &c1 is no better: 18...&b5 19 ℤa3 ℤxa3 20 bxa3 ℤg8! 21 g3 ₩c6 22 ₩b8+ &e7 23 ₩xg8 &d3 whereupon Black consolidated and won smoothly in Davis-Ghizdavu, USA 1975.

18...&xb5 19 ℤ3d1 &c6 20 ℤhe1 &xe4!

The bishop is safe: 21 ♖xe4 ♖a1+ 22 ♔b2 ♖xd1.

In the coming play Black expertly combines attack and defence to notch up an impressive victory.

21 ♕d4 ♗g6 22 g4 0-0 23 h4 g5! 24 fxe5 ♖c8 25 ♖d2 ♖a2 26 e6 fxe6! 27 ♕xf6 ♖axc2 28 ♖xc2 ♖xc2 29 ♕xe6+ ♗f7 30 ♕xf7+ ♔xf7 31 ♔xc2 ♕g2+! 32 ♔d3 ♕xg4 33 ♖e4 ♕f3+ 34 ♖e3 ♕d5+ 35 ♔c3 ♕c5+ 36 ♔d3 ♕b4 37 ♖e4 ♕xb3+ 38 ♔d4 ♕f3 39 ♔e5 ♕f6+ 40 ♔d5 h6 41 ♔c4 ♔g6 0-1

Part Three: The Modern Thinking

7 Garry Kasparov's influence on modern opening theory

It is quite normal for a world champion to leave a mark on chess development and chess theory. Of course, the extent of the influence is determined by the longevity and domination of his reign as well as his own particular interests. There is no question that the two exceptional world champions in their knowledge of and influence on opening theory are Robert J. Fischer and Garry Kasparov. They proved this early on. Bobby Fischer was 29 when he became world champion; Garry Kasparov is 33 as I write. There are many other parallels between them:

(1) Both are very hard workers, enjoy doing their theoretical digging and feel that it is extremely important to get as large an advantage as possible out of the opening.

(2) Both aim for opening variations having excellent prospects for the initiative.

(3) Both have a wider opening repertoire with White than with Black.

(4) Both are ready to take on more risk as Black than as White.

Therefore, their Black openings are sharper, more double-edged and complicated.

(5) Despite their recognised excellence and creativity in opening play, neither has a variation – much less an opening – named after him.

The major difference is that Bobby Fischer lived in much simpler and less demanding times. The 1980s and 1990s overflow with talented young beavers. Kasparov faces much more competition than Fischer ever did. Due to the quantity and quality of opening theory developments, it is very hard to just keep up with progress. Kasparov is not only keeping up but is at the leading edge of so much that he touches. Moreover, the "playing life" of a variation is getting shorter and shorter before it is abandoned as having been "played out" and attention shifted to a new idea.

To be on top under such working conditions it is not only necessary to be hard working, talented, curious, creative and imaginative. You have to be a searcher for the ultimate truth as well as forever growing in chess maturity. I well remember a question that I asked Kasparov in December 1983 in London after his victory in the Semi-Final Candidates' Match against Korchnoi. The question was: "You became a very strong grandmaster by opening with 1 e4. Yet well before your reaching your 20th birthday you had switched over to 1 d4. Why the switch?" After a few brief moments came this very well phrased answer: "I have learned that after 1 d4 there are more opportunities for richer play." In fact in the Korchnoi match Garry only played 1 d4. Yet as time went on he returned to 1 e4 part of the time and also added 1 c4 to his repertoire. Thus Kasparov is a virtuoso with 1 c4, 1 d4 and 1 e4 – truly a man for all seasons.

I shall now discuss two of the many openings where his influence on modern opening theory has been particularly significant.

(A) *Nimzo-Indian Defence*
In the first game of his 1985 World Championship Match vs. Anatoly Karpov, Garry Kasparov surprised his opponent three times within the first five moves.

(1) After **1 d4 ♘f6 2 c4 e6** Kasparov played **3 ♘c3**.

In his marvellous book *New World Chess Champion*, Kasparov comments as follows about this routine enough move: "In

recent times I have avoided the Nimzo-Indian Defence, giving preference to 3 ♘f3 or 3 g3."

(2) Karpov responded with the expected **3...♗b4**, whereupon came the unexpected **4 ♘f3**, a sound move, yet with a reputation for stodginess. This is how Kasparov describes the moment: "A surprise! Earlier I normally used to play 4 e3, for which Karpov had undoubtedly prepared before the unlimited (i.e. 1984 – EM) match."

(3) Black chose the most common reply **4...c5** and White replied **5 g3**. Karpov now took 29 minutes on his move and during the first five moves had already used 48 minutes.

Let us now take a quick look at the whole game:

5...♘e4 6 ♕d3 ♕a5 7 ♕xe4 ♗xc3+ 8 ♗d2 ♗xd2+ 9 ♘xd2 ♕b6?!

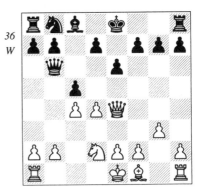

36
W

Kasparov demonstrates that Black cannot afford the loss of time which results from this move. Better are 9...♘c6 or 9...0-0 even though in either case Black is quite far from equality.

10 dxc5! ♕xb2 11 ♖b1 ♕c3 12 ♕d3! ♕xd3 13 exd3

White has a large advantage due to his superior development, active piece placement and spatial superiority. He makes use of these factors in impressive style. When Karpov neglects a few opportunities for minimising his difficulties, he is swept off the board. The rest of the game – with some brief comments based on Kasparov's analysis – is:

13...♘a6 14 d4 ♖b8 15 ♗g2 ♔e7 16 ♔e2 (stronger is 16 0-0!) **16...♖d8 17 ♘e4 b6 18 ♘d6 ♘c7?** (drawing chances are offered by 18...bxc5!) **19 ♖b4! ♘e8 20 ♘xe8** (the accurate capture for White is 20 ♘xc8+!) **20...♔xe8?** (20...♖xe8 is correct) **21 ♖hb1 ♗a6 22 ♔e3 d5 23 cxd6 ♖bc8 24 ♔d3 ♖xd6 25 ♖a4 b5 26 cxb5 ♖b8 27 ♖ab4 ♗b7 28 ♗xb7 ♖xb7 29 a4 ♔e7 30 h4 h6 31 f3 ♖d5 32 ♖c1 ♖bd7 33 a5 g5 34 hxg5 ♖xg5 35 g4 h5 36 b6 axb6 37 axb6 ♖b7 38 ♖c5 f5 39 gxh5 ♖xh5 40 ♔c4 ♖h8 41 ♔b5 ♖a8 42 ♖bc4 1-0**

What Kasparov brought to the 4 ♘f3 variation was a dynamic search for the initiative. This emphasis turned out to be much more important than such static considerations as quality of pawn structure. Overall, the 1985 match saw six Nimzo-Indians, all starting with 4 ♘f3. White scored 3 wins and 3 draws, with the early

course of the game indicating an even greater White advantage. In the other five games the significant developments in the opening phase were as follows (after 1 d4 ♘f6 2 c4 e6 3 ♘c3 ♗b4 4 ♘f3):

Game 7: 4...0-0 5 ♗g5 d6 6 e3 ♘bd7 7 ♕c2 b6 8 ♗d3 ♗xc3+ 9 bxc3! h6 10 ♗h4 ♗b7 11 ♘d2! g5 12 ♗g3 ♘h5.

Now instead of the "unnecessary subtlety" 13 ♕d1, Kasparov gives as much stronger 13 f3! (13...f5 14 ♗f2 ♘df6 15 h3 f4 16 0-0-0; 13...♘xg3 14 hxg3 ♔g7 15 g4! c5 16 ♘f1 ♘f6 17 ♘g3).

Game 11: 4...0-0 5 ♗g5 c5 6 e3 cxd4 7 exd4 h6 8 ♗h4 d5 9 ♖c1! dxc4 10 ♗xc4 ♘c6 11 0-0 ♗e7 12 ♖e1 b6 13 a3 ♗b7 14 ♗g3 ♖c8 15 ♗a2 ♗d6. Here, instead of the liquidating 16 d5, White could have retained his initiative with 16 ♗h4! or 16 ♗e5! (Kasparov)

Games 13 and 17:

Unhappy with the results of the normal type of development of Games 7 and 11, Karpov aimed for long term strategic advantages: **4...c5 5 g3 ♘c6 6 ♗g2 ♘e4 7 ♗d2 ♗xc3 8 bxc3 0-0 9 0-0** *(D)*

White's advantage derives from the dynamic factors of superior development and the powerful central diagonal of his g2-bishop. Black should look for counterplay against White's centre.

(A) Game 13: **9...f5?! 10 ♗e3!! ♘xc3 11 ♕d3 cxd4 12 ♘xd4**

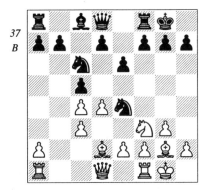

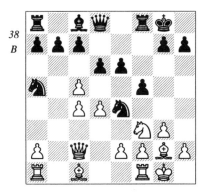

♘e4 13 c5! with very strong pressure for White against Black's position (note that 13...♘xc5? loses a piece after 14 ♘xc6).

(B) Game 17: Thus **9...♘a5** is an improvement. However, if instead of the clumsy **10 dxc5?!** **♕c7!**, White had played **10 ♗f4!**, his opening advantage would have been maintained, e.g. 10...♘xc3? 11 ♕c2! or 10...♘xc4 11 dxc5!.

Game 19: Again dissatisfied with the openings of the previous two examples and being a point behind in the match, Karpov chose a strategically very unbalanced and demanding plan: **4...♘e4 5 ♕c2 f5 6 g3! ♘c6 7 ♗g2 0-0 8 0-0 ♗xc3 9 bxc3 ♘a5 10 c5 d6 11 c4!** *(D)*

White is ready to open up the position to take advantage of his active development and the bishop pair. According to Kasparov, Black should have taken the pawn with 11...dxc5 although White has more than enough compensation after 12 ♗a3 or 12 ♖d1. As played, Black gets nothing for his troubles.

11...b6?! 12 ♗d2! ♘xd2 13 ♘xd2 d5 14 cxd5 exd5 15 e3

As so often happens, the immediate dynamic elements have been transformed into long-term strategic ones: White has the superior bishop, Black has a permanent weakness on e5 and an offside knight. Kasparov shows total maturity (at the age of 22!) to take full advantage of these factors.

15...♗e6 16 ♕c3 ♖f7 17 ♖fc1 ♖b8 18 ♖ab1 ♖e7 19 a4 ♗f7 20 ♗f1! h6 21 ♗d3 ♕d7 22 ♕c2 ♗e6 23 ♗b5 ♕d8 24 ♖d1 g5?! 25 ♘f3 ♖g7 26 ♘e5 f4 27 ♗f1 ♕f6 28 ♗g2 ♖d8 29 e4 dxe4 30 ♗xe4 *(D)*

The position has been opened up so that White's more active forces can take advantage of Black's weakened kingside.

30...♖e7 31 ♕c3 ♗d5 32 ♖e1 ♔g7 33 ♘g4! ♕f7 34 ♗xd5 ♖xd5 35 ♖xe7 ♕xe7 36 ♖e1 ♕d8 37 ♘e5 ♕f6 38 cxb6! ♕xb6 39 gxf4! ♖xd4?! 40 ♘f3 ♘b3 41 ♖b1 ♕f6 42 ♕xc7+ 1-0

After this game, Karpov had had enough of "Kasparov's 4 ♘f3". In

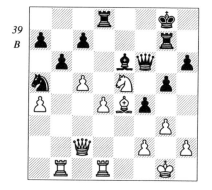

39
B

game 21, he avoided the Nimzo-Indian by playing 3...d5 and in game 23 he decided to take "no chances" and responded to 1 d4 immediately with 1...d5.

The above discussion tells "all" about Garry Kasparov's use of 4 ♘f3 and its resulting influence on the 1985 World Championship Match. How about the effect on the rest of the world? First, some numbers. The "openings code" for the variations with 4 ♘f3 is largely E20 and E21. In the first edition of the *Encyclopedia of Chess Openings E* (ECO E) published in 1978, the 4 ♘f3 variations took up 3 columns and 17 notes under E20 and 10 columns and 62 notes under E21. In the second edition (1991 publication) the references under E20 had exploded to 17 columns and 103 notes and under E21 increased substantially to 12 columns and 84 notes.

The impact on opening theory has also been substantial. Because Kasparov demonstrated that 4

♘f3 is a high-class developing move against the Nimzo-Indian, Black players began to recognise that smooth, efficient development is also the correct plan for Black. Thus, in the sequence from Games 13 and 17 (1 d4 ♘f6 2 c4 e6 3 ♘c3 ♗b4 4 ♘f3 c5 5 g3 ♘c6 6 ♗g2 ♘e4 7 ♗d2), the strategically ambitious 7...♗xc3 has been replaced with the simpler 7...♘xd2 8 ♕xd2 cxd4! 9 ♘xd4 0-0.

More importantly, Black's most reliable continuation has become (after 4...c5 5 g3) cxd4! 6 ♘xd4 0-0 7 ♗g2 d5. Black has usefully exchanged off his secondary central c-pawn for White's primary central d-pawn, has rushed his king to safety by castling and is establishing further central influence with 7...d5. Black's prospects for full, healthy equality are bright.

What is Kasparov saying about these developments? Well, he's not playing 4 ♘f3 any more. Garry is into 4 ♕c2 now, significantly advancing the theory of that variation.

(B) *Scotch Opening*

The starting position of the Scotch results after **1 e4 e5 2 ♘f3 ♘c6 3 d4 exd4 4 ♘xd4**

Though White's position is a good one, the opening has never established much respect with either theoreticians or top players. The reason is that Black was not perceived to be under any particular challenge since his immediate development prospects were

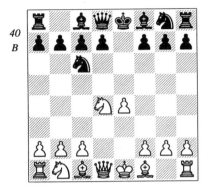

40
B

judged to be equivalent to White's (both sides have open diagonals for the queen and king's bishop, one knight is developed, no point in Black's position is under pressure, etc.). Even Bobby Fischer – who did not shrink from playing the King's Gambit (scoring three wins in three games!) – never ventured it. In the *Chess Informant* (No. 49) leading up to the 1990 World Championship Match only one game with the Scotch appeared.

Yet a marked interest has developed since the match, since in Games 14 and 16 Kasparov chose a characteristically ambitious plan. After the "standard" 4...♘f6, he selected 5 ♘xc6 bxc6 6 e5 ♕e7 7 ♕e2 ♘d5 8 c4. In Game 14, Karpov responded 8...♗a6; in Game 16 he switched to the more modest 8...♘b6. In either case, a dynamic fight is in store. This suits the World Champion just fine; he

won Game 16 and drew Game 14. Again the chess world quickly took notice. While in *Chess Informant* 50 the only two games were the Kasparov-Karpov ones, by No. 54 already 12 full games (and many partial ones) appeared. Moreover Kasparov has continued to play the Scotch, for example in the world championship matches against Nigel Short in 1993 and Viswanathan Anand in 1995. In the Short match the variation that was employed was 4...♗c5 5 ♘xc6 ♕f6 6 ♕d2 dxc6 7 ♘c3 ♗e6 8 ♘a4 (Games 11 and 17). In Kasparov-Anand, Game 8, Black chose the main line, 4...♘f6 5 ♘xc6 bxc6 6 e5 ♕e7 7 ♕e2 ♘d5 8 c4 ♗a6 9 b3. In Kasparov-Karpov, 1990 Match, Game 14, Black played 9...0-0-0. Anand ventured the theoretical novelty 9...g5!?. The brief and exciting game was called a draw after 10 ♗a3 d6 11 exd6 ♕xe2+ 12 ♗xe2 ♗g7 13 cxd5 ♗xe2 14 ♔xe2 ♗xa1 15 ♖c1 0-0-0 16 ♖xc6 ♖he8+ 17 ♔d3 ♖d7 18 ♘c3 ♗xc3 19 ♔xc3 ♖e5 20 ♔c4 ♖e4+ 21 ♔d3 ♖e5 22 ♔c4 ♖e4+.

Of course, the Scotch is only in the early stages of its rigorous scientific investigation. I expect the creative theoretical and practical work to continue at a rapid pace and look forward to the World Champion's rich new contributions.

8 Rehabilitation of opening systems

We are in the scientific age of chess. Perhaps the most visible evidence lies in the opening phase, where an apparently never-ending stream of discoveries is vastly increasing our knowledge and understanding. While it is true that a number of "genuine discoveries" are made, it is hardly surprising that it should be so. I mean, this is occurring throughout the sciences – why not in chess, too? However, what is much less appreciated is that a large number of opening systems have been rehabilitated over the past 20 years. It is this "quiet work" that to me is the most significant development because it has caused a revolution as far as our previous conclusions are concerned. Simply put, a large number of previously "unplayable" systems have turned out to be quite playable now that we understand how to take advantage of their good points.

In this chapter I shall consider two opening systems for Black where this has occurred and three important recent developments in the rehabilitation of White systems. In addition, I will give some guidelines to decide whether or not the underlying conditions required for rehabilitation are present.

Rehabilitation of Black opening systems

The single most important principle to remember is that Black cannot afford as much as White. Whether it involves delaying development, leaving his king in the centre, weakening his position etc., the risk is very great that Black will be punished for his audacity. Black must be far more careful about executing a plan than White would have to be.

(A) Benoni Defence/System
The basic pawn formation in the Benoni results after the moves: 1 d4 ♘f6 2 c4 c5 3 d5.

Black has gladly "forced" the white d-pawn forward so that he can hope to gain certain advantages, e.g. to start undermining the d-pawn with ...e6, to undermine the base (c4) with ...b5, develop the f8-bishop on the now nicely open a1-h8 diagonal. Often these ideas occur in combination.

Let us consider two ways of accomplishing the most radical plan: undermining the d-pawn's base with an early ...b5.

(1) The Blumenfeld Counter-Gambit
This is the old way, and runs:
1 d4 ♘f6 2 c4 c5 3 d5 e6 4 ♘f3
(this same position can occur with

the move-order 1 d4 ♘f6 2 c4 e6 3 ♘f3 c5 4 d5) and now **4...b5**.

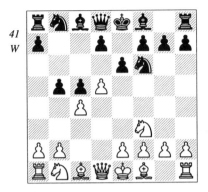

Black is using a double-barrelled approach to try to eliminate White's d5 outpost: first by challenging the pawn with 3...e6 and then by attacking its base with 4..b5. But there are serious problems in its wake: both the kingside and the queenside are weakened and development is delayed. Black cannot afford so many concessions. White gains a clear advantage with **5 ♗g5!**:

(a) **5...♕a5+** 6 ♕d2! ♕xd2+ 7 ♘bxd2 bxc4 8 ♗xf6 gxf6 9 e4 f5 10 ♗xc4 ♗b7 11 0-0 ♗h6 12 ♖fe1, Grünfeld-Rabinowitz, Moscow 1925. Black has weaknesses galore, while also being behind in development.

(b) **5...bxc4** 6 e4! ♕a5+ 7 ♗d2 ♕b6 8 ♘c3 ♗a6 9 ♘e5. Black's position is a mess.

(c) **5...exd5** 6 cxd5 d6 7 e4! a6 8 a4 ♗e7 9 ♗xf6 ♗xf6 10 axb5 ♗xb2 11 ♖a2 ♗f6 12 ♘bd2 0-0 13 ♗d3 ♗b7 14 0-0 axb5 15 ♖xa8

♗xa8 16 ♗xb5, Vaganian-K.Grigorian, USSR (ch) 1971. White has more space and nimble knights; Black's queen's bishop is poorly placed and the d-pawn is a permanent weakness.

The plain fact is that the Blumenfeld is played little in tournaments and I do not expect any rehabilitation. Black simply cannot get away with what the Blumenfeld aims to do.

(2) Benko Gambit

Despite this, the idea of undermining the c4 base is sound. What is needed is an approach that Black can afford. The answer is the Benko Gambit:

1 d4 ♘f6 2 c4 c5 3 d5 b5!

Rather than trying to do two things simultaneously, Black is satisfied to do just one but to do it well. He starts aiming at his main goal one move earlier, while not giving White any chances on the kingside. For instance, 4 ♗g5 is parried by 4...♘e4.

Therefore, to try to "refute" the Benko Gambit, White might as well take the pawn with **4 cxb5 a6! 5 bxa6**. The main lines now continue **5...g6 6 ♘c3 ♗xa6** *(D)*

Already here we see the successful execution of the ...b5 pawn sacrifice. Black will have the open a- and b-files to press against White's queenside, aided by the fianchettoed bishop. Black's only disadvantage will be the missing pawn. He has no really vulnerable

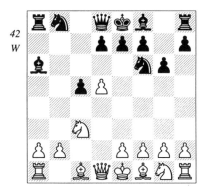

points anywhere. Thus White's major task will have to be the defensive husbanding of the extra pawn. His hopes for near-term active play are scant. The two main lines from diagram 42 are:

(a) 7 e4 ♗xf1 8 ♔xf1 d6 9 ♘f3 ♗g7 10 g3 0-0 11 ♔g2 ♘bd7

(b) 7 ♘f3 ♗g7 8 g3 d6 9 ♗g2 ♘bd7 10 0-0 0-0.

In each case Black has sufficient compensation. I refer to John Fedorowicz's excellent book *The Complete Benko Gambit* (Summit Publishing, 1995) for a detailed discussion of the above variations.

The Benko Gambit move-order was first played by Swedish IM Erik Lundin against Laszlo Szabo in Saltsjobaden 1948. Yet there was no follow-up until 1967, when Pal Benko started playing it with great success. Benko became the true pathfinder and the opening deservedly carries his name. it is my opinion that the Benko Gambit will continue to stand the test of time.

B) Closed Ruy Lopez – main line

In the Closed Ruy Lopez, the main line position results after 1 e4 e5 2 ♘f3 ♘c6 3 ♗b5 a6 4 ♗a4 ♘f6 5 0-0 ♗e7 6 ♖e1 b5 7 ♗b3 d6 8 c3 0-0 9 h3

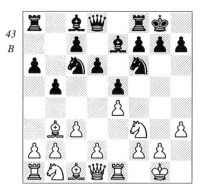

White's last move is strictly preventive: he wants to play d4, without being bothered by ...♗g4. It should be clear to Black that d4 cannot be prevented. Therefore, the important question becomes: how to prepare for it? I will now take a brief look at the historical main line move and three important alternatives, all from the viewpoint of our current understanding of them.

(1) The historical main line: 9...♘a5 10 ♗c2 c5 11 d4

For close to one hundred years this has been considered to be the main line position. With 11...♕c7 Black enters the Chigorin Variation; other important variations include 11...♘c6, 11...♗b7 and 11...♘d7.

The past 20 years has seen a marked diminution of its use. Black's problem is simple: the a5-knight, being on the edge of the board, is poorly placed. No fully satisfactory method has as yet been found to bring it back into the game.

(2) Breyer's Variation: 9...♘b8

When the brilliant young Hungarian master and opening theoretician Gyula Breyer (1894-1921) suggested this move more than 70 years ago, it was met with little else than derision. How can it be correct to undevelop a well-developed knight, thereby losing two tempi? However, there is another side to the coin, i.e. the knight's location on c6: the knight prevents the use of the c-pawn for central purposes and blocks the b7-e4 diagonal for a fianchettoed bishop on b7. The Breyer idea can be seen much more clearly after the normal 10 d4 ♘bd7. Compared to the on-the-edge location on a5, the knight is now centralised and smoothly protects the key e5 point. Moreover, the c-pawn has been freed and from b7 the bishop will have an excellent diagonal. Breyer reasoned that, since in the Closed Ruy Lopez White's build-up is a slow one, Black is fully justified in investing two tempi to improve the co-ordination and placement of his queenside forces. The positive points of this variation were rediscovered around 1965 and in the early to middle 1970s, the "Breyer" was the rage of international play. The main line play within it develops as follows: 11 ♘bd2 ♗b7 12 ♗c2 ♖e8 13 ♘f1 ♗f8 14 ♘g3 g6 15 a4 c5 16 d5

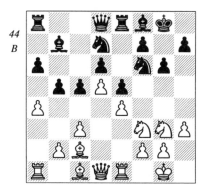

44
B

Here we also see the negative side of the Breyer: White has been able to harmoniously develop his queen's knight and the dark-squared bishop can be developed at his leisure. White has a considerable space advantage and Black is without prospects for counterplay. In my opinion, the Breyer variation will always be strategically sound, yet require laborious defending.

(3) Smyslov's Variation: 9...h6

Former World Champion Vassily Smyslov introduced this into tournament practice in the late 1950s and it was the major alternative to 9...♘a5 until the Breyer Variation came to the fore. If Black wants to be flippant, he can explain his move as follows: "If White can play 9 h3, why can't I play 9...h6?" Well, as I said at the beginning, Black often cannot afford what White can. In our case, 9 h3 was the preparation for the thematically strong 10 d4 advance, whereas Black only prepares for the modest regrouping of his kingside forces via 10...♖e8 and 11...♗f8, without having to worry about White's ♘g5.

The thematic line now goes: 10 d4 ♖e8 11 ♘bd2 ♗f8 12 ♘f1 ♗d7 13 ♘g3 ♘a5 14 ♗c2 ♘c4 15 b3 ♘b6

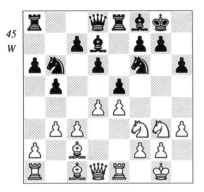

45
W

The results: White has smoothly completed the critical development of his queen's knight and has a superior centre; Black is in a not particularly harmonious defensive crouch. The immediate 9...h6 is obsolete and I'm confident that it will not be rehabilitated.

I think this is a good time to step back for a few moments from the specifics of variations and review again what the opening is supposed to accomplish. (Refer also to Chapter 1) In brief, the three areas of greatest significance for opening play are king safety, piece development and centre control. We can formulate these principles into the following specific objectives:

(1) Bring your king into safety by castling.

(2) Develop your pieces toward the centre so that they are ready for middlegame action.

(3) Control the centre, either by actual possession, or by short-range or long-range action of pieces or pawns.

Good opening moves will be those which help further at least one of those objectives. If you feel like selecting a move which is of no help in any of these areas, you should realise that the chances are excellent that it will not be a good move. There must be some specific (and very good) reason to be able to successfully violate the above priorities. (For a more detailed explanation of the theory of modern opening play see my book *How To Play Good Opening Moves*, David McKay, 1982.)

Let us see how the previous three Ruy Lopez variations conform to the above principles:

(1) 9...♘a5 has the serious shortcoming of being decentralising. This is partially redeemed by the effect of chasing White's bishop back to c2 and enabling the c-pawn to help with central influence.

(2) 9...♘b8 brings about excellent central redeployment, albeit at the cost of two tempi.

(3) 9...h6 just wastes a tempo. In summary, I expect that the lines after 9...♘a5 and 9...♘b8 will retain a certain level of playability; 9...h6 will remain extinct.

Yet, isn't there a move for Black which is absolutely "perfect", but has not yet been mentioned? I think that we can use the "Man from Mars" analogy. If such a person would know the above principles and be a generally good chess player, while at the same time not knowing anything about the theory of the Ruy Lopez, are not the chances excellent that from Diagram 43 he/she would play...

(4) 9...♗b7!

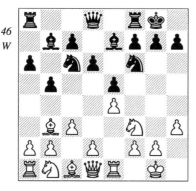

What a fantastic move! Black smoothly completes the development of his minor pieces by placing the light-squared bishop on the h1-a8 central diagonal. The most vulnerable point in White's position is the e4-pawn and Black immediately gets ready to apply pressure on it.

It is only within the last decade years that this variation has become fully respectable, i.e. "playable". Before that, it was either ignored or criticised. Thus Leonard Barden in the 1963 edition of his excellent book *The Ruy Lopez* states: "9...♗b7 is refuted by 10 d4" and gives the following sequence as proof: 10...exd4 11 cxd4 ♘a5 12 ♗c2 d5 13 e5 ♘e4 14 ♘c3 f5 15 exf6 ♗xf6 16 ♘xe4 dxe4 17 ♗xe4 ♗xe4 18 ♖xe4 c5 19 ♖g4! cxd4 20 ♗g5 d3 21 ♗xf6 ♕xf6 22 ♕xd3 ♕xb2 23 ♕d5+ ♔h8 24 ♖e1 ♖ad8 25 ♖f4! "with a very strong attack", Tal-Dr.Lehmann, Hamburg 1960.

The first edition of the *Encyclopedia of Chess Openings C* (1974) does not even consider the correct 10...♖e8, nor does Paul Keres in his German language *Ruy Lopez to French*, published in 1974. For journalistic purposes, an important question is: how to call this variation? Often the names of Salo Flohr or Igor Zaitsev are attached to it, yet that does not seem appropriate to me since they did not understand the correct follow-up. I would propose that Gligorić, Belyavsky and Balashov as the most deserving patron saints. Anyway, back to chess theory:

10 d4 ♖e8!

This move/plan/idea is what validates 9...♗b7. By rapidly developing his pieces towards the centre (remember the e4-point!), Black prevents the smooth development of White's queenside. It turns out that 11 ♘g5 is no threat, because of 11...♖f8. Considerable – frustrating for White – experience has shown that White has nothing better than 12 ♘f3 after which Black returns with 12...♖e8. This can be considered a drawing line for White and a considerable number of GMs have taken advantage of it to draw with Anatoly Karpov.

The alternatives to the text have failed because they did not measure up against the standard of opening principles:

- 10...exd4 hands over control of the centre to White after 11 cxd4.
- 10...♘a5 is decentralising,
- 10...♕d7 lacks any clear objective.

11 ♘bd2 ♗f8!

This completes the initial regrouping started with 9...♗b7.

Because Black has not wasted a crucial tempo with 9...h6, he is ready to capture on e4 if White continues with the desired knight redeployment: 12 ♘f1? ♘a5 13 ♗c2 exd4 14 cxd4 ♘xe4. And if White cannot move his knight away from d2, then he has problems developing the queenside ... and if White can't complete his queenside development, why should he be able to retain his opening advantage? This is the logical thinking behind the above move-order

which has completely rehabilitated the move 9...♗b7. There is even a defensive "bonus" for Black in the position after 11...♗f8!: because the e8-rook protects the e-pawn, the queen's knight is free to move away from c6. This feature can come into effect in positions where it is important to open the b7-bishop's diagonal.

Since this variation is currently the main line in the Ruy Lopez, theoretical developments are coming thick and fast. White moves which are being explored in depth are 12 a3, 12 ♗c2 and 12 a4. I will conclude my discussion with the following active, popular, unbalanced – and in my view, very controversial, main line:

12 a4 h6 13 ♗c2 exd4

In the late 1980s this centrally disadvantageous capture became very popular. Black voluntarily gives up the centre in the hope of getting sufficient counterplay. The purely strategic continuations include 13...♘b8 and 13...♕d7.

14 cxd4 ♘b4 15 ♗b1

47
B

According to "sound principles of strategy", the only way to justify 13...exd4 is now to challenge White's centre with 15...c5 and, after the indicated 16 d5, to continue with 16...♘d7. The position is extremely double-edged and it is still too early to make definitive conclusions. Anatoly Karpov went back to this sequence in games 4, 20 and 22 of his 1990 World Championship Match against Garry Kasparov after the debacle he experienced in Game 2 with ...

15...bxa4?!

Karpov (and others) had been quite successful with the text during the years 1988-1990. Yet I have always been incredulous about these successes: how can it be correct to first give up the centre then follow it up by ruining your queenside pawn formation – especially as there is no immediate compensation? But, of course, the text does have a point: Black hopes to keep White off-balance by continually exerting pressure against White's e-pawn.

16 ♖xa4 a5 17 ♖a3 ♖a6 18 ♘h2!

Not a new idea, but in conjunction with White's next, the correct plan. Previously the text had been played with the idea of quick kingside action with f4 and/or ♘g4. Black has sufficient resources against that.

18...g6 19 f3!!

The plan that "refutes" the line with 15...bxa4. By safeguarding

e4, White pre-empts any Black counterplay and thereby leaves Black with no compensation for his severe central inferiority and split queenside pawns. Just the next few moves show the power of the idea:

19...♕d7 20 ♘c4 ♕b5 21 ♖c3 ♗c8 22 ♗e3

White is fully mobilised, has only strengths and no worries. Kasparov went on to win brilliantly in 44 moves:

22...♔h7 23 ♕c1 c6 24 ♘g4 ♘g8 25 ♗xh6!! ♗xh6 26 ♘xh6 ♘xh6 27 ♘xd6 ♕b6 28 ♘xe8 ♕xd4+ 29 ♔h1 ♕d8 30 ♖d1 ♕xe8 31 ♕g5 ♖a7 32 ♖d8 ♕e6 33 f4 ♗a6 34 f5! ♕e7 35 ♕d2! ♕e5 36 ♕f2 ♕e7 37 ♕d4 ♘g8 38 e5 ♘d5 39 fxg6+ fxg6 40 ♖xc6 ♕xd8 41 ♕xa7+ ♘de7 42 ♖xa6 ♕d1+ 43 ♕g1 ♕d2 44 ♕f1 1-0

My final prognostications regarding this variation are: 9...♗b7 will remain fully viable as long as Black can defend the Ruy Lopez; the sub-variation with 15...bxa4?! has very little prospects of being rehabilitated.

Rehabilitation of White opening systems

It is very important to realise that the immediate goal of the opening phase is quite different for Black and White: Black can be satisfied to equalise, whereas White should be aiming to retain his characteristic opening advantage. This means that when we speak of rehabilitation of Black systems, we expect that Black will be no worse off than in the recognised "good" variations. A rehabilitated White system should lead to some advantage. It would hardly be a big deal to improve a system from inferiority to equality.

In this section I will consider three important recent developments in the rehabilitation of White systems. It should also be noted that there are openings where I feel the chances for theoretical rebirth are extremely poor. An obvious example is the Blackmar-Diemer Gambit: 1 d4 d5 2 e4. Sacrificing a prime central pawn for a tempo in the face of a healthy, solid Black position cannot be sound. Just a bit more promising is the Smith-Morra Gambit against the Sicilian: 1 e4 c5 2 d4 cxd4 3 c3 dxc3 4 ♘xc3. Since 1...c5 is not a primary developing move, White gains slightly more compensation than in the Blackmar-Diemer. Yet in all the main lines of the Sicilian, White is able to work up a dangerous attack for nothing. Why should he handicap himself at the very start by being a pawn down?

(A) *Grünfeld Defence: Exchange Variation*

The Grünfeld Defence, **1 d4 ♘f6 2 c4 g6 3 ♘c3 d5**, got its start in 1922 when the Austrian master and theoretician Ernst Grünfeld introduced it into international

tournament play. From its very beginning right up to the present, the most thematic attempt at its "refutation" has been the Exchange Variation: **4 cxd5 ♘xd5 5 e4 ♘xc3 6 bxc3 ♗g7**

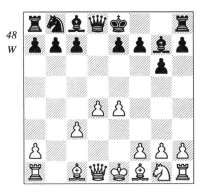

48
W

White has built up a very strong centre, with each of his primary central pawns on the fourth rank. Moreover, Black will never be able to rival White in the centre, because – in effect – Black has allowed his d-pawn to be exchanged off for White's b-pawn. Black's general strategy is to challenge White's centre, usually with ...c5, then to undermine it and hopefully to annihilate it. Therefore, the Grünfeld leads to very unbalanced, fighting chess.

(1) Old Exchange Variation

For well over 50 years from its birth, the only correct deployment of White's kingside minor pieces from Diagram 48 was considered to be 7 ♗c4 c5 8 ♘e2. This formation stood the test of time and I expect that it will remain fully playable for a long time to come. Yet there are also two negative factors in the formation: the c4-bishop's unprotected location gives Black the opportunity to play ...♕c7 and/or a later ...♘a5 with gain of time and, more importantly, the e2-knight is strictly a defensive piece, supporting d4 without having to worry about a ...♗g4 pin.

But the gospel was that White had no choice, because ♘f3 was "obviously" wrong. Contemporary literature, of course, reflected this "common knowledge". For instance, the first edition of the *Encyclopedia of Chess Openings D*, published in 1976, only had two columns devoted to (from Diagram 48), 7 ♘f3 c5, one on the careful 8 ♗e2 and the other on the passive 8 h3. The two moves which are now played almost exclusively (8 ♗e3 and 8 ♖b1) were not even mentioned in a footnote.

(2) Modern Exchange Variation

Starting in the second half of the 1970s, the world's top players began exploring the centrally active development with 7 ♘f3. They reasoned: why should such a good, healthy normal move be as bad as its reputation? They questioned the relevance of previous games such as: 7...c5 8 ♗c4?! ♘c6 9 ♗e3 0-0 10 h3?! ♕a5! 11 ♕d2?! cxd4 12 cxd4 ♕xd2+ 13 ♔xd2 ♖d8 14 ♗d5, Dr.M.Vidmar-A.Alekhine, Nottingham 1936, when 14...♘xd4! would have led

to a clear advantage for Black. In the forefront of this investigation was World Champion Anatoly Karpov.

By now the Modern Exchange Variation is a main line method against the Grünfeld. The second edition of *ECO D* (published in 1987) gives 43 variation-packed columns. Currently the two most popular White continuations after **7 ♘f3 c5** are:

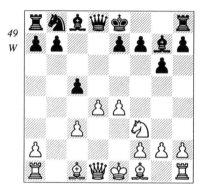

49
W

a) **8 ♗e3** – White overprotects d4 and gets ready to develop the queen's rook to c1. This was the first "high quality" sub-variation. By its very nature, it seems like quite an obvious way of continuing from Diagram 49. However, to even "bother" looking at it, the GMs had to start believing that Diagram 49 is even worth a look.

For over 50 years we did not think so. Once careful investigation of 8 ♗e3 started, it was rather quickly determined that the Black counterplay based on an early ...♗g4 led to nothing special after either 8...0-0 9 ♖c1 ♗g4 or the immediate 8...♗g4. Currently 8...♕a5 is Black's most common response.

b) **8 ♖b1** – Over the past 6 -7 years this has become the main line within the Modern Exchange Variation. White removes the rook from exposure to Black's g7-bishop and positions it to apply pressure against Black's queenside. Such a flexible approach is very much in the spirit of modern opening play. As White is threatening "nothing", Black can afford to complete his kingside development with 8...0-0. White then works on the same goal with 9 ♗e2, giving Black a wide choice of plans. The most common is 9...cxd4 10 cxd4 ♕a5+; however, work continues on 9...♘c6, 9...b6 and 9...♗g4.

All in all, a rich field of exploration still awaits us.

The discovery that the knight development to f3 is completely satisfactory in the Exchange Variation is particularly important as these positions can arise from a number of opening schemes. This implies that both sides be completely aware of the science of move-orders. (See Chapter 4 in my book *How To Be A Complete Tournament Player*). In particular Black must be ready to face the Modern Exchange Variation from the following characteristic move-orders:

- From 1 d4 openings: 1 d4 ♘f6 2 ♘f3 g6 3 c4 ♗g7 4 ♘c3 d5 5 cxd5 ♘xd5 6 e4 ♘xc3 7 bxc3 c5.

- From 1 ♘f3 openings: 1 ♘f3 ♘f6 2 c4 g6 3 ♘c3 d5 4 cxd5 ♘xd5 5 e4 ♘xc3 6 bxc3 ♗g7 7 d4 c5.

- From 1 c4 openings: 1 c4 ♘f6 2 ♘c3 d5 3 cxd5 ♘xd5 4 ♘f3 c5 5 d4 g6 6 e4 ♘xc3 7 bxc3 ♗g7.

My overall conclusion is that both the Old Exchange Variation and the Modern Exchange Variation will remain highly respected methods of facing the Grünfeld Defence. Both offer White a consistent way of trying to capitalise on his superior centre.

(B) *Nimzo-Indian Defence: Capablanca Variation*

The Nimzo-Indian Defence arises after **1 d4 ♘f6 2 c4 e6 3 ♘c3 ♗b4**. In its early days, the most popular White response was **4 ♕c2** – the Capablanca or Classical Variation. White prevents the doubling of his pawns and protects the important e4-square. This remained White's main weapon until the 1949 match between Max Euwe and Yugoslav Vasja Pirc. However, instead of being "perfect", there are negative factors associated with 4 ♕c2: White delays primary development by a move and leaves d4 unprotected. Pirc showed that both of these factors can be exploited by the move-order **4...c5 5 dxc5 0-0** *(D)*

For well over 30 years the Pirc Variation was the main reason why the classical 4 ♕c2 was not an important part of the international tournament scene. The

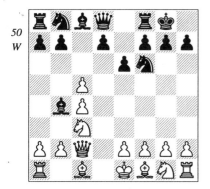

50
W

contemporary viewpoint was well expressed by *Modern Chess Openings*, 12th edition, published in 1982: "The absence of a threat (other than P-K4, if that can be regarded as one), as well as the premature development of White's queen, holds little future for this system if White wants to avoid drawish set-ups."

The main line moves explored for White from Diagram 50 were 6 ♘f3, 6 ♗f4 and 6 ♗g5 but in all cases Black replied 6...♘a6! followed by an early ...♘xc5, and was able to show that his superior development allowed comfortable equality. The course of Euwe-Pirc, Ljubljana 1949 match was thematic: 6 ♗g5 ♘a6! 7 a3 ♗xc3+ 8 ♕xc3 ♘xc5 9 ♗xf6 ♕xf6 10 ♕xf6 gxf6 11 b4?! ♘a4 12 0-0-0?! a5 13 ♔c2 d5! 14 e3 axb4 15 axb4 ♗d7, with a strong attack and superior chances for Black.

Among the 6th move alternatives tried for White on an occasional basis was **6 a3**, in order to force **6...♗xc5**, thus preventing

Black's powerful 6...♘a6 followed by ...♘xc5 plan. The consistent follow-up **7 ♘f3 ♘c6 8 ♗g5** was considered harmless because of the sequence **8...♘d4 9 ♘xd4 ♗xd4 10 e3 ♕a5** when White has nothing better than **11 exd4 ♕xg5**, leading to Diagram 51.

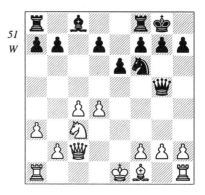

51
W

Ever since the van Scheltinga-O'Kelly game at Amsterdam 1950, this position had been rated as fine for Black: his queen is powerfully placed and how is White to get his king to safety?

The correct solution to the position was first demonstrated by World Champion Anatoly Karpov in his game against Lajos Portisch, Amsterdam 1981. Noting that 11 exd4 has led to a significant central superiority and that Black's queenside remains undeveloped, he reasoned that what is necessary is to remove Black's only trump – the active queen. Therefore he played **12 ♕d2!** giving Black the following unappetising choices:

a) To retreat his queen with **12...♕g6**. After 13 f3! followed by 14 ♗d3 White has a large middle-game advantage.

b) Exchange queens by means of **12...♕xd2+** 13 ♔xd2. The endgame is pleasantly favourable for White: he has a powerful centre, a significant space advantage on the queenside, a useful queenside majority and the centralised king is a strength.

The game continued: 13...b6 14 f3 ♗a6 15 ♖c1 ♖ac8 16 b3 ♖fd8 17 ♗e2 ♔f8 18 ♖he1 d6 19 ♖c2, with a continuing advantage for White. Portisch did succeed in gaining a 48-move draw.

Perhaps because White did not succeed in winning the endgame, there was no immediate follow-up to it in top-level play. But when Yasser Seirawan resurrected Karpov's idea in 1986 to win some brilliant endgames, the whole world took notice.

A typical example is Y.Seirawan-Y.Grünfeld, Zagreb Interzonal 1987: 13...d6 14 ♗d3 ♗d7 15 b4! b6 16 ♖hb1 ♗c6 17 f3 ♖fc8 18 a4 a5 19 bxa5 bxa5 20 ♖b2 ♔f8?! 21 ♖ab1 h6 22 ♖b6 ♔e7 23 d5! exd5 24 ♗f5 ♖c7? 25 ♘b5 ♗xb5 26 cxb5 ♘e8 27 ♖a6 ♖ca7 28 ♖xa7+ ♖xa7 29 b6 ♖b7 30 ♗c8 ♖b8 31 b7 ♔d8 32 ♖b5 ♘f6 33 ♖xa5 ♔c7 34 ♖b5 ♘g8 35 ♖b1 ♘e7 36 a5 g5 37 ♖c1+ ♔d8 38 a6 ♘xc8 39 ♖xc8+ ♖xc8 40 a7 1-0

Black's endgame prospects are so unpleasant after 13 ♔xd2 that the whole Pirc Variation (5...0-0) has become unplayable at the higher level. What the above implies is that 4 ♕c2 has been completely rehabilitated as a viable method for striving for the normal White opening advantage and over the past seven years has again become a mainstay on the international circuit. Black players who still believe in 4...c5 are, after 5 dxc5, exploring the alternatives 5...♕c7 and the immediate 5...♘a6. There are also attempts to return to the old 4...d5 and much work is taking place on the flexible 4...0-0. White's most ambitious plan then is 5 a3 ♗xc3+ 6 ♕xc3. The more modest 5 ♘f3 allows 5...c5, when after 6 dxc5 ♘a6! Black has transposed into a fully satisfactory line of the Pirc Variation. (See also the discussion in Chapter 2.)

(C) *Caro-Kann Defence: Advance Variation*

After **1 e4 c6 2 d4 d5** White has the choice of three perfectly reasonable approaches regarding what to do about his e-pawn: (1) protect it by 3 ♘c3 or 3 ♘d2, (2) exchange it by 3 exd5, or, (3) advance it. The last possibility, **3 e5**, brings about the Advance Variation. It has always had something of a naive reputation. Yes, it's true that the advanced e-pawn cramps Black's position, but – unlike the same move in the French defence – Black's light-squared bishop can be readily developed. Moreover, Black can later challenge White's centre, just as in the French, by ...c5. Therefore, White's chances for an advantage are scant. Let us take a brief look at some historical moments and a very intriguing recent development. The basic starting point of the variation results after 3...♗f5

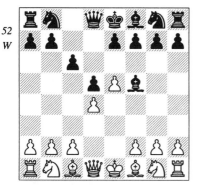

White has various plans:

(1) Exchange the f5-bishop

Because Black's light-squared bishop is actively placed, it seems logical to exchange it off with 4 ♗d3 ♗xd3 5 ♕xd3. The disadvantage of this is that after 5...e6 Black achieves a favourable "French Defence" position since he does not have the burden of the bad light-squared bishop. For instance, 6 ♘f3 ♕a5+! 7 ♘bd2 ♕a6 gives Black full equality, whether White exchanges queens or not. It is important to note that Black's remaining bishop is the superior one, since White's is hemmed in by his own central pawns.

(2) Immediate central activity with 4 c4

Unlike the same move in the Panov Attack (3 exd5 cxd5 4 c4), here 4 c4 offers little prospects of an initiative since the d5-square is bound to remain safely in Black's hands. A good defensive method for Black is 4...e6 5 ♘c3 dxc4 6 ♗xc4 ♘d7 7 ♘f3 ♘b6 8 ♗b3 ♘e7 9 0-0 ♘ed5 10 ♕e2 ♗e7 11 ♘e4 0-0, Johannessen-Porath, Leipzig Olympiad 1960, when Black was solid, safe and equal.

(3) Tal's kingside pawn storms

In the 1961 return match for the world championship, Mikhail Tal surprised Mikhail Botvinnik with pawn storms on the kingside, starting with 4 h4. The passage of time has led to a better understanding of White's most effective move-orders. For the past fifteen years the main lines have started with 4 ♘c3 e6 5 g4 ♗g6 6 ♘ge2. For Black 6...♗e7, 6...f6 and, in particular, 6...c5 have the best reputation. Yet little is absolutely clear. The second edition of *Encyclopedia B* (1984), gives "unclear" as the evaluation for the main lines and that is still the most accurate description for the situation today.

In my opinion, White's chances for some advantage are good. The reasons are: the space gained on the kingside comes with gain of time by attacking Black's bishop and Black's counterplay with ...c5 is a move late since the c-pawn has needed two moves to get to c5. However this variation is only for those fearless White players who excel in murky violent attacks.

(4) Quiet play with Short's 4 c3

The English GM Nigel Short has recently come up with a very sophisticated insight into the basic nature of Diagram 52: Black's ♗f5 is no problem since it cannot do any particular damage and, moreover, Black's thematic counterplay with ...c5 will be a tempo behind the related French Defence lines. Therefore, White can just play "normally" and retain the advantage of the superior central space gained by 3 e5. This theme is well demonstrated by the course of N.Short-Y.Seirawan, Manila Interzonal 1990: **4 c3 e6 5 ♗e2 c5 6 ♘f3 ♘c6 7 0-0**

Here we already see the first advantages of the "Short System". White's d4-pawn is secure and, therefore, Black's counterplay is basically stillborn. Moreover, the ♗f5 takes away that important square from Black's king's knight. In Short-Hjartarson, Manila Interzonal 1990, Black followed in true "French fashion" with 7...♖c8 8 a3 c4 9 ♘bd2 ♘h6, yet after 10 b3 cxb3 11 ♕xb3 White was still a full tempo ahead of "French lines".

7...h6 8 ♗e3! cxd4 9 cxd4 ♘ge7 10 ♘c3 ♘c8

As can be seen Black has certain problems in completing his kingside development.

11 ♖c1 a6
According to Short, better is 11...♘b6.

12 ♘a4 ♘b6 13 ♘c5 ♗xc5 14 ♖xc5

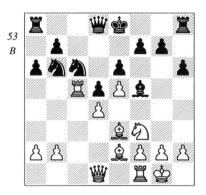

53
B

The logic behind White's build-up is now clear: he has more space, superior development, an initiative on the queenside, potential for the characteristic play on the kingside and the bishop pair; White's advantage, although not huge, is clear and pleasant.

14...0-0 15 ♕b3! ♘d7 16 ♖c3 ♕b6 17 ♖fc1! ♕xb3 18 ♖xb3 ♖fb8 19 ♘d2 ♔f8 20 h4! ♔e8 21 g4 ♗h7 22 h5! ♘d8?

Black cannot afford such a waste of time. Short suggests 22...♔d8, with White retaining a substantial spatial advantage after 23 f4.

23 ♖bc3! ♘b6 24 ♘b3! ♘a4 25 ♖c7 ♘xb2 26 ♘c5 b5 27 g5! ♘c4 28 gxh6 gxh6 29 ♘d7 ♘xe3 30 fxe3 ♗f5 31 ♔f2 ♖b7 32 ♘f6+ ♔f8 33 ♖g1! 1-0

It is of course too early to make a definitive conclusion regarding the "Short System". But I feel confident that its chances are bright for it to generate a normal opening advantage. In ambitious central variations, such as 3 e5 here, the difference of a tempo can have a major effect on the ultimate results. White here has that tempo and with it a safeguarded superior centre.

In any new strategic variation it takes a while to establish what is the most effective move-order. By 1996 it had become clear that 4 ♘f3 e6 5 ♗e2 is White's "perfect" move-order. Those two moves are required, while c3 can be delayed or even omitted, depending on Black's particular sub-variation.

9 How to avoid bad variations

Most of us surely do not want to intentionally play a variation which is considered to be bad. Yet it seems to happen much too often that just a few moves after playing something that we have confidence in, we suddenly realise that our position is poor. Why did this happen and what can be done to avoid such unpleasant episodes?

Your chances of avoiding a bad variation are greatly enhanced if you observe the following principles:

(a) if the variation seems to ignore at least some of the principles of opening play (king safety, central control, piece development towards the centre), be sceptical.

(b) if the variation does not seem to follow the spirit of the opening, be sceptical.

(c) if published theory gives its OK to a variation which is questionable under (a) or (b), be sceptical.

I will illustrate the above points with the help of the following two theoretically important examples.

1) *Sicilian Defence:*

1 e4 c5 2 ♘f3 ♘c6 3 ♗b5

White's third move, 3 ♗b5, has become popular in master play for two reasons: (1) A whole slew of Black variations are prevented, (2) The variations tend to be more strategic than tactical in nature. A well-regarded response for Black now is

3...g6 4 0-0 ♗g7 5 ♖e1 e5

White's most common strategic variation is 6 ♗xc6 dxc6 7 d3. Also important is the following quasi-gambit:

6 b4!?

The threat is simply to capture on c5. Therefore Black must take on b4. Theory considers both 6...♘xb4 and 6...cxb4 as satisfactory. I have had much more confidence in the latter and it has always been part of my repertoire

6...cxb4 7 a3

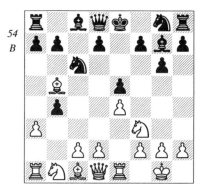

54
B

This is the tactical/strategic idea behind White's sacrifice. He expects to either get a very strong attack for the pawn or to recover it with an enhanced centre. Here Black has three important responses:

(A) **7...bxa3?**

Because of his backward development and weakness on d6, Black cannot afford such greediness. His position quickly becomes critical after 8 ♗xa3 (also good is 8 ♘xa3 followed by 9 ♘c4) ♘ge7 9 ♗d6 0-0 10 ♘c3 ♖e8 11 ♗c4 a6 12 ♕b1! ♗f6 13 ♕a2, A.Kapengut-E.Paoli, Kecskemet 1972.

(B) **7...♘ge7?! 8 axb4 0-0**

Theory has considered this to be the main line and to be perfectly satisfactory for Black. The game references given continue with 9 ♗a3, 9 ♗b2, 9 c3 and all end with equality for Black. Yet, particularly in hindsight, White's moves look rather clumsy.

This is a good moment to take a more basic look at the position after 8...0-0. The pawn exchange on b4 has resulted in a considerable enhancement of White's relative central influence because, in effect, White's a-pawn has been exchanged for Black's c-pawn. Moreover, this exchange has led to a sound seven-pawn chain for White, whereas Black's pawns are split into two parts and are therefore less self-supporting. White also has pressure along the a-file, while Black has an inactive g7-bishop and a potential weakness on d6. In conclusion: White has achieved real gains and Black has no compensation for these. What is still needed, however, is a way of demonstrating how to build on White's advantages. The answer

was provided by the game B.Filipović-E.Mednis, Lugano 1987.

9 d3!!

This is the strategic refutation of Black's "bad variation". Again 9...♘xb4? is poor because of 10 ♗a3 and otherwise White will work on his advantages. The game continued 9...♕c7 10 ♗xc6! bxc6?! (this leads to a new weakness on a7, so 10...dxc6 or 10...♕xc6 would have been better) 11 ♗e3 f5 12 ♘c3! f4 13 ♗c1 h6 14 b5 d6 15 ♗a3 c5 16 ♘d2 ♗e6 17 ♘c4 f3 18 g3 g5 19 ♗b2 ♘g6 20 ♖e3 g4 21 ♖a6 ♖ad8 22 ♕a1 ♖f7 23 ♕a5

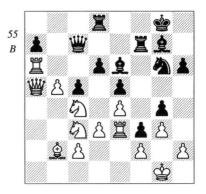

55
B

and White went on to win in 46 moves. It was quite impressive how the Yugoslav IM infiltrated into my weak squares. Later, when I reviewed in detail the game, it became clear that the 7...♘ge7 variation is simply bad (for the reasons explained earlier) and can't be fixed. After consulting my personal notes it became obvious that the only correct method is ...

(C) **7...b3!**

My notes carried the following reference of the first use of 7...b3!: A.Menvielle-L.Polugayevsky, Las Palmas 1974: 8 cxb3 ♘ge7 9 ♗b2 0-0 10 ♘c3 d6 11 h3 h6 12 ♗c4 ♔h7 13 d4 ♘xd4 14 ♘xd4 exd4 15 ♘b5 ♘c6 16 ♕d2 ♘e5 17 ♗xd4 a6 18 ♘c3 ♕g5 with equality and a draw on move 26 (19 ♕xg5 hxg5 20 ♗xe5 ♗xe5 21 ♖ac1 b5 22 ♗d5 ♖a7 23 a4 ♗d7 24 axb5 axb5 25 ♘e2 b4 26 ♖ed1).

It is hardly surprising that it was a world class GM who "intuitively" understood the correct way of handling Diagram 54 for Black. 7...b3! 8 cxb3 brings about the exchange of the two c-pawns and yields no central advantage for White at all. Since the other possible advantages (open a-file, opportunity to exploit the weakness on d6) are also denied White, Black can expect full equality. I found it disappointing that the second edition *of Encyclopedia of Chess Openings, Volume B* (published in 1984) still did not carry the Polugayevsky game. Yet curiously, under reference B31, note 28, the following item appears: 7...b3?! 8 cxb3 ♘ge7 9 ♗b2 0-0 10 ♗c4 d6 11 b4 ♗g4 12 h3 ♗xf3 13 ♕xf3 ♘d4 14 ♗xd4 exd4 15 d3 ± Cuartas-Szilagyi, Bern 1976. It is obvious that White is clearly better in the final position of this variation, but that should not be blamed on the correct 7...b3!. The error was that Black created his own "bad variation" by unaccountably voluntarily exchanging off his good bishop for White's king's knight by 11...♗g4?! 12 h3 ♗xf3?! and then compounded his problems by taking on an isolated doubled pawn with 13...♘d4?! 14 ♗xd4 exd4. If instead Black plays 11...a6! followed by the normal ...♗e6, he should retain approximate equality.

After doing the above work, I felt confident about facing 6 b4 again. The opportunity came less than four months later in the Andorra International 1977. In the game A.Ozsvath-E.Mednis, the Hungarian FM seemed to be surprised by 7...b3! and after some ten minutes of thinking decided to continue actively with 8 ♘c3?! bxc2 9 ♕xc2 ♘ge7 10 ♘d5 0-0 11 a4?!

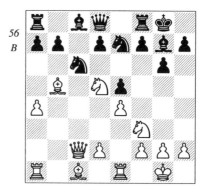

The idea is 12 ♗a3, yet compared to the position arising after 7...bxa3? White is many tempi behind and therefore nothing can come from it. Moreover, Black can even take White's offered material with 11...♘xd5 12 exd5 e4 13 ♕xe4 ♗xa1. Because Ozsvath is a dangerous attacking player I was reluctant to do so in a practical game and decided to first continue with queenside development, thereby ensuring a good and secure position.

11...d6 12 ♖b1 ♘xd5 13 exd5 ♘e7 14 ♗a3?! ♘xd5 15 ♕e4 ♘f4

White has no compensation for his missing pawns and Black won without particular problems:

16 ♕b4 ♗g4! 17 ♖b3 ♗e6! 18 ♖bb1 ♗d5! 19 ♖e3 ♗a2! 20 ♖d1 ♘d5 21 ♕e4 a6! 22 ♗f1 ♖c8! 23 ♖c3 ♖xc3 24 dxc3 ♘xc3 25 ♕c2 ♘xd1 and White resigned on move 46.

2) *Slav Defence, Main Line*

For well over half a century the main line in the Slav Defence has been

1 d4 d5 2 c4 c6 3 ♘c3 ♘f6 4 ♘f3 dxc4 5 a4 ♗f5

The logic behind Black's move is clear: before playing ...e6 he develops his light-squared bishop; on f5 it will make it harder for White to build a strong centre with e4. Up until some 25 years ago, an important variation was the following:

6 ♘e5 e6 7 f3 ♗b4 8 e4 *(D)*

White's 7th move prepared this direct advance, though at the cost of development; Black's 7th move envisioned a tactical way of coping with it.

8...♗xe4! 9 fxe4 ♘xe4 10 ♗d2 ♕xd4 11 ♘xe4 ♕xe4+ 12 ♕e2

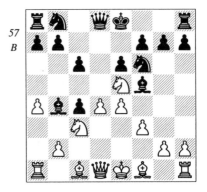

♗xd2+ 13 ♔xd2 ♕d5+ 14 ♔c2 ♘a6 15 ♘xc4

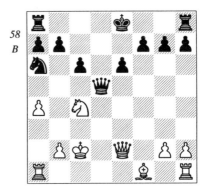

The earlier complications have led to the emergence of a strategically most unbalanced position.

Black has three good pawns for the sacrificed bishop and, moreover, White's kingside development is backward and his king seems insecure. It is, therefore, hardly surprising that there was little appetite on the part of White players to continue exploring this position. As far as top-level chess was concerned, it lay dormant for some 20 years.

Yet in 1988 the slumbering giant awoke with a roar. Former World Champion Anatoly Karpov was the chief "arouser". This is a brief chronology of his exploits:

(a) In Karpov-Tukmakov, Gijon 1988, he demonstrated that the highly rated **15...♕f5+** can be met successfully by the audacious 16 ♔c3!. After the further moves 16...0-0 17 ♕e5 ♕f2 18 ♗d3 ♖ad8 19 ♖hf1 ♕h4 20 ♕e4 ♕h6 21 ♕e3 ♕h4 22 ♖f4 White's extra piece was much more effective than Black's pawns.

(b) In Karpov-Hübner, Tilburg 1988, Round 4, Black just was able to equalise after **15...0-0-0 16 ♕e5 f6 17 ♕e3!** c5 18 ♗e2 ♘b4+ 19 ♔b3 ♘c6 20 ♔c3 ♘d4 21 ♗f3 ♘xf3 22 gxf3 ♕d4+.

(c) Yet just a few rounds later, in Round 8, in the game Karpov-J.Hjartarson, he improved with **18 ♔b3!** (instead of 18 ♗e2) and scored the following most impressive victory: 18...♘b4 19 ♖c1 ♘c6 20 ♔a3 ♘d4 21 ♘a5! e5 22 ♕c3! b6 23 ♘b3 ♕xb3+ 24 ♕xb3 ♘xb3 25 ♔xb3 ♖d4 26 h4! ♖hd8 27 ♗c4 ♔c7 28 h5 ♖g4? (better 28...a6) 29 h6! ♖xg2?! (29...g6 is required) 30 hxg7 ♖xg7 31 ♖cf1 ♖d6 32 ♖h6 e4 33 ♖hxf6 h5 34 ♖6f4 ♖d4 35 ♖f7+ ♖d7 36 ♖xg7 ♖xg7 37 ♖f4 ♖g3+ 38 ♔c2 ♖g2+ 39 ♔c3 ♖g3+ 40 ♔d2 ♖g4 41 ♖f7+ ♔d6 42 ♔e3 a6 1-0

What Karpov (and his "followers") demonstrated was that, with a modicum of care, White's king is safe enough while, on the other hand, Black's pawn formation, though sound, is not compact – therefore White's extra bishop offers excellent chances for the initiative both in the middlegame and endgame.

The "natural" consequence was that many Black players panicked and decided that the fault must be in Diagram 58. They therefore indulged in a number of "bad variations" just to avoid Diagram 58. Three instructive examples are:

(i) In Round 10 at Tilburg 1988, in Karpov-J.Timman Black varied on move 12 with **12...♕h4+?!** (instead of 12...♗xd2+) and after 13 g3 ♗xd2+ 14 ♔xd2 ♕e7 15 ♕e3! ♘a6 16 ♗xc4! ♘b4 (16...0-0-0+ 17 ♔e2) 17 ♖ad1 found himself in a position where White's development is much superior to that in diagram 58. If "your variation" allows the opponent superior development over that in the normal line, be very sceptical of your variation.

(ii) From Diagram 57 Black played **8...♘xe4?** in A.Greenfeld-J.Granda, Thessaloniki Olympiad 1988. After 9 fxe4 ♕h4+ 10 ♔e2 ♗xe4 11 g3! ♕h5+ 12 g4 ♗d3+ 13 ♔f3 ♕h4 14 ♗xd3 cxd3 15 ♔g2! ♘d7 16 ♘xd3! ♗e7 17 ♗f4 ♘f6 18 ♘e5 ♖d8 19 h3 White has a won position: Black has only two pawns for the piece, while White is well developed, secure and even threatens 20 ♘f3. If "your variation" calls for an obvious piece sacrifice in a very well-known line and this sacrifice has not appeared in 50 years, be very sceptical of it. The Peruvian GM should have been more sceptical.

(iii) From Diagram 57 Black played **8...♗g6?** in M.Petursson-E.Meduna, Gausdal 1988. He was annihilated after 9 ♗xc4 ♘bd7 10 h4! ♕a5 11 ♕b3 0-0-0 12 ♗f4 ♘xe5 13 ♗xe5 h5 14 0-0! ♘d7 15 ♗g3 ♗e7 16 ♖ac1 ♕b6 17 ♘b5! e5 18 ♗xf7 ♔b8 19 ♗xg6 cxb5 20 ♗f5 ♕xd4+ 21 ♔h2 1-0.

Meduna is a recognised expert on the Slav and he knew that the point of the variation 5...♗f5 and 7...♗b4 is to prevent White from playing e4 trouble-free. There is no way that after 8 e4 the abject retreat 8...♗g6 will work out well. If "your variation" requires that you ignore the theme of the opening, be very sceptical of it.

Rather than looking for bad variations to find the salvation of the short-term troubles that Diagram 58 was causing Black, it was Diagram 58 itself that required work for Black. Just as Karpov had provided the necessary insight into White's opportunities, so the need was for Black to discover the correct piece and pawn configurations. Once this was

fully appreciated, Black's results started improving. A sound way of handling Diagram 58 was demonstrated in I.Novikov-E.Bareev, USSR Championship 1990:

15...0-0-0 16 ♕e5 f6 17 ♕e3 ♔b8!

Rather than the weakening 17...c5, Black improves his king position.

18 ♔b3 e5 19 ♗e2 ♘c5+ 20 ♔b4 ♘e6 21 ♗f3 ♕d7

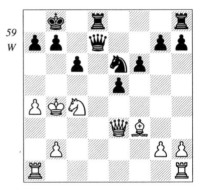

Bareev rates this position as giving equal chances. Black has good central influence, a safe king and well-placed pieces: White has a extra piece, but no particular objects of attack in Black's camp. The side playing better has realistic winning chances. Black won an interesting endgame in 62 moves.

10 Opening traps: fact or fiction?

Among the best-selling opening books are those on opening traps. This is not because the person doing the buying is afraid of falling into such a trap. No, he/she has a much more "positive" outlook, i.e. to catch the opponent in a trap and thus score an easy win. It is important to be familiar with the potential traps in your opening repertoire so that you do not blunder yourself while being able to take advantage of gaffes by the opponent. However, do not have your hopes too high for scoring loads of points this way. In real life, real people fall into opening traps much less often than authors of such books make you think. Still, a genuine opening trap is a trap all the same and it is in your interest to be familiar with it. Yet, the expression "a little bit of knowledge can be very dangerous" can easily come into play if you see the same trap, but the position is slightly different. You think it makes no difference – but the difference can be huge. This is the important practical subject that I will be discussing here. My examples will be basically those that can result from the Dragon Variation of the Sicilian Defence. The particular theme will be: White has played an early ♗e3; Black can bother the bishop by

responding with ...♘g4. Should Black do so? I will first look at some examples with Black's king still in the centre and then with Black castled.

(I) *Black's king is in the centre*

The modern move-order for achieving the Dragon Variation is 1 e4 c5 2 ♘f3 d6 3 d4 cxd4 4 ♘xd4 ♘f6 5 ♘c3 g6. White's most flexible move for reaching a number of main line variations is 6 ♗e3

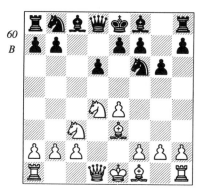

But does not Black have now have the nasty-looking 6...♘g4, attacking the bishop? The answer is "No", because after the "unexpected" 7 ♗b5+!, White wins by force:

a) 7...♘d7? or 7...♗d7? allows 8 ♕xg4;

b) 7...♘c6 8 ♘xc6 bxc6 9 ♗xc6+ ♗d7 10 ♗xa8 puts White up the exchange and a pawn.

Thus, after 6...♘g4? 7 ♗b5+!, Black has fallen into a genuine opening trap. From the standpoint of theory, this is an important trap. Yet, how significant is it in real life? I mean, I have been playing 6 ♗e3 for well on 40 years and, up to now, not a single opponent has ventured 6...♘g4?.

What is more important is how the above information can be used or misused in "similar" situations. Let us now continue from Diagram 60 as follows:

6...♗g7

If White is aiming for the Yugoslav Attack variations with ♗c4, the usual move-order now is 7 f3, 8 ♕d2 and 9 ♗c4. But why not the immediate ...

7 ♗c4

and the answer is: "because of..."

7...♘g4! 8 ♗b5+ ♚f8

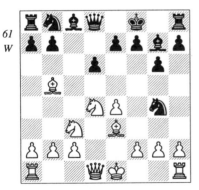

61
W

The trap has not sprung since Black's king had a safe escape square. While it is true that Black has been denied castling, both the white bishops are now awkwardly scattered about and in this unbalanced position Black's chances are fully equal:

(1) **9 ♗c1?** ♕b6 gives Black a clear advantage.

(2) **9 ♕d2** a6 10 ♗c4 ♘c6 with full equality for Black, Skold-M.Botvinnik, Stockholm 1962. Black, at his convenience, will play ...♘xe3 and the bishop pair will compensate for the uncastled king.

(3) **9 0-0** ♘xe3 (here too 9...a6!? 10 ♗c4 ♘c6 is possible, delaying White's attack along the f-file) 10 fxe3 e6 11 ♗c4 ♕e7 12 ♘cb5 ♗e5!. Black looks OK in this unclear position (13 ♘f3 ♚g7).

(4) **9 ♗g5** (this method is probably White's soundest approach.) 9...h6 10 ♗h4 g5 11 ♗g3 ♕b6 12 ♘de2 h5! (Black must try to exploit the awkward location of White's bishops – otherwise his weaknesses will start to tell, as for instance after 12...♘c6? 13 h3) 13 h4 gxh4 14 ♖xh4 ♘c6 15 ♕d2 ♘d4! 16 ♘xd4 ♕xd4 17 0-0-0 ♕xd2+ 18 ♖xd2 ♗f6, led to an approximately balanced position in Ljubojević-Sosonko, Buenos Aires Olympiad 1978.

In the previous examples what Black had to be concerned about was ♗b5 with check. But what if that move doesn't come with check? To take a look at this important question, let us use the old move-order for the Dragon: 1 e4 c5 2 ♘f3 ♘c6 3 d4 cxd4 4 ♘xd4 ♘f6 5 ♘c3 d6. When the Dragon variation earned its respectability in the early 1930s, these were the early moves and only after the "standard" 6 ♗e2 did Black start the fianchetto with 6...g6. The Richter-Rauzer Attack (6 ♗g5) and the Sozin Attack (6 ♗c4) were both introduced to prevent the feared Dragon. However, White can also choose:

6 ♗e3

In one sense this is a flexible developing move and also gives Black another chance to enter the Dragon with 6...g6. Moreover, the move is also a challenge to Black: what are you going to do about me?

6...♘g4

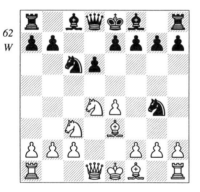

If Black is intent on "refuting" 6 ♗e3, this is the way. Alternatives are: aiming for the Dragon with 6...g6, the Scheveningen with 6...e6, or a quasi-Boleslavsky with 6...e5.

White's choices are clear: should I move the attacked bishop or should I ignore the attack and go for a counter-attack myself? This then leads to the following two lines:

(1) 7 ♗g5

The young English GM Michael Adams was the first to show the potential of the text-move. He demonstrated that the dangerous looking 7...♕b6 can be readily met with 8 ♗b5 ♗d7 9 0-0!, when the endgame after 9...♕xd4 10 ♗xc6 ♕xd1 11 ♗xd7+ ♔xd7 12 ♖axd1 is pleasantly favourable for White, e.g. Adams-Muir, London 1984.

I believe that the critical variation starts with 7...h6 8 ♗h4 g5 9 ♗g3 ♗g7. We are, however, in the very infancy of it.

(2) 7 ♗b5

The traditional line: White aims at rapid mobilisation of his forces against Black's uncastled king. For this he is willing to ruin his pawn formation and hand over the bishop pair.

7...♘xe3 8 fxe3

White may as well be consistent. After the scared 8 ♘xc6?! ♘xd1 9 ♘xd8+ ♔xd8 10 ♖xd1 a6! Black's king is secure and the potential of the bishop pair already gives him the slightly superior endgame, Fyllingen-Mednis, Gausdal 1990.

8...♗d7 9 0-0 e6

Because White's edge in development is nothing to be sneezed at, Black cannot afford 9...♘e5? 10 ♘f3! ♘xf3+ (10...♗xb5 11 ♘xb5 is no better for Black) 11 ♕xf3 f6 12 e5! with a devastating attack.

10 ♗xc6 bxc6 11 e5 ♗e7

Again Black should rush to complete his development. After 11...dxe5?! 12 ♕h5 ♕e7 13 ♕xe5 White has the advantage.

12 ♕h5 0-0 13 exd6 ♗xd6

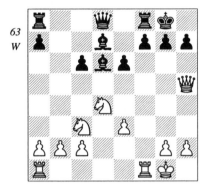

63
W

White must look for attacking chances to compensate for Black's bishop pair and extra central pawn. I am now giving what is considered to be the main line:

14 ♘e4 ♗e7 15 ♖ad1 ♕b6 16 ♖f3 ♗e8 17 ♖h3 h6 18 ♖g3 ♔h7 19 ♖f1

White now threatens 20 ♖f6!! e.g. 19...c5? 20 ♖f6!! ♗xf6 21 ♘xf6+ ♔h8 22 ♕g5!!. The obvious response, 19... f5, is supposed to lose because of 20 ♖xg7+ ♔xg7 21 ♘xe6+, but it doesn't seem so clear to me after 21...♔h7. After 22 ♘xf8+ ♗xf8 Black parries both 23 ♕xf5+ ♗g6 24 ♘f6+ ♔g7 25 ♕d7+ ♔h8 and 23 ♘f6+ ♔h8! 24 ♕xf5 (24 ♘xe8 ♕xe3+ followed by 25...♖xe8.) 24...♕xe3+ 25 ♔h1 ♕e7. In each case, Black is better.

19...♕d8

The text is, according to theory, the only correct move.

20 c4 a5 21 ♕e5 ♖g8 22 ♘f3!

The unsound 22 ♘xc6? ♗xc6 23 ♖xf7 was refuted in Gipslis-Tukmakov, Parnu 1977: 23...♕d1+ 24 ♔f2 ♕c2+ 25 ♔g1 ♕b1+ 26 ♔f2 ♗f8!! 27 ♘f6+ ♔h8 28 ♘xg8 ♖d8 29 ♕c3 ♕d1 30 e4 ♖d2+ 31 ♔e3 ♕e1+ 0-1.

The text leads to an interesting draw by repetition of moves.

22...f6! 23 ♕xe6 ♗d7 24 ♕f7 ♗e8 Draw

So, what can we say about the "naive", obvious 6...♘g4? It is fully playable, yet does require a substantial amount of theoretical knowledge.

(II) *Black has castled kingside*

Of course, when Black has castled kingside, he does not have to worry about ♗b5 in response to ...♘g4. Yet the important point is that just because ...♘g4 can be played, it does not follow that therefore it should be played.

In its early years, the main line of the Dragon was: **1 e4 c5 2 ♘f3 ♘c6 3 d4 cxd4 4 ♘xd4 ♘f6 5 ♘c3 d6 6 ♗e2 g6 7 ♗e3 ♗g7 8 0-0 0-0 9 f4** *(D)*

With his last move White starts his attack against Black's kingside and is ready for an opportune e5 or f5 advance. If Black is lackadaisical, White will be able to build up a very powerful attacking formation. His last move, however, has loosened his position

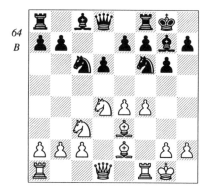

along the a7-g1 diagonal and also the g4-square remains vulnerable. Black's chances for counterplay must come from these features. The moves worth trying are therefore 9...♘g4 and 9...♕b6. Let us see how they work out:

(1) **9...♘g4?!**

Tactically fine, but it leads to a strategically unsatisfactory situation.

10 ♗xg4 ♗xd4

Not 10...♗xg4? and Black loses material after 11 ♘xc6.

11 ♗xd4 ♗xg4 12 ♕d2! ♗e6 13 f5 ♗c4 14 ♖f3 ♘xd4 15 ♕xd4 ♗a6 16 ♘d5 with a large advantage to White. Because of his absent dark-squared bishop, Black's kingside has become seriously weakened. White threatens 17 f6, so 16...f6 is forced, weakening the kingside still more. The game reference is Emanuel Lasker-Golmayo, Havana (match) 1893.

(2) **9...♕b6!**

The move that has made 9 f4 obsolete in modern tournament play. Black threatens 10...♘xe4!,

winning a pawn, while White lacks a way to "punish" the audacious text. For instance:

(a) 10 ♘f5? ♕xb2 11 ♘a4 ♕a3 12 c3 ♘xe4!.

(b) 10 ♘a4?! ♕b4 11 c3 ♕a5 12 b4 ♕c7 13 ♗f3 ♗d7 and White's queenside is compromised.

10 e5?! dxe5 11 fxe5 ♘xe5 12 ♘f5 ♕xb2 13 ♘xe7+ ♔h8 14 ♗d4 ♕b4! 15 ♗xe5 (15 ♘xc8 ♖d8!) 15...♕xe7 16 ♕d4 ♘h5. White has insufficient compensation for the pawn.

10 ♕d3 ♘g4! 11 ♘d5

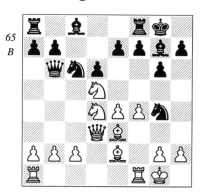

Looks dangerous, but it leads only to an equal endgame. A more routine route to that is 11 ♗xg4 ♗xd4 12 ♗xd4 ♕xd4+ 13 ♕xd4 ♘xd4 14 ♗d1.

11...♗xd4! 12 ♗xg4

Capturing the queen is good only for Black: 12 ♘xb6?! ♗xe3+ 13 ♔h1 ♗xb6 14 ♗xg4 ♗xg4 15 f5 ♘e5 16 ♕g3 ♔h8 17 ♕h4 ♗d8, Bosch-Landau, Amsterdam 1939. The three active pieces are more effective than White's queen.

12...♗xe3+ 13 ♕xe3 ♕xe3+

Dubious is 13...♕xb2?! 14 ♗xc8 ♖axc8 15 ♖ab1 ♕xa2 16 ♖xb7, with a strong initiative for White.

14 ♘xe3 ♗xg4 15 ♘xg4

This endgame is completely equal.

Yes, do learn the traps important in your opening, yet be careful about applying the same theme in "similar" situations. It may not work or – at the very least – require a substantial amount of preparatory research.

11 Opening novelty: good or just interesting?

Consider this scenario: *Chess Life* publishes a game where a strong GM uses a new move in a variation of interest to you and scores an impressive win. You can't wait for your next tournament to start so that you can get a "free point" by using the novelty yourself. Should you?

Well, it mostly depends on whether the novelty is in fact a good one or just an interesting one. How can you tell this ahead of time? Unfortunately, foresight is a lot harder than hindsight. Yet, some guidelines will help. Firstly, do some checking yourself. Does it make strategic sense for the variation? Is there some thematic tactical response that must be explored? Do not choose to play it unless you both believe in it and understand what the idea is about. Still, it will be difficult for just one person to come up with the truth. To minimise risk (although at the cost of opportunity) you may want to wait for the "inventor" to play it again. In the 1950s and 1960s a good approach was: "watch Bobby". Not only in his time, but for all times, Robert J. Fischer has been recognised as the greatest explorer of openings. In the course of these explorations

he discovered many interesting ideas and was willing to try out a number of them at least once. Yet this hardly meant automatically getting the "Fischer stamp of approval". For instance, in the game R.Fischer-E.German, Stockholm Interzonal 1962, Round 13, he dared an old move of dubious reputation against the Petroff Defence (C 43): 1 e4 e5 2 ♘f3 ♘f6 3 d4 exd4 4 e5 ♘e4 and here, instead of the normal 5 ♕xd4, Fischer essayed 5 ♕e2!?

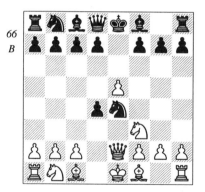

66
B

Caught by surprise, the Brazilian IM decided not to challenge his opponent and settled for the insipid 5...♘c5 6 ♘xd4 ♘c6 7 ♘xc6 bxc6 8 ♘c3 ♖b8 and after 9 f4! ♗e7 10 ♕f2 d5 11 ♗e3 ♘d7 12 0-0-0 Fischer demonstrated the power of his kingside pawn majority and won on move 30. Yet Bobby would not praise his 5th move and in his next encounter with the Petroff (8 years later!) went back to 3 ♘xe5. He, no doubt, was sure that after the theoretically important reply, 5...♗b4+, Black has no problems at all, no matter whether White plays 6 c3, 6 ♘bd2 or Steinitz's 6 ♔d1.

The principle to follow is that when a strong GM uses a new idea for the second time, that generally means that you also are on rather strong ground. Not much confidence should be placed on just a single event. A truly scintillating example comes from the creative mind of another World Champion, Garry Kasparov. I consider it the most exhilarating opening idea ever seen in World Championship play. The scene was the 1985 Karpov-Kasparov Match, Games 12, 14, 16 and 18:

In the Taimanov variation of the Sicilian Defence, after the normal moves **1 e4 c5 2 ♘f3 e6 3 d4 cxd4 4 ♘xd4 ♘c6 5 ♘b5 d6 6 c4 ♘f6 7 ♘1c3 a6 8 ♘a3** Kasparov shocked chess theory and his opponent with the audacious **8...d5!!?** *(D)*

Black breaks loose from the cramp by simply throwing away an important central pawn: 9 exd5 exd5 10 cxd5 ♘b4. Karpov chose 11 ♗c4, but after 11...♗g4 12 ♗e2?! ♗xe2 13 ♕xe2+ ♕e7 14 ♗e3 ♘bxd5 Black had his pawn back and readily equalised (15 ♘c2

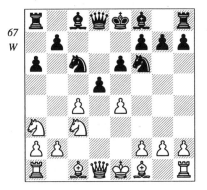

67
W

♘xe3 16 ♘xe3 ♕e6 17 0-0 ♗c5 18 ♖fe1 0-0 ½-½).

(2) Karpov-Kasparov, Game 14, October 10.

Karpov's team obviously was not yet ready to cope with the innovation and he side-stepped with 5 ♘c3 (Draw in 32).

(3) Karpov-Kasparov, Game 16, October 15.

Karpov felt ready and varied from the 11 ♗c4 of Game 12 with 11 ♗e2. Yet after 11...♗c5 12 0-0 0-0 13 ♗f3 ♗f5 14 ♗g5 ♖e8 15 ♕d2 b5 16 ♖ad1 ♘d3! Black had full compensation for the pawn and went on to win brilliantly in 40 moves. (The game was chosen as the best one of *Chess Informant* 40).

(4) Karpov-Kasparov, Game 18, October 22.

It was now Kasparov who varied on move 2! He explains his choice – 2...d6 – quite enlighteningly in his wonderful book on the 1985 match: "The gambit variation had brought its dividends, and I did not wish to tempt fate..."

Kasparov did not play 8...d5 again. But those who followed him blindly soon were to rue their naivety. For example, in A.Karpov-J.van der Wiel, Wijk aan Zee 1986, played less than two months after the end of the Karpov-Kasparov match, White improved on the 12 0-0 of Game 16 with 12 ♗e3! and soon obtained a significant advantage: 12...♗xe3 13 ♕a4+! ♘d7 14 ♕xb4 ♗c5 15 ♕e4+ ♔f8 16 0-0, with Black having no compensation for the pawn.

The moral, again, is to watch the inventor. Moreover, keep going back to the fundamentals. Can it really be that Black can afford to play something like 8...d5? The odds for that are poor – probably no better than one in a hundred!

After this lengthy "introduction", I will now give three more examples regarding the good vs. "interesting" discussion.

Interesting Move/Idea

In the fall of 1974 Arthur Bisguier and I were invited to play in an International Tournament held at Sombor, Yugoslavia. The only other westerners present were from Holland: the young GM Jan Timman and the experienced IM Rob Hartoch. Knowing that against 1 e4 e5 2 ♘f3 ♘c6 3 ♗c4, Bisguier invariably chose the Two Knights' Defence, 3...♘f6, Timman had prepared a new idea

in one of the main variations (C59):

4 ♘g5 d5 5 exd5 ♘a5 6 ♗b5+ c6 7 dxc6 bxc6 8 ♗e2 h6 9 ♘f3 e4 10 ♘e5 ♗d6 11 f4 exf3 12 ♘xf3 0-0 13 d4 c5 14 dxc5 ♗xc5 15 ♕xd8 ♖xd8 16 ♗d2!?

This is the attempted improvement over 16 c3 ♖e8 17 ♔f1 ♖xe2 18 ♔xe2 ♗a6+ 19 ♔d1 ♘g4 20 ♔c2 ♘f2 21 ♖d1 ♘xd1 22 ♔xd1 ♖d8+ 23 ♗d2 ♘c4 24 b4, E.Mednis-A.Bisguier, US Championship 1957/58. White went on to survive and the game ended a draw on move 40.

Timman's plan is to castle on the queenside as quickly as possible. What struck me most during the post-mortem was his characterisation of the idea: "It is an interesting idea. I don't claim that it is a good one, but it is an interesting one."

16...♘c6 17 ♘c3

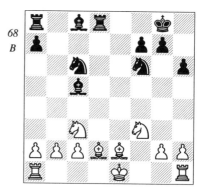

68
B

17...♘b4?

This brute force move is easily repulsed. For the correct 17...♘g4!

see the following illustrative game Hartoch-Bisguier.

18 0-0-0 ♗f5 19 ♘e1 ♘g4 20 a3 ♘c6 21 ♘d3 ♗b6

21...♗xd3 fails to 22 ♗xg4.

22 h3! ♘e3 23 ♗xe3 ♗xe3+ 24 ♔b1 ♘d4 25 ♗g4 ♗g6 26 ♖he1

White has consolidated his material advantage and went on to win without difficulty: **26...♗g5 27 ♘e2 h5 28 ♘xd4 ♖xd4** (28...hxg4 29 ♘e5!) **29 ♗f3 ♖c8 30 ♖e5 f6 31 ♖d5 ♖xd5 32 ♗xd5+ ♔h7 33 b4 ♗e3 34 c4 ♔h6 35 ♔b2 f5 36 ♘e5 f4 37 c5 ♗f5 38 ♘f7+ ♔g6 39 ♘d6 ♖c7 40 ♘xf5 ♔xf5 41 ♗f3 g6 42 ♖d5+ ♔f6 43 ♔c3 ♖e7 44 a4 1-0**

Timman and Hartoch were staying together in the same hotel room. I was therefore quite surprised that in R.Hartoch-A.Bisguier, Round 6, the position shown in Diagram 68 arose again. Bisguier was ready and improved with:

17...♘g4! 18 ♘e4

Now, of course, 18 0-0-0?! loses the exchange to 18...♘f2.

18...♗b6 19 h3

19 0-0-0?! fails to the same motif as in the previous note: 19...f5 followed by 20...♘f2.

19...♘e3 20 ♗xe3 ♗xe3

With White's king stuck in the centre and the Black bishop pair and rooks ready to rake him there, Black has more than sufficient compensation for the sacrificed pawn. While it is true that throughout the C59 complex Black has good compensation, what White has wrought here is worse than usual. Why did Hartoch blindly follow Timman's idea? In any case, a natural attacking player like Bisguier had no problem handling this position and won impressively:

21 ♗d3 ♖b8 22 b3 ♘b4 23 ♔e2 ♗b6 24 ♖hd1 ♗b7 25 ♘f2 ♘d5 26 ♖e1 ♘e3 27 ♖g1 ♖e8! 28 ♔d2 ♘d5! 29 ♘d1 ♗xg1 30 ♘xg1 ♘f4 31 g3 ♘xd3 32 cxd3 ♖e6 33 ♘c3 ♖d8 34 ♘ce2 ♗a6 35 d4 ♖de8 36 ♘f4 ♖e3 37 g4 ♖3e4 0-1

Good Move/Idea

The odds that an interesting move/idea will also be fundamentally good are greatly increased if at least one of the following conditions is present: (1) The very specific problem in the position is solved, and (2) The strategic need(s) of the position are furthered.

In the game V.Epishin-G.Sosonko, Ter Apel 1992, Black came up with a significant novelty to rehabilitate an important sub-variation within the Queen's Gambit Declined, Ragozin Variation complex (D38):

1 d4 d5 2 c4 e6 3 ♘c3 ♘f6 4 ♗g5 ♗b4 5 cxd5 exd5 6 ♘f3 h6 7 ♗h4 (7 ♗xf6 is generally considered good enough for a normal opening advantage) **7...g5** (prior to this game the text was generally thought to be inferior to 7...c5) 8 ♗g3 ♘e4 9 ♘d2! ♘xc3 10 bxc3 ♗xc3 11 ♖c1

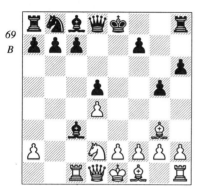

69
B

What is Black to do about his attacked bishop? 11...♗xd4? loses to 12 ♕a4+ while 11...♗a5 places it out of play for the coming storming of Black's kingside (for example 12 ♕c2 ♘c6 13 e3 0-0 14 h4). 11...♗xd2+?! 12 ♕xd2 ♘c6 13 h4!, A.Adorjan-B.Kurajica, Sarajevo 1982, demonstrated the porosity of Black's kingside.

11...♗b2!

Problem solved! Now 12 ♖c2 (and 12 ♖b1) allows 12...♗xd4. If 12 ♗xc7, Epishin in *Chess Informant* 54 gives 12...♕d7 13 ♗e5 ♗xc1 14 ♗xh8 ♗a3 as "unclear".

12 ♖xc7 ♘a6! 13 ♖c2 ♗xd4 14 e3 ♗g7 15 ♗xa6 bxa6 and Black has full equality (the game was eventually drawn).

I will conclude this section with a more complicated example. A very double-edged position results from the following variation of the Queen's Gambit Declined (D37):

1 d4 d5 2 c4 e6 3 ♘c3 ♘f6 4 ♘f3 ♗e7 5 ♗f4 0-0 6 e3 c5 7 dxc5 ♗xc5 8 ♕c2 ♘c6 9 a3 ♕a5 10 0-0-0 (very demanding; safer is 10 ♖d1) 10...♗d7 11 g4 ♖fc8 12 ♔b1

Before continuing the kingside attack, White takes time out for king safety. Black players have been responding with 12...dxc4, 12...♗e8 or 12...♗f8 – with varying degrees of successes. Yet the key question remains: what should Black do to further his attacking prospects? In B.Gelfand-A.Belyavsky, Linares 1991, Black answered with the electrifying:

12...b5!!

Losing no time! White's possibilities now include:

(1) 13 cxd5? b4! 14 dxc6 ♗xc6 15 axb4 ♗xb4 16 ♗e2 ♗xc3 17 bxc3 ♗e4 18 ♖d3 ♖ab8+! and Black wins (Ftačnik).

(2) 13 ♘xb5?! and Black gains the advantage after both 13...♘e7 (Ftačnik) and 13...a6 (Mikhailjchisin).

(3) 13 g5 ♘h5 14 cxb5 ♘xf4 15 exf4 ♘e7 16 ♘e5 ♗e8 with advantage to Black (Mikhailjchisin).

It is worth noting that Belyavsky's idea received the prize for the most important theoretical novelty of *Chess Informant* 51.

13 cxb5 ♘e7 14 ♘d2 ♕d8! 15 ♘b3

Ivanchuk and Ftačnik draw attention to 15 ♗e2, planning 16 g5.

15...♘e4! 16 ♘xc5 ♖xc5 17 ♗e5 ♘xc3+ 18 ♗xc3 ♗xb5

Here the Latvian magazine *Sahs Baltija*, No. 4, 1992 quotes Ivanchuk as saying "the chances are approximately equal". In the game Black went on to win convincingly – see *Chess Life*, June 1991, p. 25 or *Chess Informant* 51, Game 415.

My evaluation of 12...b5!! is that it is "good" since Black's thematic counterplay is furthered. This means that White should look for improvements earlier. Currently both 11 ♔b1 (V.Akopian-Gi.Garcia, World Open, Philadelphia 1994 – see *Chess Informant* 61, Game 440) and 11 cxd5 (J.Piket-J.Timman, Amsterdam 1995 – see *Inside Chess*, No. 19, 1995, p.35) are leading to an advantage for White.

12 The advantage of the move in symmetrical positions

Apart from the special and important exception of zugzwang positions, it is advantageous to be on the move. This is especially so in the opening. I shall be discussing the interesting and theoretically important situation where the position is absolutely symmetrical, but White is to move. The opportunities and risks are of course greatest in open games, i.e. where White has played 1 e4.

It may seem intuitively that a move-on-move symmetrical development in open games must be greatly in White's favour, yet under normal conditions this generally isn't so. The reason is that if White is playing good moves, so is Black and therefore nothing is possible. Moreover, since the position is inherently open, Black knows that he must be careful and break off the symmetry in time. I shall look at three important openings: Petroff Defence, Four Knights Opening and Vienna Opening. In Chapter 14 I shall discuss the currently fashionable Exchange Variation in the French Defence.

(1) *Petroff Defence (C42)*
The following symmetrical sequence is usually considered to be an opening blunder by Black:

1 e4 e5 2 ♘f3 ♘f6 3 ♘xe5 ♘xe4?!
Of course, correct is 3...d6 4 ♘f3 ♘xe4. Yet the text is nowhere as bad as its reputation. For instance, the first edition of the *Encyclopedia of Chess Openings*, Volume C (1974) claims a won position for White.

4 ♕e2 ♕e7
Black cannot play 4...♘f6?? 5 ♘c6+ or 4...d5? 5 d3 ♘f6?? 6 ♘c6+ – two continuations I run into in simuls.

5 ♕xe4 d6 6 d4 dxe5 7 dxe5
Black has good compensation for the pawn after 7 ♕xe5 ♕xe5+ 8 dxe5 ♗f5! 9 c3 ♘d7 10 f4 ♗c5, due to his active, superior development.

7...♘c6 8 ♘c3!
Not holding on to the pawn, but aiming for superior development, is the only way to show up the flaw in 3...♘xe4?!. Black gains approximate equality after the other moves: 8 f4 ♗d7 9 ♘c3 0-0-0 followed by ...f6, 8 ♗f4 g5! and 8 ♗b5 ♗d7 9 0-0 0-0-0.

8...♕xe5 9 ♕xe5+ ♘xe5 10 ♗f4 ♗d6 11 ♗g3!
Now that White's dark-squared bishop is protected (11 ♘b5? ♘f3+!), White threatens 12 ♘b5 or 12 ♘e4.

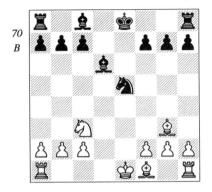

11...♗d7 12 0-0-0 0-0-0 13 ♘e4 ♗c6 14 ♘xd6+ cxd6 15 f3 ♖he8 16 ♖d4 ♔c7 17 a4

I have been following E.Vasyu-kov-V.Chekhov, USSR Championship (First League) 1975. White has the dual advantage of superior pawn formation and the bishop pair. Vasyukov went on to win on move 51. Though there can be no talk of White having a "won position", his advantage is clear and pleasant. There is no rational reason, therefore, for Black to choose 3...♘xe4?! in favour of the correct 3...d6.

(2) *Four Knights Opening (C49)*
The normal position results after:

1 e4 e5 2 ♘f3 ♘c6 3 ♘c3 ♘f6 4 ♗b5

There are two main reasons why the Four Knights has over the past six years again become an important guest in grandmaster repertoires. The first has to do with the desire for some respite from the overanalysed Ruy Lopez, a factor which is abetted by the emergence of the Marshall Gambit as a tough nut for White to crack. The other reason is that Rubinstein's "drawing ...♘d4" has lost its teeth as far as drawing is concerned. That is, while a draw would result after 4...♘d4 5 ♘xd4 exd4 6 e5 dxc3 7 exf6 ♕xf6! 8 dxc3 ♕e5+ 9 ♕e2, White can thwart Black's hopes with the modest retreat 5 ♗a4. This can and does lead to very unbalanced play. (An excellent treatise on the Four Knights is *New Ideas In The Four Knights* by John Nunn.)

Therefore, Black players interested in keeping the game in more strategic channels are returning to the symmetrical line

4...♗b4 5 0-0 0-0 6 d3 d6 7 ♗g5

This is the moment of truth for Black. He can not continue the symmetry with 7... ♗g4? because White comes first with the attack, e.g.:

(1) 8 ♗xf6 gxf6 (8...♕xf6? 9 ♘d5 followed by 10 ♗xc6 will cost

Black a piece) 9 ♘d5 ♗c5 10 ♕d2, K. Schlechter-Leonhardt, Hamburg 1910. White has the horrible threat of 11 ♕h6 and Black's kingside is already permanently weakened.

(2) 8 ♘d5 ♘d4 9 ♘xb4 ♘xb5 10 ♘d5 ♘d4 11 ♕d2! c6 12 ♘xf6+ gxf6 13 ♗h4 ♗xf3 14 ♕h6 ♘e2+ 15 ♔h1 ♗xg2+ 16 ♔xg2 ♘f4+ 17 ♔h1 ♘g6 18 ♖g1 with a very strong attack for White (*ECO* C Revised, 1981). Indeed, White's immediate threat is 19 f4.

7...♗xc3 8 bxc3

The exchange has given White the potential of the bishop pair in case the centre gets opened up and the b-pawn's move to c3 has enhanced White's centre. There is, however, a cost: doubled c-pawns and the offside position of the light-squared bishop. Thus an interesting, strategically unbalanced, situation has arisen, where whoever plays better has excellent prospects for the win.

8...♕e7

The start of a regrouping: the queen's knight will travel to e6 to force White's pinning bishop to declare its future intentions.

9 ♖e1 ♘d8 10 d4 ♘e6 11 ♗c1

A strategic retreat whereby White keeps the options of later redeployment along the c1-h6 diagonal as well as the potential trip to a3 to take advantage of the pin on the d-pawn. Instead 11 ♗h4 ♘f4 leaves White's bishop largely offside, whereas the passive 11

♗d2 just limits White's options. I shall now be following the game N.Short-V.Anand, Linares 1992.

11...c5

The text has been the most popular main line variation. Black puts d4 under serious challenge, though at the potential cost of losing control of d5. The second most popular line is 11...♖d8, with a recent game going: 12 ♘h4 g6 13 a4 c6 14 ♗f1 d5! 15 ♘f5! gxf5 16 exf5 e4! 17 fxe6 ♕xe6 with roughly equal chances, J.Nunn-D.Prasad, Manila Olympiad 1992.

12 a4 ♖d8 13 dxe5

A radical decision: White leaves himself with isolated doubled c-pawns, while enhancing the prospects of his light-squared bishop and stopping Black's central counterplay.

**13...dxe5 14 ♕e2 ♕c7 15 ♗c4!
h6**

Black will now wind up in a passive situation. Anand subsequently suggested 15...♖e8! 16 ♘h4 ♘f4 "with counterplay" as a more attractive course.

16 ♘h4 ♖e8 17 ♘f5 ♘f4 18 ♕f3 ♗xf5?!

Black is too optimistic regarding the position. Strategically sounder is 18...♗e6 19 ♗f1 (19 ♗b5 ♖ed8) 19...c4 with Black close to equality.

19 exf5 ♖ad8 20 a5! *(D)*

A strategically unbalanced and deceptive position of which Short's evaluation was much superior. Though White's pawn formation

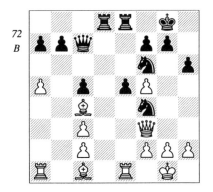

72
B

seems to be in a shambles (isolated doubled c-pawns, doubled f-pawns), his compensation is more than adequate: initiative on the queenside, excellent potential for his bishops in an open position, lack of opportunities for Black's knights. The recurrent theme to the end will be the power of the bishop pair. White has a small yet pleasant advantage here and he never lets go of it.

20...♘4d5 21 ♕g3 ♔h7 22 h3 ♖e7 23 ♗f1!

Preparing for activation of the queen's rook via a4. Anand considers Black's best defensive plan to be 23...c4 24 ♖a4 b5, with White retaining a slight edge after 25 axb6 ♘xb6 26 ♖a1.

23...♕c8?! 24 ♖xe5 ♖xe5 25 ♕xe5 ♖e8 26 ♕g3 c4

Preparing to capture on f5. After the immediate 26...♕xf5?, the reply 27 ♗d3! is a decisive pin, e.g. 27...♖e1+ 28 ♔h2 ♘e4 29 ♗xh6! ♘xg3 30 ♖xe1 ♔xh6 31 ♗xf5 ♘xf5 32 ♖e5 with a won endgame for White (Anand).

27 ♗b2 ♕xf5 28 ♗xc4 ♘e4 29 ♕f3 ♕xf3 30 gxf3 ♘exc3 31 ♔f1! ♖c8 32 ♗d3+

Works like a charm, yet according to Short more of a permanent bind would result from 32 ♗b3!

32...♔g8 33 ♖a3 b5??

The kind of error that in uncomfortable positions comes easily to humans. In order is the careful 33...♖c7, with White holding the initiative after 34 ♖b3.

34 axb6 1-0

After 34...axb6 35 ♗f5!, protecting the c3-knight by retaining the rook on the c-file allows 36 ♖a8+ ♖c8 37 ♖xc8#.

(3) Vienna Opening (C25)

1 e4 e5 2 ♘c3 ♘c6

The most common response is 2...♘f6, though White can then safely choose the challenging 3 f4. The symmetrical text has been preferred by strategists to avoid that advance because for a long time theory considered the variation 3 f4 exf4 4 ♘f3 g5 to be good for Black. However, recent successes by Arnason and Motwani have left matters truly unclear.

3 ♗c4 ♗c5

Because of Black's equally high-quality development, White has few prospects of gaining an advantage with 4 d3 or 4 ♘f3. However, there is an audacious way of trying to exploit Black's last two moves. I am now following the game B.Larsen-L.Portisch, Santa Monica 1966.

4 ♕g4! g6

An unavoidable weakening of the kingside. There is no reason to give up the right of castling with 4...♚f8?!. Moreover, Black generally cannot afford the same kind of outlandish behaviour in early opening play as White, e.g. 4...♕f6? is bad because of 5 ♘d5! ♕xf2+ 6 ♚d1 ♚f8 7 ♘h3 ♕d4 8 d3. One example is 8...♗b6 9 ♖f1 ♘d8 10 c3 ♕c5 11 ♘g5 ♘h6 12 ♕h5 and Black resigned in Alekhine-Lugovsky, 1931 (12...d6 13 ♘f6!).

5 ♕f3 ♘f6 6 ♘ge2 d6 7 d3 ♗g4 8 ♕g3 h6

Preventing the pin on g5. According to Portisch, he also evaluated 8...♗e6, 8...♕d7 and 8...♗xe2, before concluding that the text is flexible and good.

9 f4 ♕e7 10 ♘d5 ♘xd5 11 ♕xg4

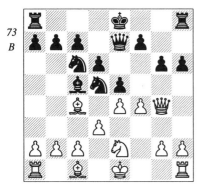

73
B

At the moment White has the more active queen whereas Black is ahead in minor piece development. White's prospects for the initiative are based on the attack along the f-file, aiming at f7. Who is better?

11...♘f6?!

Played with a sharp counterattacking plan in mind, but since Black doesn't carry it through, the text just leads to a very strong attacking position for White. Both Larsen and Portisch agree that best is 11...♘e3 12 ♗xe3 ♗xe3 when Larsen considers 13 ♕g3 ♘d4! and adds that "White's advantage must studied under a microscope". Portisch analyses 13 f5 ♕g5 14 ♕f3 ♘d4 15 ♘xd4 exd4 16 fxg6 ♕xg6 17 ♖f1 ♖f8 as leading to equality.

12 ♕h3! ♘a5?

Leads to nothing but weaknesses. Black should have continued with the planned 12... d5! 13 exd5 ♘b4 when best play for both sides is 14 fxe5! ♕xe5 15 ♚d1 ♘bxd5 16 ♖e1 0-0! which Portisch calls "extremely wild, but still playable for Black".

13 ♗b5+ c6 14 ♗a4 b5 15 ♗b3 d5 16 fxe5 ♕xe5 17 c3!

White threatens 18 d4 and is also ready to chase away Black's queen with 18 ♗f4, as well as attacking along the half-open f-file with ♖f1. Larsen feels that Black's lesser evil now is 17...♗e7, with White having a large advantage after 18 0-0.

17...♘xb3 18 axb3 ♗b6 19 ♖f1 ♗d8

If 19...dxe4, White wins with 20 d4 ♕e7 21 ♗g5! (Portisch).

20 ♗f4 ♕e6

The endgame is poor, but no worse than the middlegame after 20...♕e7 21 ♘d4.

21 ♕xe6+ fxe6 22 ♘d4! dxe4

After 22...♔d7 23 ♗e5 ♖f8 White brings his last piece into the game with 24 ♖a6, winning absolutely everything.

23 ♘xc6 ♖h7 24 ♘xd8 ♖xd8 25 ♖a6 exd3 26 ♗xh6

Because in such a open position the bishop is much superior to Black's knight, the win would have been much simpler after either 26 ♖xe6+ or 26 ♗e5 – in either case retaining the bishop.

26...♖xh6 27 ♖xe6+ ♔d7 28 ♖fxf6 ♖xh2 29 ♖d6+ ♔e7 30 ♖xd8 ♔xf6 31 ♔f2 ♖h1 32 ♖xd3 ♖b1 33 ♖d2

From a horrible position Black has reached a rook and pawn endgame where he is only a doubled pawn down. Even though Black does have real practical chances for a draw, Larsen – at his prime around the time of this game – takes care of the technical problems with exceptional skill. Since the following is outside the scope of this chapter, I'll make no further comments.

33...♔e5 34 ♔f3 a6 35 b4 ♔f5 36 ♔e3! ♔g4 37 ♔d4 ♔g3 38 ♔c5 g5 39 ♔b6 ♖a1 40 b3 ♖c1 41 ♔xa6 ♖xc3 42 ♖b2 g4 43 ♔xb5 ♔h2 44 ♔a5 ♖c8 45 b5 ♖a8+ 46 ♔b4 ♖b8 47 ♔c5 ♖c8+ 48 ♔d6 ♖b8 49 ♔c6 ♖c8+ 50 ♔b7 ♖f8 51 b6 g3 52 ♔a6 ♖f2 53 ♖b1 1-0

Part Four: The Modern Approach in the Selection of Your Opening Repertoire

13 Building a systematic opening repertoire against the Sicilian

The previous parts have presented various important aspects of general principles of modern opening play. Now it is time to be more specific. This chapter is not meant for the chess professional who both needs and has the time to arrange his openings so as to follow the very latest grandmaster evaluations. For instance, such a player as White against the Sicilian Defence, may at the same time have as his repertoire: the Yugoslav Attack against the Dragon, Richter-Rauzer Variation against the Classical Variation, 6 f4 against the Najdorf, the Keres Attack (6 g4) against the Scheveningen, etc. Conceptually there is nothing wrong with such a repertoire. The only disadvantage is that every system for White is specific unto itself and therefore requires a tremendous effort to keep learning new systems as well as to keep up with each of them.

This chapter is aimed at the player for whom the time for study is strictly limited. He or she needs some rhyme or reason for selecting something that fits more than just one variation. Let us assume that you "like" to play 1 e4 as White. What should you play against the Sicilian Defence?

Most importantly, you should select an active approach, striving for an open game. A number of students have told me that they like to play 1 e4 except when faced with the Sicilian. Such a "complaint" makes no chess sense to me. I mean, 1 e4 is for those who like active, attacking play. Because the Sicilian delays Black's kingside development while ignoring White's active development, attacking players should jump for joy when they see Black play 1...c5. If you don't like playing against the Sicilian, you should quit playing 1 e4. Try 1 d4, which is also an active move, but does not require speedy mobilisation for attacks. If you still want to play 1 e4, read on. Let me assume that you like active, attacking play, yet do not feel comfortable with your own king in imminent danger. I suggest open systems with ♗c4, in conjunction with kingside castling. Let us see how this works out for the following four important Black variations: Classical, Najdorf, Dragon and Scheveningen. Of necessity, all that I will be able to give is what I consider to be the current main line in each variation.

(1) *Classical Variation*

1 e4 c5 2 ♘f3 d6 3 d4 cxd4 4 ♘xd4 ♘f6 5 ♘c3 ♘c6

This is the basic position of the Classical Variation. White has a large number of playable moves including 6 ♗g5, 6 ♗e3, 6 f4, 6 g3, 6 ♗e2 and 6 ♗c4. I am selecting the last of these.

6 ♗c4

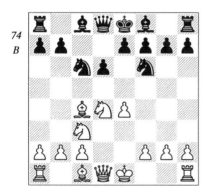

74
B

This is the Sozin variation, named after the Soviet master

who played it a few times (unsuccessfully) in the early 1930s. The true father, however, is Robert J. Fischer, who worked it into a successful system in the second half of the 1950s. In open games the light-squared bishop's most powerful early diagonal is a2-f7, bearing down on Black's vulnerable f7-point. Already White has an immediate threat, e.g. 6...g6?! 7 ♘xc6 bxc6 8 e5 dxe5?? 9 ♗xf7+. Black has three satisfactory defences.

6...e6

By far the main line: Black shortens the White bishop's diagonal, gets ready to complete kingside development and controls d5. The alternatives are:

(a) 6...♗d7: Black is now ready to follow up with 7...g6, establishing the Dragon Variation. But, of course, he could have done so immediately with 5...g6.

(b) 6...♕b6: The Benko Variation, with the main line being 7 ♘b3 e6 8 0-0 ♗e7 9 ♗e3 ♕c7 10 f4 a6 11 ♗d3 b5.

Good references for the Sozin Variation include *ECO B* Revised, *The Sicilian Sozin* by Harding, Botterill and Kottnauer, and *Bobby Fischer's Chess Games* by Wade and O'Connell.

7 ♗b3 ♗e7 8 ♗e3 0-0 9 0-0

The Fischer variation. Instead, 9 ♕e2 followed by 10 0-0-0 brings about the Velimirović Variation, a much more double-edged method. After the text White also will have good attacking chances, yet his king remains safe.

9...a6

The best way to start mobilising Black's queenside. Considerable practice has shown that it is not worth the time to exchange off White's light-squared bishop with 9...♘a5?!: 10 f4 b6 11 e5 ♘e8 12 f5! dxe5 13 fxe6 ♘xb3 14 ♘c6! ♕d6 15 ♕xd6 ♗xd6 16 axb3 with the superior endgame for White because both of Black's queenside pawns are vulnerable.

10 f4 ♘xd4 11 ♗xd4 b5 12 e5!

White must not tarry with his attack. After 12 a3?! ♗b7 White cannot hope for more than equality – see, for instance, Fischer – Spassky, Match Game 4, 1972.

12...dxe5 13 fxe5 ♘d7 14 ♘e4!

The queen's knight must be activated before Black gets in ...♗b7. The active-looking 14 ♕f3?! works out poorly because of 14...♘c5!, with advantage to Black.

14...♗b7 15 ♘d6 ♗xd6 16 exd6 ♕g5 17 ♖f2!

The critical position for the variation where White castles kingside. White has the bishop pair in an open position and a far advanced passed d-pawn; Black has a sound kingside pawn majority plus active queen and bishop.

Important alternatives for Black are:

a) **17...e5?**. Opening the diagonal for the b3-bishop is simply

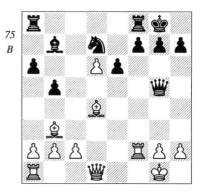

suicidal: 18 ♗c3 ♘f6 19 ♕f1!, Kudrin-Dahlberg, Lone Pine 1981, when Black lacks a satisfactory continuation.

b) **17...♗d5?!** gives White time to safeguard his passed pawn. After 18 ♖d2 ♗xb3 19 axb3 e5 20 ♗f2! ♖fc8 21 ♕e2 ♖c6 22 c4 White had a clear advantage in Bangiev-Chernikov, USSR 1975.

c) **17...a5**. It is unclear whom, if anyone, this weakening of the queenside benefits. Oll-Loginov, USSR 1987 continued: 18 a4 b4 19 ♕d2 ♕xd2 20 ♖xd2 ♖ac8 21 ♖e1 ♗a6 22 c3 ♗c4 with – most likely – dynamic equality.

d) **17...♖ad8** is Black's soundest plan: the d-pawn can become vulnerable both in the middlegame and endgame. Now there is no time for 18 ♕e2?! because of 18...♗d5!; after 18 ♕d2 ♕xd2 19 ♖xd2 ♘f6! 20 ♗xf6 gxf6 the endgame is equal. H.Olafsson-E.Mednis, New York International 1977 was drawn in 24 and R.Henry-Mednis, Badger Open 1986, was drawn in 28.

(2) *Najdorf Variation*
1 e4 c5 2 ♘f3 d6 3 d4 cxd4 4 ♘xd4 ♘f6 5 ♘c3 a6

White has a number of high-quality methods of trying to refute the Najdorf: 6 ♗g5, 6 f4, 6 ♗e2 and 6 ♗c4. As part of my systematic approach, I will be discussing 6 ♗c4. Good references for additional study are *The Najdorf for the Tournament Player* by John Nunn, *ECO B* Revised and My *60 Memorable Games* by Bobby Fischer.

6 ♗c4

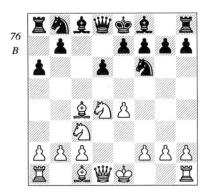

76
B

Another "invention" by Bobby Fischer. He reasoned that if 6 ♗c4 is fine against the Classical Variation, it should also be good when facing the Najdorf. This was his weapon – with very few exceptions – against the Najdorf throughout his chess career. White gets ready to attack Black's king, with his own king castled kingside.

6...e6

By far Black's most reliable plan. He can, however, also play first 6...b5 and only after 7 ♗b3, 7...e6.

7 ♗b3 b5

This active advance ensures that the variations will have the character of the Najdorf. Instead 7...♘c6 transposes into the Sozin. Too passive is 7...♗e7?! 8 f4 0-0 because White can immediately make good use of his b3-bishop with 9 f5.

8 0-0

The king is safe, the king's rook can be mobilised for work – and the text has no dark side. Its tactical justification is that 8...b4?! 9 ♘a4 ♘xe4 10 ♖e1 ♘f6 11 ♗g5 ♗e7 12 ♘f5! gives White an attack which is close to decisive (12...exf5? 13 ♗xf6 gxf6 14 ♕d5 wins).

8...♗e7 9 ♕f3

Currently White's most popular plan. Rather than going for an early pawn storm, White will try for a quick piece attack.

9...♕c7

An important alternative is 9...♕b6 when White keeps good attacking chances after 10 ♗g5!? 0-0 (not 10...♕xd4?, which loses to 11 e5) 11 ♖ad1 ♗b7 12 ♖fe1 ♘bd7 13 ♕g3.

10 ♕g3 ♘c6

Or 10...0-0 11 ♗h6 ♘e8 12 ♖ad1 ♗d7 13 f4, with a slight edge for White in the game A.Sokolov-B.Gelfand, USSR (ch) 1989.

11 ♘xc6 ♕xc6 12 ♖e1 0-0 13 ♗h6 ♘e8 14 ♘d5 ♗d8 15 ♖e3! ♕b7 16 ♘f4 ♔h8 17 ♗g5

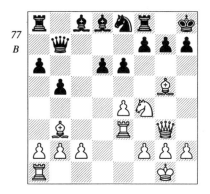

77
B

Because of his edge in development, White has a very strong attack. For instance, 17...f6? is refuted by 18 ♗xe6! fxg5? 19 ♘g6+ hxg6 20 ♕h3#. According to de Firmian, Black's only defence is 17...♗xg5 with a continuing normal opening advantage to White. Instead, N.de Firmian-W.Browne, US Championship 1989 continued:

17...♗b6?! 18 ♖f3! ♕xe4 19 ♔f1!! e5! 20 ♘d5 ♗a5 21 ♘e7 ♘c7 22 ♘xc8 ♖axc8 23 ♗e7 f5! 24 ♗xf8 ♖xf8 25 c3 f4 26 ♕g4 b4 27 ♖e1 ♕c6 28 ♖h3 ♕e8 29 ♕f3 h6? (necessary is 29...bxc3 30 bxc3 g6 – de Firmian) 30 ♕e4! bxc3 31 ♗c2 ♕b5+ 32 ♗d3 1-0

(3) *Dragon Variation*
1 e4 c5 2 ♘f3 d6 3 d4 cxd4 4 ♘xd4 ♘f6 5 ♘c3 g6 6 ♗c4

In conjunction with 7 h3, the text forms the Jansa Variation, named after the Czech Vlastimil Jansa, who played it very successfully for well over fifteen years. It has never been particularly popular, yet offers good chances for an opening advantage. Its theme again is: White wants to attack by having an actively placed king's bishop, yet with his king safe on the kingside. Probably the most reliable theoretical sources on this variation are *ECO B* Revised and recent *Chess Informants*.

6...♗g7 7 h3
A necessary part of White's system: in case of Black's ...♘c6, he can protect his knight with ♗e3. White does not play 7 f3 because he wants to be in the position to play a later f4 without loss of time.

7...0-0 8 0-0 ♘c6
The normal continuation. White is also slightly better after 8...a6 9 ♗b3 b5 10 ♘d5 ♗b7 11 ♘xf6+ ♗xf6 12 ♗h6 ♖e8 13 ♖e1, Jansa-Petursson, Gausdal 1988.

9 ♗e3 ♗d7
Black doesn't have full equality after either 9...♘xe4 10 ♗xf7+ ♖xf7 11 ♘xe4, or 9...♘a5 10 ♗b3 b6 11 ♕d3 ♘xb3 12 axb3, in the latter case because Black's c6-knight is more important for control of key central squares than is White's light-squared bishop.

10 ♗b3 (D)
Black's choices now include:
(1) 10...♘xd4 11 ♗xd4 ♗c6 12 ♕d3 ♘d7 13 ♗xg7 ♔xg7 14 ♕d4+ f6 15 ♔h2 ♕b6 16 ♕d2. White has a slight edge because of his greater central space and attacking chances after f4.
(2) 10...♕a5 11 ♖e1 ♖ac8 12 ♘d5 ♕d8 13 ♘b5! ♘xd5 (not

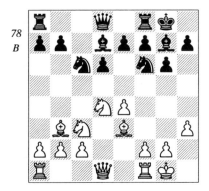

13...♘xe4? losing to 14 ♘xa7! ♘xa7 15 ♗b6 ♕e8 16 ♗xa7) 14 exd5 ♘a5 15 ♘d4 b5 16 c3. Here White's spatial advantage and pressure along the e-file give him a slight plus, Hennings-Kapengut, Lublin 1973.

(3) **10...♖c8 11 ♖e1! ♖e8?! 12 ♕d2 ♕a5?! 13 ♘f3! a6 14 ♖ad1.** White has completed the active development of his forces and is ready to start the attack. Jansa-W.Watson, Gausdal 1988 is an ideal example of how to carry it out: 14...b5 15 ♗h6 ♗h8 16 ♘g5 ♘e5 17 f4 ♘c4 18 e5! ♘h5 19 ♕f2 ♘g7 20 g4 b4 21 ♘d5 ♘e6 22 f5! ♘xg5 23 ♗xg5 ♘xe5 24 ♘xe7+ ♖xe7 25 ♗xe7 ♗c6 26 ♖e3 ♕b6 27 ♗xd6 ♗f3 28 ♗xe5! ♗xd1 29 ♗xh8 ♔xh8 30 ♖e8+ 1-0.

(4) Scheveningen Variation

1 e4 c5 2 ♘f3 d6 3 d4 cxd4 4 ♘xd4 ♘f6 5 ♘c3 e6 6 ♗c4

Black can now transpose into the Sozin with 6...♘c6 or into the Najdorf with 6...a6. These same opportunities also exist over the next 2-3 moves. However, it is my opinion that Black has an easier time equalising if he embarks on a different route. Good references for this are *The Sicilian Scheveningen* by Pritchett and *ECO B* Revised.

6...♗e7 7 ♗b3

The bishop's location on c4 is not a stable one, e.g. 7 0-0 0-0 8 ♗e3 ♘xe4! 9 ♘xe4 d5 and with the disappearance of White's centre, his advantage has also gone.

7...0-0

The immediate 7...♘a6 followed by 8...♘c5 is also good.

8 0-0

After either 8 ♗e3 or 8 f4 Black also plays 8...♘a6.

8...♘a6! 9 f4 ♘c5 10 ♕f3

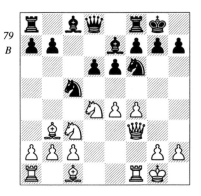

Black now has two major alternatives:

(a) Play on the queenside starting with **10...a6**. After 11 f5 ♔h8 (11...♕c7 12 g4 d5!? is unclear) 12 g4 ♘fd7 13 ♗e3 ♘e5 14 ♕g3 ♗d7 15 ♖ad1, Honfi-Vogt, Trnava 1982, White's attacking chances give him a slight edge.

(b) Counterplay in the centre starting with **10...e5!**. White's best is then probably 11 ♘de2 b5 12 fxe5 dxe5 13 ♗g5, most likely with equal chances. This variation deserves more practical tests.

14 The not-so-harmless Exchange Variation of the French Defence

The aptly named Exchange Variation of the French Defence results after the moves **1 e4 e6 2 d4 d5 3 exd5 exd5**

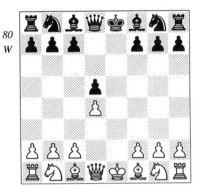

80
W

Just a momentary look tells us that the situation is as clear and symmetrical as possible. The popularity of, and respect for, this variation has fluctuated widely over the past century and a half. It was Paul Morphy's method against the French and was wonderfully suited to the style of the "apostle of rapid development". The advent of improved defensive skills started by Wilhelm Steinitz soon turned the variation into a toothless tiger good only for safe draws. This "reputation" endured for well over 100 years. Yet over the past half-dozen years the Exchange Variation has enjoyed a genuine renaissance, helped along no doubt by World Champion Garry Kasparov's success with it at Tilburg 1991. My two overall conclusions/recommendations are as follows:

I) *Do not play the Exchange Variation to gain a sure draw.*

Because Black's position has no flaws both in terms of ease of development and soundness of pawn structure, any pussyfooting around by White can easily lead to an initiative for Black. I would like to demonstrate this by the following two examples, one from "long ago" and the other quite recent.

(1) In the early 1950s I was the strongest player in New York City's high schools and my only defence to 1 e4 was the French. Therefore many of my opponents selected the Exchange Variation and not once did they score. A typical game is S.Daniels-E.Mednis, New York City High School Championship 1954, French Defence C01:

1 e4 e6 2 d4 d5 3 exd5 exd5 4 ♘f3 ♗d6 5 ♗d3 ♘e7 6 ♗e3 ♘bc6 7 ♘c3 ♗g4 8 h3 ♗h5 9 g4 ♗g6 10 ♗xg6 hxg6 11 ♕d2 ♕d7 12 ♗f4 f6 13 ♗xd6 ♕xd6 14 ♘b5 ♕d7 15 ♕f4 0-0-0 16 0-0-0 g5 17 ♕d2 ♘g6

18 ♕c3 a6 19 ♘a3 ♘f4 20 ♖he1
♖xh3 21 ♘b1 ♕xg4 0-1
(2) A key game in the last
round of the Manila 1990 Interzonal was M.Gurevich-N.Short.
Gurevich needed only a draw in
order to qualify for the Candidates
Matches, whereas Short needed a
win. See what happens:
1 d4 e6 2 e4 (even though Gurevich is a consistent queen's pawn
player, the false lure of the Exchange Variation lead him to
change his opening repertoire)
2...d5 3 exd5 exd5 4 ♘f3 ♗g4 5 h3
♗h5 6 ♗e2 ♗d6 7 ♘e5 ♗xe2 8
♕xe2 ♘e7 9 0-0 0-0 10 ♗f4 ♖e8 11
♕g4 ♗xe5! (unbalances the position and has the strategic basis of
aiming for a good knight vs. inferior bishop conflict) 12 ♗xe5 ♘g6
13 ♗g3 ♘d7 14 ♘d2 ♘f6 15 ♕f3
c6 16 ♕b3 ♕b6! (continuing to
have faith in the superiority of his
knight over White's bishop)17
♕xb6 axb6 18 a3 ♘e4 19 ♘xe4
♖xe4 20 ♖fd1 b5 21 ♔f1 f6 22 f3
♖e6 23 ♖e1 ♔f7 24 ♖xe6 ♔xe6 25
♖e1+ ♔f7 *(D)* 26 ♔e2 (Short suggested 26 ♗f2! h5 27 g4 ♘f4 28
♗e3! as a more effective set-up for
aiming for the draw) 26...h5! 27
♔d3 h4 28 ♗h2 ♘e7 29 ♗f4 ♘f5
30 ♗d2 b6 31 ♖e2 c5 32 ♗e3 b4!
33 axb4 c4+ 34 ♔c3 ♘d6 35 ♖e1
♖a4 36 ♔d2? (required is 36 ♖b1!
– Short) 36...♖xb4 37 ♖a1? ♖xb2
38 ♖a7+ ♔e6 39 ♖xg7 b5 40 ♗f2
b4 41 ♔c1 c3 42 ♗xh4 ♘f5 0-1
(II) *If the idea of energetic play
in clear-cut, almost symmetrical*

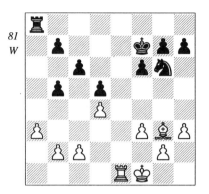

*positions appeals to you, then con-
sider the Exchange Variation as
a viable approach in going for the
win.*

White has two ways to aim to
exploit his "Move 1" advantage
from Diagram 82: (1) Establish
pressure on d5 with 4 c4, and (2)
Go for rapid development a la
Morphy. It is important to stress
that because of the quite recent
respectability of the Exchange
Variation, we are at the beginning
of our theoretical investigation.

(A) **4 c4 ♘f6 5 ♘c3 c6**
There are two reasons why I
have selected the text as the main
line: (1) It is quite logical to over-
protect the menaced d5-point,
and (2) This position can (and
often does!) arise from the Slav
Defence as follows: 1 d4 d5 2 c4 c6 3
♘c3 e5 4 e3 exd4 5 exd4 ♘f6. The
alternatives consist of first developing the dark-squared bishop.
Two logical examples are:
(1) 5...♗e7 6 ♗d3 dxc4 7 ♗xc4
0-0 8 ♘ge2 ♘bd7 9 0-0 ♘b6 10
♗b3 c6 11 ♖e1 ♗f5?! (the bishop

soon winds up exposed on g6; normal would be 11...♘bd5 followed by 12...♗e6 with a slight spatial advantage to White) 12 ♘g3 ♗g6 13 f4! ♗d6 14 ♖f1! ♕c7 15 ♔h1 h6 16 f5, with a strong initiative to White, P.Wolff-A.Dreev, Biel Interzonal 1993.

(2) 5...♗b4 6 ♗d3 c5 7 ♘ge2 ♘c6 8 cxd5 ♘xd5 9 dxc5 ♗g4? (playing for complications boomerangs; according to Tangborn, Black equalises after 9...♘xc3 10 bxc3 ♗xc5) 10 0-0 ♗xc3 11 bxc3 ♘xc3 12 ♕c2! ♗xe2 13 ♖e1! ♕d4 14 ♗b2 0-0-0 15 ♗f5+ ♔c7?! 16 ♗xc3 ♗d3 17 ♕c1 ♕c4 18 ♖e4!! ♘d4 19 ♕f4+ ♔c6 20 ♗xd4 ♖d5 21 ♗xg7 ♕xc5 22 ♖c1 1-0 M.Ashley-A.Shabalov, New York (Marshall) 1993.

6 ♘f3

This natural developing move is my main line. We will follow the game M.Gurevich-P.Nikolić, Belgrade 1991, which was played approximately five months after the debacle versus Short and arose out of the Slav move-order mentioned earlier. Normal alternatives are:

(1) 6 cxd5 ♘xd5 7 ♗d3 ♗e7 8 ♘f3 ♗g4 9 0-0 0-0 10 ♖e1 ♘d7?! (better is 10...♗f6 – Speelman) 11 ♘xd5! cxd5 12 ♗f4 ♖c8 13 h3 ♗h5 14 ♗f5 ♗g6 15 ♗xg6 hxg6 16 ♗g3 ♗f6 17 ♕b3, J.Speelman-V.Salov, Linares 1991. White's more active pieces give him a slight and pleasant advantage.

(2) 6 ♗d3 ♗e6 7 cxd5 ♘xd5 8 ♘ge2 ♘d7 9 0-0 ♘7f6 10 ♘g3 ♗e7

11 ♖e1 0-0 12 a3 ♖e8 13 ♗g5 h6 14 ♗d2 ♕b6 15 ♘ge2 ♖ad8 16 ♕c2 ♗f8 17 ♘a4 ♕c7 18 ♘c5, J.Benjamin-H.Stenzel, New York State Championship 1993. White's spatial plus gives him a slight edge.

6...♗d6 7 c5

White changes the nature of the position to one where he will be playing for superior piece activity on the kingside.

7...♗e7 8 ♗d3 b6 9 cxb6 axb6 10 0-0 ♗a6 11 ♗xa6 ♖xa6 12 ♕d3 0-0 13 ♗g5 h6 14 ♗h4 ♘h5 15 ♗xe7 ♕xe7 16 ♖fe1 ♕d8 17 ♘e5

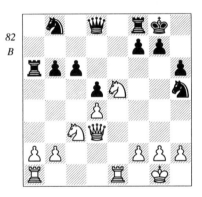

82
B

White's more active piece positioning as well as Black's incomplete queenside development gives White the "usual" slight plus. Gurevich now suggests that Black should get the a6-rook into the game with 17...♖a7 followed by 18...♖e7.

17...b5?! 18 a3! ♘d7 19 ♘xd7 ♕xd7 20 ♘a2! ♘f4 21 ♕f3 ♘e6 22 ♘b4 ♖aa8 23 ♕c3! ♖ac8 24 ♖ac1 c5 25 dxc5 ♖xc5 26 ♕f3

≅xc1 27 ≅xc1 ≅c8 28 ≅d1 d4 29
h4! ≅c5 30 g3 ♕c8?

The legacies of White's kingside initiative are the isolated
Black b- and d-pawns. Black is too
complacent in regard to their vul-
nerability. As Gurevich points out,
he has to look for middlegame
counterplay with 30...g5! 31 ♘d3
≅d5, with fair chances of holding
the game.

**31 ♘d3! ≅c7 32 ♕d5! ♕b7 33
♕xb7 ≅xb7 34 ≅e1! ♔f8 35 ≅e5
♘d8 36 ♘b4! f6 37 ≅d5 ♘f7**

Voluntarily giving up the d-
pawn must be hopeless. However,
if 37...♘e6 Gurevich gives 38
♘d3! following by the king jaunt
to b4 as the winning method.

**38 ≅xd4 ♘e5 39 ♔g2 ♔f7 40
♘d3 ♘c4 41 a4! ♔e7 42 axb5
♘d6 43 ≅b4 ♘xb5 44 ♘c5 ≅b8
45 ♘b3 ≅b7 46 ♘d4 ♘d6 47
♘f5+ ♔f8 48 ≅xb7 ♘xb7 49 h5!
♔f7 50 b4 g6 51 hxg6+ ♔xg6
52 ♘d4 ♔g5 53 b5 f5 54 f4+
♔f6 55 b6 ♘d6 56 ♔h3 ♔g6 57
♘c6 ♘b7 58 ♘e5+ 1-0**

(B) **4 ♘f3 ♘f6**

Black should recognise that
when White is playing good developing moves, so should he. The alternatives are unimpressive:

(1) **4...♗g4?! 5 h3 ♗h5 6 ♕e2+!**
♕e7 (6...♗e7? 7 ♕b5+) 7 ♗e3 ♘c6
8 ♘c3 0-0-0 9 g4! ♗g6 10 0-0-0 f6
11 a3 ♕d7 12 ♘d2! f5?! 13 ♘b3
♘f6 14 f3 ♗d6 15 ♕d2 ≅he8, so
far G.Kasparov-N.Short, Tilburg
1991. Kasparov now suggests 16
♔b1! with the follow-up 17 ♗g5 as

White's most accurate way to enhance his advantage.

(2) **4...♘c6 5 ♗b5 ♗d6 6 c4**
dxc4 7 d5 a6 8 ♗a4 b5 9 dxc6 bxa4
10 0-0 ♘e7 11 ♕xa4 0-0 12 ♘bd2!
≅b8 13 a3 c3 14 bxc3 ≅b6 15 ≅e1!
♘xc6 16 ♘c4 ≅b5 17 ♘xd6 was
M.Chandler-E.Bareev, Hastings
1991/92. At the moment White's
pieces are more active, thereby
leading to some advantage.

(3) **4...♗d6 5 c4!? c6 6 ♘c3 ♘e7
7 ♗d3 0-0 8 0-0 dxc4 9 ♗xc4 ♘d7
10 ♗g5 ♘b6 11 ♗b3 h6 12 ♗h4**
♕c7 13 ♗xe7 ♕xe7 14 ≅e1, G.Kai-
danov-P.Nikolić, Groningen 1993.
For the "usual reasons" (more
space, piece activity) White has a
normal plus.

There is another important
reason why the position after
4...♘f6 is a significant one: it can
and often does result from the following main line sequence in the
Petroff Defence: 1 e4 e5 2 ♘f3
♘f6 3 ♘xe5 d6 4 ♘f3 ♘xe4 5 d3
♘f6 6 d4 d5.

5 ♗d3

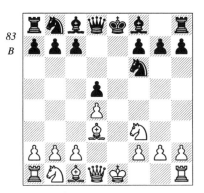

(1) 5...♗e7

Black realises that prompt and safe development should in due course lead to approximate equality. Thematic play now is: 6 0-0 0-0 7 ♗g5 ♗g4 8 ♖e1 ♖e8 9 ♘bd2 ♘bd7 10 c3 h6! (it is important to force the g5-bishop to immediately declare its intentions; after 10...c6 11 ♕c2 h6 12 ♗f4! ♘h5 13 ♗e5 ♘xe5 14 ♗h7+! followed by 15 ♘xe5 White had a clear advantage in the game Glek-S.Dolmatov, Dortmund 1992) 11 ♗xf6 (now after 11 ♗f4 ♘h5 12 ♗e5 ♘xe5 White can't recapture with the king's knight; if he cannot activate that piece with gain of time then White has nothing) 11...♗xf6 12 ♕b3 ♘b6 13 h3 ♗e6 14 ♖e3 ♕d6 15 ♖ae1 c5! 16 ♕a3 ♗e7 17 dxc5 ♕xc5 18 ♕xc5 ♗xc5. Here the players agreed to a draw in A.Kosten-Y.Piskov, Nuoro 1993. Kosten adds that after 19 ♖3e2 ♗d7 20 ♘e5 ♔f8 21 ♘b3 ♗d6 22 ♘d4 the position remains equal. I think that White should have a tiny edge due to Black's isolated d-pawn.

(2) 5...♗g4

What White didn't dare to do (pin Black's knight), Black decides to do. I don't have full confidence in such rambunctiousness. A good example to follow is the game S.Hohelj-I.Glek, Porz 1991: 6 0-0 ♗e7 7 h3 ♗h5 8 c3 0-0 9 ♗f4 c5!? 10 dxc5 ♗xc5 11 ♘bd2 ♘c6 12 ♕c2 ♖c8 13 ♗f5 ♗g6 14 ♘b3 ♗b6 15 ♖ad1 (structurally this

position is similar to that in the Classical Defence to the Tarrasch Variation, i.e. 1 e4 e6 2 d4 d5 3 ♘d2 c5 4 exd5 exd5; there Black must strive very hard to justify the isolated d-pawn and the same applies here also) 15...♘e4! 16 ♗xg6 fxg6!? 17 ♗h2 ♕e7 18 ♕d3 ♖cd8 19 ♘fd4! ♕h4 20 ♕e2! (the idea is 21 ♕g4!), with a continuing advantage for White.

(3) 5...c5!? was played in G.Kasparov-V.Korchnoi, Tilburg 1991. This double-edged move comes from the creative mind of Korchnoi. It has two points: if 6 dxc5 ♗xc5, then Black has recaptured on c5 without having first played ...♗e7/♗d6 and therefore will have saved an important tempo; otherwise Black will play ...c4, chasing back White's d3-bishop. Of course, there is also another side to this: time for development is lost and the d5-pawn can turn out to be vulnerable.

6 0-0 c4 7 ♖e1+ ♗e7 8 ♗f1 0-0 9 ♗g5 ♗g4

The pin doesn't really work out well. Perhaps 9...♘c6!? should be given a more careful investigation. In H.Hamdouchi-D.Komarov, Cannes Grand Prix 1992, White did not gain an advantage after 10 ♘e5 ♗e6 11 ♘xc6 bxc6 12 b3 c5! 13 bxc4 dxc4 14 ♘d2 h6 15 ♗f4 cxd4 16 ♗xc4.

10 h3 ♗xf3

White will now have the two bishops, a light-square superiority and attacking prospects against the d-pawn. Yet after 10...♗h5 11 ♘c3 ♘c6 12 g4! ♗g6 13 ♘e5 White had a strong initiative in S.Makarychev-M.Ulybin, USSR Championship 1991.

11 ♕xf3 ♘c6 12 c3 ♕d7

In E.Kengis-M.Gurevich, Tilburg 1992 Black tried 12...♘e8!? as an improvement, so as not to be left with an impotent bishop after a later ♗xf6 by White. After 13 ♗xe7 ♘xe7 14 ♘a3! ♘c7 15 ♘c2 ♕d6 16 g3 ♖ad8 17 ♖e2 White had a slight edge (control of e-file, play against d5, kingside attacking chances) and went on to win on move 45 – see *Chess Informant* 56, game 284.

13 ♘d2

According to Kasparov, 13 ♘a3! followed by 14 ♘c2 would have been a better idea.

13...♖ae8 14 b3?!

Beginning with this move, Kasparov starts to severely criticise the play of both sides. The only legacy of the text is that after Black's obvious reply White is left with a vulnerable c-pawn.

Instead he gives the following convincing variation for maintaining and enhancing White's advantage: 14 ♖e3! ♗d8 15 ♖ae1 ♖e6!? 16 h4! ♖fe8 17 ♗xf6 ♗xf6 18 g3 ♖xe3 19 ♖xe3 ♖xe3 20 fxe3!. Not only is the d-pawn a fundamental weakness, but via the e4-break White can create a strong protected passed d-pawn.

14...b5 15 bxc4 bxc4 16 ♖ab1 ♗d8 17 h4?!

84
B

According to Kasparov, now Black could even gain a slight edge with 17...♖e6!? due to his coming control of the e-file. Instead, necessary is 17 ♖xe8 when 17...♖xe8?! 18 h4! is slightly in White's favour, whereas 17...♘xe8! equalises. The rest of the game will be given just with Kasparov's move marks; his full analysis appears in *Chess Informant* 53, game 243.

17...♖xe1? 18 ♖xe1 ♖e8 19 ♖b1! h6 20 ♗xf6 ♗xf6 21 g3 ♘e7 22 ♕d1! g5?! 23 hxg5 hxg5 24 ♗g2 g4 25 ♘f1? ♗g5 26 ♖b2 ♔g7 27 ♕b1?! ♖c8 28 ♖e2 ♖c6 29 ♖e5 f6 30 ♖e2 ♖b6 31 ♕d1 ♘f5 32 ♖e1 ♘h6 33 ♕e2 ♔f7 34 f4?! gxf3 35 ♕xf3 ♖d6 36 ♖e5 ♔g7 37 ♖xd5 ♖xd5 38 ♕xd5 ♕a4?? 39 ♕b7+ ♔g6? 40 ♗c6! ♕a5 41 ♗e8+ ♔f5 42 ♕h7+ ♔g4 43 ♕e4+ ♔h3 44 ♗d7+ f5 45 ♕g2+ 1-0

(4) 5...♗d6

This is Black's most popular response. He trusts his position to be sound enough to be able to imitate White's active moves. Now we will follow D.Gurevich-V.Ivanchuk, Biel Interzonal 1993.

6 0-0 0-0 7 ♞g5

The two important alternatives are:

(1) **7 h3 h6 8 ℁e1 ℁e8 9 ℁xe8+ ♛xe8 10 ♞c3 a6 11 ♟e3 ♞c6 12 a3 ♞e7!** 13 ♞h4 ♞g6 14 ♞xg6 fxg6 15 ♛f3 ♛f7 16 ♟f4 ♟xf4 17 ♛xf4 g5 18 ♛e5 ♟e6 19 ♟g6 ♛xg6 20 ♛xe6+ ♛f7 with equality and a draw agreed in Pe.H.Nielsen-L.B.Hansen, Taastrup 1992.

(2) **7 ♞c3** was always Paul Morphy's choice. Three characteristic examples are:

(a) **7...c6 8 ♟g5 h6?!** 9 ♟h4 ♟g4 10 h3 ♟xf3 11 ♛xf3 ♞bd7 12 ♟f5 ♛c7 13 ℁ae1 ℁ae8 14 ℁e3 ♟f4 15 ℁e2, with a slight edge, P.Morphy-Lowenthal, Match Game 10, 1858.

(b) **7...♟g4 8 h3 ♟e6?!** 9 ♟e3 (9 ♟g5!) 9...♞c6 10 ♛d2 ♛d7 11 ♟f4 ℁fe8 12 ℁ae1 ℁ad8 13 ♞e5 ♛c8 14 ♟b5 ♟xe5! 15 ♟xe5 ♞xe5! 16 dxe5 ♞e4!, with equality, P.Morphy-Walker, London 1859.

(c) **7...c5?!** 8 dxc5 ♟xc5 9 ♟g5 ♟e6 10 ♛d2 ♞c6 11 ℁ad1 ♟e7 12 ℁fe1 a6 13 ♛f4, Morphy-Allies, Paris 1858. White's pieces are very active and Black has no compensation the isolated d-pawn.

7...♟g4 8 c3 ♞bd7 9 ♞bd2 c5?!

In playing for the win Black risks being left with an isolated d-pawn with little to show for it. The normal move is 9...c6, continuing with the symmetry.

10 ♛c2 h6?!

The active 10...♛b6 is more useful.

11 dxc5! ♞xc5 12 ♟h4 ℁e8 13 ♟b5?!

Instead of the unmotivated text, the normal 13 ℁fe1!, with the idea 14 ♟f5, would give White a small but comfortable plus.

13...♟d7 14 ♟xd7 ♞cxd7 15 ♞d4 a6?! 16 ♞f5 ♟f8 17 ℁ad1 ♛b6 18 ♞b3

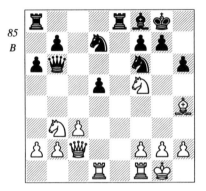

85 B

In Classical Tarrasch Variation positions, b3 is a poor square for the queen's knight and in this structurally similar position the same principle applies. Gurevich suggests instead 18 ♞f3! ♟c5 19 b4 ♟f8 20 ♞e3 with good chances for the advantage. By playing too passively White runs into trouble, yet Ivanchuk doesn't take advantage of the opportunity and the game ends up drawn. I am concluding this chapter by just giving Gurevich's move markings. For complete analysis consult *Chess Informant* 58, game 300.

18...♖e4! 19 ♗xf6? ♘xf6 20 ♘e3 ♖e5 21 ♖d3 ♖ae8 22 ♘d4 ♗c5 23 g3 h5! 24 b4 ♗xd4 25 ♖xd4 ♕e6? (25...♖xe3!) 26 ♕d3 g6 27 a4 ♖c8 28 ♖d1 ♖c6 29 a5 ♔h7 30 ♔g2 ♕c8 31 c4 dxc4 32 ♘xc4 ♖ee6 33 ♘b6 ♕c7 34 ♕f3 ♖c3 35 ♖d7 ♕xd7 36 ♘xd7 ♖xf3 37 ♔xf3 ♖c6 38 ♘c5 ♖c7 39 ♖d4 ♔g7 40 h3?! ♔f8 41 g4 hxg4+ 42 hxg4 ♔e7 43 g5 ♘d7! 44 ♘xd7 ♖xd7 45 ♖xd7+ ♔xd7 46 ♔e4 ♔e6 47 ♔d4 ♔d6! 48 f3 ♔c6 49 ♔e5 ♔d7 ½-½

15 For fans of closed openings: should you play 1 d4 or 1 g3?

If as White you like open positions, active development and prospects for an early attack, the choice for your first move is clear: 1 e4 is the way to go. But the choice in the 1990s is considerably harder for those who prefer a more closed system, delayed contact between the forces, increased king safety and play based on longer-term strategic objectives. 1 d4 was the strategist's choice 100 years ago. The hypermoderns in the 1920s successfully argued the merits of 1 c4 and 1 ♘f3. In addition, since the early 1960s, 1 g3 has been recognised as playable. Thus there are four excellent first moves within the closed systems repertoire to choose from: 1 d4, 1 c4, 1 ♘f3, and 1 g3. Which shall it be?

The first point to note is that in terms of early active play, 1 d4 is the most suitable move, followed by 1 c4, 1 ♘f3 and with 1 g3 bringing up the rear. To help the reader gain a better insight into the modern theory of closed systems, I will take a closer look at the two extremes of the above group.

(1) 1 d4 (D)

Main characteristic: White aims for early active central play, with

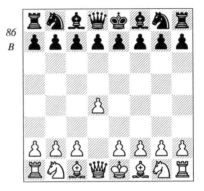

86
B

particular emphasis on gaining an initiative on the queenside.

Advantages:

• White takes control of the d4 primary central square, and applies pressure on the important e5- and c5-squares.

• Development of the queen's bishop and some vertical development of the queen is enabled.

• The immediate movement of pieces and pawns is easy to formulate.

Disadvantages:

• Black is told immediately that d4 is the central target to eliminate in order to gain equality. Thus Black knows straight away that the ...c5 or ...e5 pawn advance will be his primary equalising tool.

Sensible Black responses:
(1) 1...d5 or 1...♘f6 under all circumstances.
(2) The following under specific conditions:
- 1...e6: if Black is ready for the French Defence (2 e4 d5)
- 1...c6: if Black is ready for the Caro-Kann Defence (2 e4 d5)
- 1...g6: if Black is ready for the Modern Defence (2 e4 ♗g7)

To illustrate the potential advantages and disadvantages of opening with 1 d4 I will now consider two games with the King's Indian Defence, where the inherent features of that opening – White's central superiority and Black's chances for counterplay – are well elucidated.

Game 1
King's Indian Defence E90
D.Piza – Alexander Wojtkiewicz
Valencia 1990

1 d4 ♘f6 2 c4 c5 3 d5 d6
Because Black delays ...e6, this opening is considered to be the King's Indian instead of the Benoni Defence.
4 ♘c3 g6 5 e4 ♗g7 6 ♘f3
White already has the central superiority characteristic of the King's Indian. With his next move he prevents the development of Black's light-squared bishop.
6...0-0 7 h3 e6 8 ♗d3 ♖e8 9 0-0 ♘a6 10 ♗g5!? h6 11 ♗e3 ♘c7 12 ♕d2 ♔h7?

The GM is careless. It was necessary to first interpolate 12...exd5 13 exd5 before playing 13...♔h7. Now White's powerful centre can be activated.
13 e5! dxe5 14 d6 ♘a6 15 ♘xe5 ♖f8 16 ♘xf7! ♖xf7 17 ♗xg6+!!

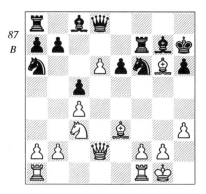

87
B

The strategic build-up has led to devastating tactics. Yet note that these tactics start with White's king in complete safety and with piece development essentially complete all across the board. The bishop is poisoned since after 17...♔xg6? 18 ♕c2+! ♔h5 19 f3! followed by 20 g4+ the king gets caught in a mating net.
17...♔g8 18 ♗xf7+ ♔xf7 19 ♗xh6
With rook and three pawns for two minor pieces and Black's king denuded, White has both a significant material and positional advantage. According to Piza, Black's relatively best defensive try now is 19...♗xh6 20 ♕xh6 ♕xd6 21 ♖ad1 (21 ♘e4!?) 21...♕e5 22 ♖fe1

♕h5, though White's advantage is clear after 23 ♕f4.

19...♗d7?! 20 ♗xg7 ♔xg7 21 ♖ae1 ♕h8 22 ♘e4! ♕h4 23 ♘xf6 ♕xf6 24 ♖e3 ♗c6 25 ♕e2 ♔f7 26 ♕h5+ ♔f8 27 ♖fe1 1-0

He has no interest in witnessing 27...♖e8 28 ♖g3 followed by 29 ♖g6 and the imminent end.

Game 2
King's Indian Defence E69
Helgi Olafsson – John Nunn
Wijk aan Zee 1991

1 d4 ♘f6 2 c4 g6 3 ♘f3 ♗g7 4 g3 0-0 5 ♗g2 d6 6 ♘c3 ♘bd7 7 0-0 e5 8 e4 c6 9 b3 exd4

In this, the Classical Variation against White's fianchetto, Black is forced to discontinue pressure against d4 since otherwise he cannot develop his queen's knight satisfactorily. As compensation for enhancing White's central superiority (Black now has no central pawn on his fourth rank), Black opens the diagonal of his g7-bishop and gets an active location for his queen's knight.

10 ♘xd4 ♖e8 11 h3 ♘c5 12 ♖e1 ♕b6 13 ♗e3 a5 14 ♖b1 ♗d7 15 ♕c2 ♖ad8 16 ♖bd1 ♕c7

White has smoothly completed his development and has a pleasant spatial and central advantage. Nunn now suggests 17 ♔h2 with a continuing White advantage. Olafsson unwisely decides to play for more.

17 f4?!

White also wants to control e5, but the upshot is a fundamental weakening of the e4-pawn and the g3-pawn. Suddenly Black has prospects for meaningful counterplay.

17...♖e7! 18 ♗f2 ♖de8 19 ♖e2 ♕c8 20 ♔h2?!

White should have risked 20 g4!? h5 21 g5 ♘h7 22 ♔h2 f6 which is unclear, according to Nunn.

20...h5! 21 ♗g1 h4! 22 gxh4

Unattractive, yet worse is 22 g4?! ♗xg4! 23 hxg4 ♕xg4 24 ♖f1 ♘h5 and Black has a large advantage (Nunn).

22...♘h5 23 ♖f1 ♗f6 24 ♖f3 ♗xh4 25 a3 ♗f6

Because of White's weaknesses on e4, f4, h3 and the kingside generally, Black has the advantage. It could be kept relatively small with the careful 26 ♔h1! (Nunn), preventing any immediate tactics.

26 ♗f2? ♘xf4!

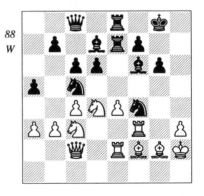

White's goose is now cooked since 27 ♖xf4 ♗e5 28 ♗g3 (28 ♗e3 g5) allows 28...♗xd4.

27 ♘xc6 ♗xc6 28 ♖xf4 ♗e5
29 ♗g3 ♘e6!! 30 ♖h4 ♗xg3+ 31
♔xg3 ♘d4 32 ♕d2 ♘xe2+ 33
♘xe2 ♕e6 0-1

The endgame after 34 ♕xa5
♕e5+ 35 ♕xe5 ♖xe5 36 ♘c3 f5 is
hopeless.

(2) 1 g3

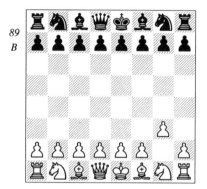

89
B

Main characteristic: White will
first complete development of the
kingside, with the fianchetto of
his light-squared bishop an inte-
gral part of this development.

Advantages:
• Almost complete flexibility
  regarding eventual piece and
  pawn deployment. The only
  fixed element is the kingside fianchetto.
• kingside castling ensures early
  safety of the king.
• White's deployment can be tai-
  lored to Black's chosen pawn
  structure.
• White does not expose any part
  of his position to ready counterplay by Black.

Disadvantages:
• Black is given a very wide
  choice of opening systems.
• Unless White's early play is
  very perceptive, he can easily
  wind up in a centrally inferior,
  passive position.

Sensible Black responses
(1) 1...c5
(2) 1...d5
(3) 1...e5
(4) 1...♘f6
(5) 1...g6
(6) The following under specific
conditions:
• 1...c6: if Black will follow up
  with ...d5
• 1...d6: if Black will follow up
  with ...c5 or ...e5
• 1...e6: if Black will follow up
  with ...d5 or ...♘f6

The next two games will illustrate how White should and should
not handle this opening.

Game 3
Réti Opening
(by transposition) A14
Anthony Miles – Andrew Muir
Ostend 1990

1 g3 d5 2 ♘f3
2 ♗g2 is perfectly playable and
if 2...e5, then 3 d3. Nevertheless,
a majority of GMs prefer not to allow Black so much of a pawn centre so early.
**2...♘f6 3 ♗g2 e6 4 c4 ♗e7 5 b3
0-0 6 ♗b2 c5 7 0-0 ♘c6 8 e3 d4**

A very ambitious plan: Black sends his d-pawn into White's part of the board and blocks off White's b2-bishop from its central diagonal. The cost is a major enhancement of the power of White's other bishop. The safe, "normal", routine move is 8...b6, followed by 9...♗b7.

9 exd4 cxd4 10 ♖e1 ♖e8 11 a3 a5 12 d3 ♗f8 13 ♘e5!

Preventing 13...e5 and opening the g2-bishop's central diagonal.

13...♘xe5 14 ♖xe5 ♘d7 15 ♖b5!? e5 16 ♘d2

White is interested in retaining strong pressure against Black's queenside as well as control of e4 and d5. The materialistic 16 ♗xb7?! ♗xb7 17 ♖xb7 gives it all up for a pawn. Black then gets good compensation for the pawn after 17...♘c5.

16...♖b8 17 b4 b6 18 bxa5 bxa5 19 a4!

White wants more than the slight routine edge after 19 ♖xb8 ♘xb8 20 ♖b1. He prefers to sacrifice the exchange for a pawn, as that gives him connected passed pawns and a wonderfully powerful light-squared bishop.

19...♗a6 20 ♘b3 ♗xb5 21 axb5 ♗b4 22 ♗a3 ♗xa3 23 ♖xa3 ♕e7 24 ♖xa5 ♕b4 25 ♖a7 ♘c5 26 ♘xc5 ♕xc5 27 ♕a4 f5 28 ♗c6!

The critical moment in the game. Black has defended well and after the careful 28...♖ec8! 29 ♗d7 White's advantage would be small, according to Miles. Instead

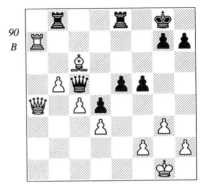

28...♖ed8?! is clearly inferior, when 29 ♖c7 threatens 30 ♗d5+ and if 30...♔h8, 30 ♕a5! is strong. Black therefore wants to exchange off White's powerful rook, but is surprised by a mating attack where White's bishop is the thematic participant.

28...♖e7? 29 ♖a8! ♖xa8 30 ♕xa8+ ♔f7 31 ♗d5+ ♔g6 32 ♕a6+ ♔g5 33 h4+ ♔g4 34 ♔g2! e4 35 f3+ ♔h5 36 ♔h3 g6 37 ♕f6 1-0

It's mate after 37...♔h6 38 ♕f8+ ♔h5 (38...♖g7 39 ♕xc5) 39 g4+ fxg4+ 40 fxg4.

Game 4
Sicilian Defence,
Closed Variation B20
Jan Kiwitter – Edmar Mednis
Metz 1990

1 g3 g6 2 ♗g2 ♗g7 3 d3 c5 4 e4

Because White has played an early e4 and Black an early ...c5, the opening is considered to be one of the variations within the Closed Sicilian complex.

4...♘c6 5 f4 d6 6 ♘f3 e6 7 0-0 ♘ge7 8 c3

The idea behind this and the next move should be to play the centrally desirable d4. By omitting the ♘c3 of the Closed Sicilian, White has enhanced his chances for that advance.

8...0-0 9 ♗e3 b6 10 ♘bd2?

Much too passive. Correct is 10 d4!. Now Black is the one who starts activity in the centre.

10...♗a6! 11 ♕c2 d5 12 ♖fd1 d4! 13 cxd4 ♘xd4! 14 ♘xd4 ♗xd4 15 ♘f1 ♗xe3+ 16 ♘xe3 ♕d4 17 ♔f2 ♖ad8

Because White tarried with the necessary d4, his position is in tatters. Black now gangs up against the vulnerable backward d-pawn.

18 ♔e2 ♖d7!

91
W

Necessary now is 19 ♖d2 ♖fd8 20 ♖ad1 ♘c6 21 a3. White's position is horrible, but there is no immediate win for Black. After White's next, there is.

19 e5? ♖fd8 20 ♘c4

The anticipated 20 ♗e4?? does not defend because of 20...♕xe4. But after the text, Black is ready to infiltrate on e3.

20...♘f5! 21 ♗h3 ♗xc4 22 ♗xf5 ♗a6! 0-1

23 ♗e4 is not playable, while 23 ♗h3 ♗xd3+ is truly resignable.

Conclusions:

(1) Is 1 d4 or 1 g3 the stronger move? Answer: The strength is the same.

(2) Which move would you play? Answer: It mostly depends on your style. Yet an admonition is also in order. The active, direct 1 d4 is easier to play, because "normal" moves will usually turn out to be good. It is my opinion that unless you have an "understanding of chess" rating of at least 2200, the risk is great that you will not realise the strengths of 1 g3, but will be caught in the disadvantages inherent in that wonderfully flexible move. That is what happened to Mr. Kiwitter in the game above.

16 Playing Queen's Pawn openings sharply

As a general principle open games – those starting with 1 e4 – are best for attacking players. This is because mobilisation of the pieces most suited for attacking Black's king (queen, king's bishop and king's knight) occurs much more rapidly after 1 e4. On the other hand, just a quick look at the position after 1 d4 shows that White's initial glance is on the queenside and that little or no attention can be paid early on to making Black's king uncomfortable.

Nevertheless, some great attacking players, including the long time US Champion Frank J. Marshall, preferred to open with 1 d4. World Champions Alexander Alekhine and Garry Kasparov have hardly been slouches in turning their closed openings into showplaces for devastating tactics. Moreover, there is one important safety factor in White's favour: because play starts from a closed opening the chances are good that White's king will be inherently safer than in most double-edged 1 e4 sequences. Black's most solid response to 1 d4 is 1...d5, when 2 c4 brings about the Queen's Gambit. This name is a historical one, but is not a very accurate description of the opening. The word

"gambit" refers to a sacrifice and we have long ago learned that White is not actually sacrificing a pawn because Black cannot afford to hold on to it. In this chapter I shall look at some important variations whereby White can strive to significantly sharpen play within the inherently safe and solid Queen's Gambit complex.

(I) *Queen's Gambit Accepted*
1 d4 d5 2 c4 dxc4

In the modern interpretation of the QGA, Black does not plan to hold on to the pawn, but will utilise the time that White spends in recovering his pawn to prepare for quick central development of his queenside forces.

3 ♘f3

White prevents any counterthrusts based on ...e5 and prepares to recover the pawn at his convenience.

3...♘f6

Black develops his king's knight to its best central square whilst preventing White's e4. Standard play now is 4 e3 e6 5 ♗xc4 c5 6 0-0 a6 7 ♕e2 b5 8 ♗b3 ♗b7 9 ♖d1 ♘bd7 10 ♘c3 ♕b6, when, in due course, with careful play Black should come very close to full equality. White, however, has an immediate way of sharpening the struggle with ...

4 ᐃc3!?

White wants to recover the pawn while building a strong centre with 5 e4. Since this would give White something for nothing, Black can't allow it. Therefore, Black's thematic approach is to threaten to hold on to the c-pawn by playing 4...a6 or 4...c6. Since the latter position is usually reached via the Slav Defence move-order, I shall consider it separately in the next section.

4...a6 5 e4 b5 6 e5 ᐃd5 7 a4

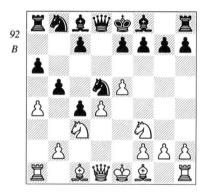

92
B

The undermining of the b5-pawn is White's usual method of handling positions where Black tries to hang on to the gambit pawn. Black can now play 7...c6, yet I don't have full confidence in that since it seems to me an inferior version of the Slav Gambit, i.e. after 1 d4 d5 2 c4 c6 3 ᐃc3 ᐃf6 4 ᐃf3 dxc4 5 e4 b5 6 e5 ᐃd5 7 e5 b5 7 a4, instead of the natural, centrally developing 7...e6, Black

plays 7...a6. 7...ᐃb7? is downright bad since after 8 e6! Black's kingside will be a mess whether he captures or plays 8...f6. Therefore, Black's next has become accepted as the standard move, yet with the unavoidable consequence that White's centre is strengthened.

7...ᐃxc3 8 bxc3 ᐃd5

This active queen posting has been Black's main line for over 40 years. The alternative 8...ᐃb7 has generally worked out badly after 9 e6!, e.g. 9...f6 10 ᐃe2 ᐃd5 11 0-0 ᐃxe6 12 ᐃe1 ᐃd7 13 ᐃh4 g6 14 ᐃg4 f5 15 ᐃf3 ᐃc6 16 ᐃg5! when White had a crushing initiative in A.Belyavsky-M.Dlugy, Tunis Interzonal 1985 – see *Chess Informant* 39, game 471. The above strategy is characteristic for this variation: White aims to exploit Black's backward kingside development. As a possible improvement for Black, instead of 12...ᐃd7, 12...ᐃb6!? has been suggested, based on the game W.Schmidt-K.J.Schulz, Prague 1987.

The evidence, nevertheless, is strong that Black should not be greedily going for White's e-pawn. Black most recent search for defensive resources has concentrated on 10...g6, as in E.Lobron-Ra-eckij, France 1994 (*Chess Informant* 62, game 427).

9 g3 ᐃe6?!

This ambitious plan is probably more than Black can afford. Safer is 9...ᐃb7 10 ᐃg2 ᐃd7!, though

White undeniably has good compensation for the pawn after 11 ♗a3, 11 0-0, or 11 ♘h4.

We now follow the game A. Chernin-A. Mikhailjchisin, Lvov 1987.

10 ♗g2 ♕b7 11 0-0 ♗d5 12 e6! ♗xe6

Neither is 12...fxe6 satisfactory: 13 ♘h4! g6 14 ♖e1 ♗g7 15 ♕g4 0-0 16 ♕xe6+ ♗xe6 17 ♗xb7 ♖a7 18 ♗g2 ♗d7 19 axb5 ♗xb5 20 ♗a3 with a large advantage for White (Gurevich).

13 ♘e5! ♗d5

White's objective in this gambit variation is to aggressively exploit his lead in development. White is therefore happy enough to exchange off Black's only developed piece. Black has no choice since 13...c6 is crushed by 14 ♕h5! g6 15 ♘xg6 fxg6 16 ♕e5.

14 ♗xd5 ♕xd5 15 axb5 f6

The end is immediate after 15...♕xb5? 16 ♕f3 with a double attack on a8 and f7. Just a bit better is 15...axb5?! 16 ♖xa8 ♕xa8 17 ♕g4! (after the immediate 17 ♕h5 Black has 17...♕d5) 17...e6 18 ♕h5 g6 19 ♘xg6 fxg6 20 ♕e5 ♖g8 21 ♕xe6+.

16 ♘g4! ♕xb5

Now 16...axb5 loses to 17 ♘e3! ♕b7 18 ♖xa8 ♕xa8 19 ♕h5+ g6 20 ♕xb5+. Notice how the loss of time with 4...a6 and the queenside weakening are taking their toll.

17 ♕f3 c6 18 ♘e3! g6 19 ♗a3 ♕h5 20 ♕e4 e5

93
W

Now White played 21 ♗xf8 and went on to win on move 42. Gurevich considers the following to be immediately decisive:

21 dxe5! ♕xe5 22 ♕xc4 ♗xa3 23 ♘g4!

and White wins, for instance 23...♕d6 24 ♖ad1 ♕c7 25 ♕e6+ ♗e7 26 ♘xf6+ ♔f8 27 ♘d7+ ♘xd7 28 ♖xd7. Again, in all these lines White's huge lead in development proved decisive.

(II) *Queen's Gambit Declined, Slav Defence*

1 d4 d5 2 c4 c6

The admirable idea behind the Slav Defence is to protect the d5 strong point with the c-pawn, thereby leaving the h3-c8 diagonal open for active development of the queen's bishop. Unfortunately, this laudable plan can only be executed at some cost.

3 ♘c3 ♘f6 4 ♘f3

Already here Black is faced with the important practical problem of how to develop the king's bishop. Of course, 4...e6 is possible, yet the whole purpose of the Slav would thereby be negated. Also 4...g6 is playable, but that would bring about variations where Black finds himself in passive versions of the Grünfeld Defence. Black's "ultimate" problem is that the desirable 4...♗f5?! is met strongly by 5 cxd5! cxd5 6 ♕b3. Therefore, to develop the queen's bishop Black must give up the centre.

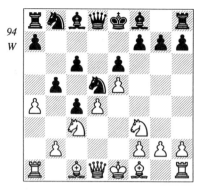

4...dxc4

It turns out that it is not at all easy for White to recover the pawn and it is on this factor that the theoretical soundness of the Slav rests. Main line play now starts with 5 a4 and after 5...♗f5 either 6 ♘e5 or 6 e3. The cost of recovering the pawn is a lost tempo and a weakening of the queenside, factors which allow Black to come close to eventual equality.

5 e4

The Slav Gambit is by far White's most aggressive option. It is important to mention that both opening theory and grandmaster practice consider the 5 e4 gambit more dangerous against the QGA than against the Slav. For this reason many GMs who have both the QGA and the Slav in their repertoire switch from the QGA to the Slav if, after 1 d4 d5 2 c4 dxc4 3 ♘f3 ♘f6, White plays 4 ♘c3, i.e. rather than going ahead with 4...a6, Black plays 4...c6.

5...b5 6 e5 ♘d5 7 a4 e6!

Black opens the diagonal of his king's bishop and, moreover, all the unpleasant possibilities of White playing e6 – as in the QGA variations – are prevented forever. These two factors, when added to the circumstance that Black's c-pawn, rather than the a-pawn, is protecting b5, makes Black's defensive task considerably easier.

8 axb5 ♘xc3 9 bxc3 cxb5 10 ♘g5 ♗b7

White did have the lethal threat 11 ♕f3, but it is easily parried by developing the queen's bishop on the long diagonal.

11 ♕h5

The threat on f7 is real and, since 11...♕e7?! makes no sense, while 11...♕c7? is refuted by 12 ♘xe6, Black only has two choices.

11...♕d7

This has developed to be the more popular choice in international play. It is my opinion, however, that Black's most effective approach is 11...g6 12 ♕g4 ♗e7. An important, little-known example from my tournament play is 13 ♗e2 ♘d7 14 ♗f3 ♕c8 15 0-0 ♘b6 16 ♘e4 a5! 17 ♗g5 ♗xe4! 18

♗xe4 ♗xg5 19 ♗xa8 ♕xa8 20 ♕xg5 ♘d5, N.Povah-E.Mednis, Ramsgate 1984. Black has a passed pawn and a colossal knight for the rook and has the slightly superior chances.

After the text, grabbing the h-pawn with 12 ♘xh7?! works out poorly after 12...♕d5 13 ♘f6+ gxf6 14 ♕xh8 b4! and it is Black rather than White who has the attack. Therefore, White should first complete his development and then work to exploit the inherent looseness in Black's position. Black's main challenge is to keep the king safe, since castling on either side is very risky. We now follow M.Illescas-A.Chernin, Pamplona 1991/92.

12 ♗e2 h6 13 ♗f3 ♘c6 14 0-0 ♘d8 15 ♘e4 a5 16 ♕g4 ♖h7 17 ♗d1!

Black, with his last move, both enabled the king's bishop to be developed as well as prevented the tactical sequence ♘d6+, ♗xd6 and ♕xg7. White therefore strives to attack the rook from c2.

17...h5 18 ♕e2 ♗d5 19 ♗c2 ♖h8 20 ♗g5

White has active minor pieces, a safe king and a spatial superiority thanks to the e5-outpost. Black suffers from the inability to co-ordinate his forces on both sides of the board. Illescas rates the position as slightly superior for White. He suggests now 20...♘c6 as Black's best plan.

20...♘b7?! 21 f4! ♖a6?!

White is starting a pawn rush on the kingside and Black should do the same on the queenside with 21...a4. The text loses a tempo.

22 h4! a4 23 ♘g3 ♘a5 24 f5! ♘b3 25 ♖ad1

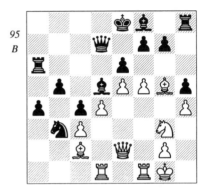

95
B

All White's pieces are properly placed for the attack and it is doubtful if Black can defend. Illescas gives 25...a3 26 fxe6 ♗xe6 27 d5 ♗g4 28 ♕e4 ♘c5 29 ♕f4! ♗xd1 30 e6! and White wins.

25...b4 26 fxe6 ♖xe6

Trying to blockade on e6, but White doesn't give Black a chance. The game concluded:

27 cxb4 a3 28 ♗f5 f6 29 ♗e3 ♕f7 30 ♕c2 ♔d8 31 ♘e2! ♖b6 32 ♘f4 ♗xb4 33 ♗e4 ♗xe4 34 ♕xe4 ♕a7 35 d5 ♗c5 36 ♘e6+ ♖xe6 37 dxe6+ ♔c8 38 ♕xc4 a2 39 ♗xc5 ♕xc5+ 40 ♕xc5+ 1-0

The game was decided by the lack of safety for Black's king.

(III) Queen's Gambit Declined, Orthodox Defence, Exchange Variation

1 d4 d5 2 c4 e6

In the Orthodox systems Black safeguards d5 with the e-pawn, develops the kingside and only later on will worry about how to bring the queen's bishop to life.

3 ♘c3 ♗e7 4 ♘f3 ♘f6 5 cxd5

In the Exchange Variation White clears the central tension, thereby enhancing Black's central influence. In return White hopes to either work on Black's queenside via a minority attack or to build, in due course, a superior centre with f3 and e4.

5...exd5 6 ♗g5 c6 7 ♕c2 g6

Because of the central pawn structure, Black's inferior minor piece is the queen's bishop. The text prepares to develop it to f5, e.g. 8 e3 ♗f5 9 ♗d3 ♗xd3 10 ♕xd3 ♘bd7! with only a small edge for White. To prevent such quiet play, White can employ a vigorous central advance.

8 e4!?

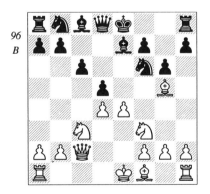

96
B

White is ready to open up the position to take advantage of his somewhat superior development and the slight weakening of Black's kingside due to 7...g6. Black's safest response now is 8...dxe4 and after 9 ♗xf6 ♗xf6 10 ♕xe4+, best is the paradoxical 10...♔f8!. Then main line play continues 11 ♗c4 ♔g7 12 0-0 ♖e8 13 ♕f4 ♗e6! 14 ♗xe6 ♖xe6 15 ♖fe1 when Black can achieve a roughly equal endgame by 15...♕d6! 16 ♕xd6 ♖xd6, as first demonstrated in Lautier-Oll, Moscow (GMA) 1989 and subsequently confirmed in the game L.B.Hansen-Smagin, Copenhagen 1990.

After the text-move we follow G.Kamsky-A.Shirov, Dortmund 1992, in which the two players are interested only in a bare-knuckled fight.

8...0-0 9 e5 ♘e4

If 9...♘h5, White keeps attacking chances and a slight plus with 10 h4! (Shirov)

10 ♗h6 ♖e8 11 ♗d3

This active, developing move is better than the slower 11 h3?! of Tal-Renet, Cannes 1989 when Black obtained sufficient counterplay to equalise.

11...♘xc3?

According to Shirov, already the losing move. He gives as correct 11...♘d6!! 12 0-0 ♘f5 13 ♗f4 ♘g7 with only a small advantage for White.

12 bxc3 c5 13 h4!

Mate is the goal! Since 13...c4 14 ♗e2 ♗f5 15 ♕c1 followed by h5 and ♘g5 doesn't slow down

White's attack, Black goes ahead with his counterplay.

13...cxd4 14 h5! g5!?

White already threatened 15 hxg6 hxg6 16 ♗xg6!. Therefore Black tries to keep the kingside as closed as possible.

15 ♗xh7+ ♔h8 16 ♗g6! ♗e6

The opening of the h-file is decisive after 16...fxg6 17 hxg6! ♔g8 18 g7! ♕c7 19 ♗xg5!.

17 ♘xd4 ♕c8 18 ♕d2!!

97
B

Kamsky's play is outstanding for both its energy and accuracy.

Shirov gives the following alternative defence for Black: 18...♘c6 19 ♗xg5 ♗xg5 20 ♕xg5 ♘xd4 21 ♕h6+ ♔g8 22 ♗h7+ ♔h8 23 ♖h3!! (an attractive finish) 23...♗xh3 24 ♗g6+ ♔g8 25 ♕h7+ ♔f8 26 ♕xf7#.

18...fxg6 19 hxg6 ♔g8 20 ♖c1!

Preventing counterplay so as to be able to fully concentrate on the attack. Throughout the game Black has been putting up the best defence. For alternative defensive tries please consult Shirov's analysis in *Chess Informant* 54, game 400.

20...♘c6 21 ♗xg5 ♕c7 22 ♗xe7! ♖xe7 23 ♔f1!! ♖ae8 24 ♖e1 ♖g7 25 ♕h6 ♔f8 26 ♖h4! ♘xd4 27 ♕h8+ ♖g8 28 ♕f6+ ♗f7 29 ♕xf7+ ♕xf7 30 gxf7 1-0

After 30...♔xf7 31 cxd4 Black is two pawns down in a hopeless endgame.

This was a fantastic game by Kamsky!

17 Playing the English Opening sharply

As already mentioned in Chapter 15, the English Opening (1 c4) is an inherently more closed opening than 1 d4. Yet, as in the saying "where there's a will, there's a way", both sides can sharpen their play even in a system as "safe" as the Symmetrical Variation. This is normally reached after the moves:

1 c4 c5 2 ♘c3 ♘c6 3 g3 g6 4 ♗g2 ♗g7

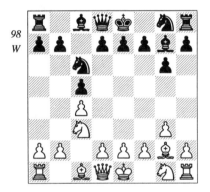

As can be seen, the position is completely symmetrical. White's only advantage derives from being on the move. Yet since the position is quite closed, it is far from easy to turn the "on the move" advantage into something more tangible. The three most important continuations for White are 5 a3, 5 ♘f3 and 5 e3.

I shall now present ways for White to sharpen the play after both 5 a3 and 5 ♘f3. Then I will show how Black can sharpen his own play after White's least ambitious continuation, 5 e3.

Variations for White after 5 a3 and 5 ♘f3

(1) **5 a3**

White prepares a strictly long-term advance on the queenside with b4. Even when that thrust is achieved, there will not be a specific threat for Black to worry about. Nevertheless, White will have gained some space on the queenside and closed, strategic openings are about such long-term ideas. Pal Benko and Yasser Seirawan have long been recognised as leading experts on this variation. Because White has as yet no "threat", Black has a number of satisfactory responses.

5...e6

Just as in the main line after 5 ♘f3, the text has had a good reputation for over 20 years: Black will develop the g8-knight to e7, preparing the ...d5 advance while keeping open the diagonal of the fianchettoed king's bishop. Other good moves include 5...a6, 5...b6, 5...d6 and 5...♖b8.

White's quiet, strategic plan now continues with 6 ♖b1, after which theory deems it advisable to prevent White's advance by 6...a5. However, White also has a more ambitious possibility:

6 b4!?

At first glance, this almost seems like a "slip of the hand", i.e. White has apparently forgotten that he has not yet played ♖b1. Yet Black's task is far from easy.

6...♘xb4!

Only this "unnatural" capture is satisfactory. Inferior is 6...cxb4?! 7 axb4, when neither greed nor forbearance are rewarded:

(1) 7...♘xb4 8 ♗a3 ♗xc3 (worse are 8...♘c6? 9 ♘b5! and 8...♗f8?! 9 d4, as pointed out by Robert Byrne) 9 dxc3 ♘c6 10 h4 ♕f6 11 ♘f3! ♕xc3+ 12 ♘d2 f5 13 0-0 ♘f6 14 ♖a2 ♕a5 15 ♕a1 ♕d8 16 e4, O.Renet -L.Yudasin, Ostend 1988. Black's backward development and dark-squared weaknesses make White's attacking prospects exceedingly bright.

(2) 7...♘ge7 8 b5 ♘e5 9 c5 d5 10 cxd6 ♕xd6 11 ♗a3 ♕d8 12 ♘h3 0-0 13 0-0 ♖e8 14 ♗c5 a6, so far A.Garcia-R.Byrne, Lugano Olympiad 1968, when instead of the game's 15 d4? Byrne suggests 15 ♕b3! with a clear advantage for White because of the large lead in development, pressure against the queenside and the extra central pawn.

Our main line follows the game V.Smyslov-W.Hartston, Hastings 1972/73.

7 axb4 cxb4 8 d4

"Relative modesty" is what White now needs. 8 ♘b5?! ♗xa1 9 ♕a4 ♗f6! 10 d4 is too ambitious because of 10...a6! 11 ♘d6+ ♔f8 12 ♘f3 ♗e7! 13 ♕xb4 a5 14 ♕c5 f6!, when White has no compensation for his pawn minus, as shown by the further course of E.Lobron-L.Kavalek, Bochum 1981: 15 h4 h5 16 0-0 ♘h6 17 e4 ♘f7 18 e5 ♗xd6 19 exd6 b6 20 ♕a3 ♗a6 21 ♘d2 ♔g7! and Black consolidated to win on move 39.

8...bxc3 9 e3!

Inferior is 9 ♘f3?! ♘e7 10 0-0 0-0 11 ♕b3 d5 12 c5 ♘c6 13 ♕xc3 ♖e8 14 ♗f4 b5! 15 cxb6 ♕xb6 16 e3 (not 16 ♖fb1? ♘xd4!) 16...♗f8, M.Bobotsov-W.Hartston, Vrnjačka Banja 1972. Black is up a sound passed a-pawn and White has no compensation. Smyslov's plan allows White to recapture on c3 while keeping a sound piece configuration.

9...♘e7 10 ♘e2 d5 11 cxd5

More ambitious is 11 ♘xc3!? as in M.Gurevich-L.Yudasin, Haifa 1995. After 11...dxc4 12 0-0 0-0 13 ♗a3 a6 (Yudasin draws attention to 13...♖b8!? 14 ♕a4 ♗d7 15 ♕xa7 ♘c6 16 ♗xc6 ♗xc6 17 ♗xf8 ♕xf8 with compensation for the sacrificed exchange) 14 ♕e2! ♕c7?! (correct is 14...♖e8 to continue after 15 ♕xc4 with 15...♘f5 or 15...b5 – Yudasin) 15 ♖fc1! White will start recovering his material while keeping a strong initiative on the queenside. For the complete game score with Yudasin's analysis please see *Informant* 63, game 40.

11...♘xd5 12 ♗a3 ♗f8!

Otherwise Black cannot castle. Hartston evaluates the resulting position as slightly better for Black; M.Taimanov in *ECO A* considers that White has compensation for the sacrificed pawn.

13 0-0 ♗xa3 14 ♖xa3 ♗d7 15 e4 ♘e7 16 ♘xc3 0-0 17 ♕a1 a5 18 ♖b1 ♘c6 ½-½!

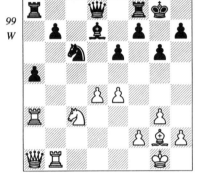

The relative fame of the players no doubt influenced the cessation of hostilities: Hartston as Black was satisfied with a draw; Smyslov wasn't all that sure what he had for the pawn. Hartston adds the following analysis: 19 ♖xb7? is bad because of 19...♘b4! when the wayward rook gets trapped; the situation after 19 ♖d1 ♘b4 20 ♕c1!? is something between slightly better for Black and unclear. It seems to me that White has fair compensation in the extra central pawn and the dark-squared weakness in Black's position. But the only way to get at the real truth of the position after Black's 18th move is for a number of top players to test it in actual play.

(2) **5 ♘f3**

This is the most important continuation, for the following two reasons: (1) White plays a natural developing move, (2) This position can readily occur from a large number of move-orders if White has played an early ♘f3. Some examples, just from the references appearing later, are: 1 ♘f3 c5 2 c4 g6 3 g3 ♘c6 4 ♗g2 ♗g7 5 ♘c3, 1 ♘f3 g6 2 c4 ♗g7 3 ♘c3 c5 4 g3 ♘c6 5 ♗g2 and 1 c4 c5 2 ♘f3 ♘c6 3 g3 g6 4 ♗g2 ♗g7 5 ♘c3.

After the text, Black cannot continue the symmetry with 5...♘f6, without being ready for White's 6 d4 when: (a) 6...cxd4 7 ♘xd4 0-0 8 0-0 ♘xd4 9 ♕xd4 d6 leads to a well-known variation which is considered to be within the English Opening, and (b) 6...0-0 7 0-0 d6 transposes into the Yugoslav Variation of the King's Indian Defence. For over 20 years, Black's strategically soundest system has been considered to be ...

5...e6

Black will follow up with ♘ge7, 0-0 and d5, obtaining good kingside development and central influence. A thematic example of traditional strategic play by White is B.Gulko-M.Dlugy, US Championship 1991, Match Game 1: 6 0-0 ♘ge7 7 d3 d5 8 ♗g5 h6 9 ♗d2 0-0 10 a3 b6 11 ♖b1 ♗b7 12 b4 dxc4

13 dxc4 cxb4 14 axb4 ♖c8 15 c5 bxc5 16 bxc5 ♘a5 17 ♘b5 ♗xf3 18 ♗xf3 ♖xc5 19 ♘xa7 ♕d7 20 ♗xa5 ♕xd1 21 ♖fxd1 ♖xa5 22 ♖d7 ♗d4 ½-½.

Over the last ten years White players have also been exploring a creative way of immediately opening the position by playing ...

6 d4!?

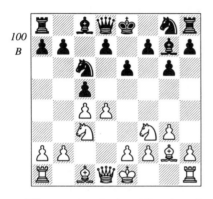

100
B

The strategic justification for this pawn sacrifice is the temporary weakening of the d6-square in Black's position as a result of 5...e6. To take advantage of this, White must open up the position. As I mentioned above, this sacrifice has only recently gained respectability. For instance, in *Encyclopedia of Chess Openings A*, published in 1979, only a single example appears: 6...cxd4 7 ♘b5 d5 8 ♕a4 ♘ge7 9 cxd5 ♘xd5 10 ♘bxd4 ♗d7 11 ♕d1 ♘xd4 12 ♘xd4 ♕b6 13 ♘b3 ♗c6 14 0-0 0-0, and Black gained a slight advantage in L.Lengyel-I.Bilek, Hungarian Championship 1964.

Black has no satisfactory way of declining the sacrifice, since, e.g. 6...♘ge7?! and 6...d6?! lead to a cramped position after 7 d5, with no compensation therefore. Also poor is 6...♗xd4? 7 ♘b5 ♗g7? 8 ♕d6, winning. This leaves Black with 6...cxd4 and 6...♘xd4. Both are currently of equal importance and each will be discussed with an illustrative game. Each game will show off White's possibilities in the best light. Of course, within the game, I will also indicate potential improvements for Black.

(A) 6...cxd4
This was played in the game A.Miles-A.Kosten, Palma de Mallorca 1989

7 ♘b5 d5!
This is universally considered to be Black's best way of preventing problems on d6. Inferior is 7...d6?! 8 ♘fxd4 when the weakness on d6 is again apparent.

8 cxd5
White must strive for active play. The inferior 8 ♕a4?! was considered earlier. It is also pointless to recover the pawn with the immediate 8 ♘bxd4?! because after 8...dxc4! 9 ♘xc6 ♕xd1+ 10 ♔xd1 bxc6 the poor location of White's king already gives the edge to Black, Levin-A.Lagunov, USSR 1989.

8...♕a5+ 9 ♕d2
It is as yet unclear whether the text-move or 9 ♘d2 is the more promising interpolation. Then the

key position results after 9...♕xb5 (9...exd5?! 10 ♘d6+ ♔e7 11 ♘xc8+ ♖xc8 12 0-0 ♘f6 13 b4! ♘xb4 14 ♘b3 ♕a6 15 ♘xd4 is good for White, C.McNab-D.Coleman, British Championship 1990) 10 dxc6 ♘e7 11 a4. Here a "GM draw" was agreed in the game A.Chernin-V.Jansa, Paris 1989. In C.McNab-A.Wojtkiewicz, London (Lloyds Bank) 1990, the players continued their fight with 11...♕b4 12 b3 ♘xc6 13 ♗a3 ♕a5 14 0-0 ♗f8 15 ♘c4 ♕d8 16 ♗xf8 ♔xf8 17 ♕d2 ♔g7 18 ♖ad1 ♕f6. Now White moved to recover his pawn by 19 ♗xc6 bxc6 20 ♕xd4 ♕xd4 21 ♖xd4 and this equal endgame was drawn on move 28.

9...♕xb5 10 dxc6 ♕xc6
Black can also hurry to complete his development with the interesting plan 10...♘e7!?. In the game A.Fishbein-V.Jansa, Herning 1991, Black gained the advantage after 11 ♘xd4 ♕b6 12 e3 bxc6! 13 b3? ♗a6 14 ♗a3 ♖c8!. Instead of 13 b3?, Jansa suggests 13 0-0 ♗a6 14 ♖d1 ♖d8 15 ♕c2 0-0 16 b4! (with the idea 16...♕xb4 17 a4, threatening 18 ♗a3) and calls the position "unclear".

11 0-0 (D)
White is now ready to recover his pawn with 12 ♘xd4 when due to his superior development in an open position he will have a clear advantage. The black queen must move and there are two possible destinations for it.
11...♕b6

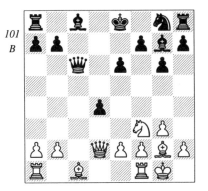

101 B

By far Black's most ambitious and riskiest way: he hopes to hold on to his valuable extra d-pawn. Considerably safer is 11...♕d6 when Black is ready to consolidate by returning the pawn. Thematic play then is 12 ♖d1 e5 (12...♘e7 13 ♘xd4 0-0 14 ♘c6 ♕c7 15 ♕a5 b6! is called unclear by Lagunov) 13 e3 ♘e7 14 exd4 exd4 15 ♕e2!? 0-0 16 ♗f4 ♕d8! (16...♕e6?! 17 ♕xe6 ♗xe6 18 ♘xd4 gives White a superior endgame, A.Lagunov-Spacek, Berlin 1990). In the game Stern-Spacek, Berlin 1990, White now erroneously played 17 ♗g5? and after 17...♖e8 was worse. A.Lagunov correctly suggests 17 ♗e5! ♗xe5 (17...♘c6 18 ♗xg7 ♔xg7 19 ♘xd4!) 18 ♕xe5 ♘c6 19 ♕c5 as the critical line and rates the position as equal. My guess is that after recovering the pawn White will have a slight edge because of his superior pawn formation.
12 b3 ♘e7
In B.Abramović-M.Matulović, Yugoslavia 1992, Black succeeded

with 12...♘f6!?, when White tried for too much with 13 ♗a3? but ended up with too little after 13...♘e4 14 ♕f4 ♘c3 15 ♖fe1 ♘d5! 16 ♕d2 a5! 17 ♖ad1 ♘b4!, with advantage to Black. Instead of 13 ♗a3? White should be satisfied with 13 ♘xd4, when 13...♘e4 14 ♗xe4 ♕xd4 15 ♕xd4 ♗xd4 16 ♖b1 leads to a slightly superior endgame for White because of the power of his king's bishop, while the position after 13...0-0 is difficult to evaluate but probably will lead to equality with best play for both sides. Positions like that always require practical tests for proper evaluation.

13 ♗a3 ♘d5?

Miles brilliantly demonstrates that this does not work. Also unattractive is 13...♗f6 when 14 ♖ac1 followed by 15 ♗c5 keeps up the pressure. Black's best seems 13...♘c6 14 ♖ac1 e5 15 e3 ♗g4, so far L.B.Hansen-V.Jansa, Kerteminde 1991, when instead of the game's 16 ♘g5, Hansen analyses 16 ♗c5! ♕d8 17 exd4 as White's most promising line and considers 17...e4!? to be Black's best defence, leading after 18 ♖fe1 ♗xf3 19 ♗xf3 f5 20 d5 ♘e5 21 ♗xe4! fxe4 22 ♖xe4 to a position where White has a very strong attack and two pawns for the sacrificed piece.

14 ♖ac1 ♘c3 15 e3!

Black attempts to keep the lines closed and White strives to open them. If now 15...♕a6 16 ♘xd4

♗xd4, White has a large advantage after both 17 ♖xc3 and 17 exd4.

15...dxe3 16 fxe3

It is this position which shows off the power behind White's pawn sacrifice: Black's king is stuck in the centre and his queenside undeveloped. If now 16...♘d5 White continues the pressure with 17 ♗c5 followed by 18 e4.

16...♕a6 17 ♗b2 ♘e4 18 ♕c2 ♘f6

18...♗xb2 19 ♕xb2 0-0 loses to 20 ♘e5! f5 21 ♗xe4 (Miles).

19 ♘g5! e5

19...♕a5 loses after 20 ♘xf7! ♔xf7 21 ♕c7+! ♕xc7 22 ♖xc7+ ♔g8 23 ♖xg7+ ♔xg7 24 ♗xf6+ ♔g8 25 ♖d1 (Miles). After the text Black plans to respond to 20 ♘xf7 with 20...0-0!, keeping some slight chances for defending. With his next move White shows that he wants more.

20 ♕c5! ♗e6 21 ♖xf6! ♗xf6 22 ♗f1 ♖c8

Black loses a lot of material after 22...♕xf1+ 23 ♔xf1 ♗xg5 24 ♕xe5; 22...♕b6 23 ♗b5+ ♗d7 24 ♗xd7+ ♔xd7 25 ♕d5+ is equally gruesome.

23 ♗b5+ *(D)*

Pinning Black into oblivion, Miles finishes with great energy and efficiency.

23...♖c6 24 ♘e4! ♗e7

If 24...♗g7, simply 25 ♗xe5!.

25 ♕xe5 f6 26 ♖xc6! fxe5

After 26...bxc6 27 ♕xe6! ♕xb5 the end comes with 28 ♘d6+.

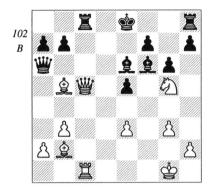

102
B

27 ♖xa6+ ♔f7 28 ♖xa7 ♗d5
29 ♗c4 1-0

(B) 6...♘xd4
Here we follow D.Gurevich-
M.Dlugy, New York Open 1989
7 ♘xd4 cxd4
Here too 7...♗xd4?! makes no
sense due to 8 ♘b5! when Black's
dark-squared bishop stands worse
on d4 than on g7.
After the text it is obvious that
White's knight must head for d6,
but is b5 or e4 the better launch-
ing square?
8 ♘e4!

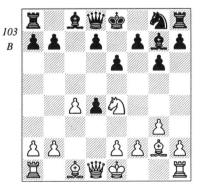

103
B

Our current knowledge says
this is the preferable route because on e4 the knight is more secure than on b5. The main line
after 8 ♘b5 is 8...♕b6 9 ♕a4 a6
(preventing the threatened 10
♕b4) 10 e3 and now:
   (1) 10...♘e7 11 ♘xd4 0-0 (after
11...♗xd4?! 12 exd4 ♕xd4 13 0-0
Black is chronically weak on the
dark squares) 12 0-0, F.Santacruz-
A.Fauland, Novi Sad Olympiad
1990. Here White has recovered
his pawn in a comfortable position, while Black will have difficulties in developing his queen's
bishop.
   (2) 10...d3! and now, in A.Cher-
nin-P.Wolff, New York Open 1989,
White was clearly in major trouble
after 11 ♕a3? ♗f8!. Instead, both
players suggest 11 0-0 ♘e7 when
Wolff gives 12 ♘c3 and adds
"White should concentrate on
equalising" while Chernin feels
that his position is satisfactory after 12 ♖d1.
   8...♘e7
Playable, yet in a certain sense
somewhat defeatist: Black gives
back the pawn and forgoes castling to ensure that he doesn't
wind up with something worse.
Other relevant tournament examples are:
   (a) 8...f5?! 9 ♘d6+ ♔f8 10 ♕b3
♗e5 11 ♕a3 ♔g7 12 ♗f4! ♗f6 13
c5 ♘e7 14 0-0 ♘c6 15 b4! b5 16
cxb6 e5? 17 ♗h6+! 1-0, D.Johan-
sen-J.Hawksworth, British Championship 1984.

(b) **8...♕c7 9 c5! ♘e7 10 ♗f4 ♕a5+ 11 ♗d2 ♕c7 12 ♘d6+ ♔f8 13 ♖c1 h5 14 ♕a4**, A.Chernin-T.Parameswaren, Bangalore 1981, when Black never got out of the queenside bind and lost on move 26.

(c) **8...d6!?** 9 ♕a4+ ♔e7 is most likely the critical line:

(c1) 10 c5 d5 11 ♘d6 ♔f8 12 0-0 ♘e7 13 e4 dxe3 14 ♗xe3 h6 15 ♖ad1 ♔g8, C.McNab-M.Chandler, Blackpool Zonal 1990. White should have compensation for the pawn here, but Black eventually consolidated to win in 51.

(c2) 10 ♗d2 a5 11 ♕a3 f5 12 ♗g5+ ♘f6 13 ♗xf6+ ♗xf6 14 ♘xf6 ♔xf6 15 0-0 ♕b6 16 ♖ad1 ♖d8 17 e3! dxe3 18 fxe3 ♕b4 19 ♕d3, G.Shwartzman-S.Fedder, Copenhagen 1990. The situation here is also rather unclear, but White won in 36.

9 ♘d6+ ♔f8 10 ♘xb7 ♗xb7 11 ♗xb7 ♖b8 12 ♗g2 ♔g8 13 0-0 h6 14 b3 d5?!

Black expects 15 cxd5? ♘xd5 with a good game for him, but the move meets a strategic refutation. He should have completed the castling by hand with 14...♔h7 when White has a slight edge due to the bishop pair.

15 ♗a3! dxc4 16 bxc4

White's bishops control most of the board, the c-pawn is passed and Black's knight has no effective square. Gurevich builds on these factors in a most instructive way.

16...♕d7 17 ♖b1 ♔h7 18 ♕c2 ♖b6 19 ♖b3 ♖c8 20 ♖xb6!

Now that Black's knight doesn't have access to c8, White is agreeable to this exchange since the b6-pawn becomes vulnerable.

20...axb6 21 ♕b3 ♕c7 22 ♖c1 ♖b8 23 ♖b1! ♗f8 24 ♕b5 ♘f5 25 ♗xf8 ♖xf8 26 ♕c6! ♕a7 27 a4!

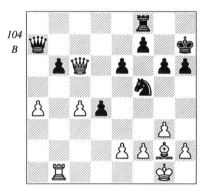

The advantage of the bishop pair has been transformed into that of more active pieces bearing down on the b-pawn. At the very least White will create a powerful passed pawn on the queenside.

27...♖b8 28 ♗e4 ♘e7?!

Short of time, Black allows the white queen to a more powerful location. According to Gurevich, necessary is 28...h5.

29 ♕d6 ♖e8 30 c5! bxc5 31 ♖b7 ♕a8 32 ♖xe7 ♕xe4 33 ♖xf7+! ♔g8 34 ♕d7 ♕b1+ 35 ♔g2 ♕e4+ 36 ♔h3 1-0

The following two questions are now appropriate:

(1) Is the gambit with 6 d4!? sound?

It is much too early to tell for sure. My best guess is that White will be shown to have sufficient compensation for the pawn.

(2) Should you play it?

a) No, if you only like sound, clear, strategic play.

b) Yes, perhaps on a occasional basis, if

• you have studied it well, and
• you don't mind complications part of the time.

It is probably most effective as a surprise weapon against a stodgy opponent.

Variations for Black after 5 e3

5 e3

The high-class idea behind this move is the same as after 5...e6 for Black in the variations after 5 ♘f3 or 5 a3: the g1-knight will be developed smoothly to e2, White will aim to get in d4, while leaving open the diagonal of the fianchetted bishop. Its only disadvantage is a practical one, i.e. because White is playing so quietly within a closed symmetrical opening, Black can afford to keep up with the symmetry. Black's simplest and soundest way of going for equality is 5...e6 6 ♘ge2 ♘ge7 7 0-0 0-0 8 d4 cxd4 9 ♘xd4 ♘xd4 10 exd4 d5 11 cxd5 ♘xd5, with equality – but no more – in full view. Yet the text also presents Black with a major problem if he/she wants or needs more than a draw, either because of being higher rated or

for tournament standing. Because White's plan is strategically sound, varying from imitating it exposes Black to potential problems. The three important non-symmetrical methods are:

(1) **5...♘f6**. The knight is developed to a "perfect" central square, yet Black's central co-ordination is nowhere as near as good as White's. Therefore White can expect a pleasant, riskless advantage. For instance: 6 ♘ge2 0-0 7 0-0 d6 8 d4 ♗d7 9 b3 a6 10 ♗b2 ♖b8 11 ♕d2 ♕a5 12 ♖fd1 cxd4 13 exd4 ♖fd8 14 d5 ♘e5 15 ♘d4 with a spatial and central advantage, So.Maus-M.Tal, Germany (Bundesliga) 1990.

I think that Black's winning chances are increased – at no increase in risk of losing – by either of the following two continuations.

(2) **5...e5**

We will follow the game I.Radulov-Angel Martin, Torremolinos 1974.

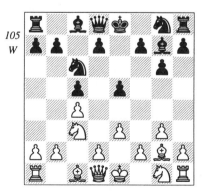

105
W

What White didn't dare to do on his previous move – advance his e-pawn two squares – Black does, thereby preventing White's d4 and gaining some central space. Of course, the disadvantages are equally obvious: permanent weakening of d5 and blocking in the g7-bishop. Even though existing theory does not provide a clear way of demonstrating a White advantage, the existence of these negative features has led to a marked loss of confidence in Black's set-up. Simply stated, the text is little seen nowadays in international play.

6 ♘ge2 ♘ge7 7 0-0 0-0 8 a3

Aiming for the b4 advance is a standard way of handling such positions, so as to gain space on the queenside and to try to undermine the central influence of Black's c-pawn. Nevertheless, the developing 8 b3 d6 9 ♗b2 is also attractive , e.g. 9...♗g4 10 d3 ♕d7 11 ♕d2 ♗h3 12 ♗xh3 ♕xh3 13 f4!, J.Bellon-L.Portisch, Madrid 1973, when the superior bishop and better central coverage give White a slight edge.

8...d6 9 ♖b1 a5

The "eternal" question in such positions is whether Black should play ...a5 to prevent White's b4 advance. There is generally no "correct" answer, but my personal opinion is that Black will find it easier to handle the positions without ...a5, as that move creates fundamental weaknesses

on both b5 and b6. A thematic example after 9...♗e6 is the game L.Pachman-M.Botvinnik, Moscow 1956: 10 ♘d5 ♗f5 11 ♘xe7+ (11 d3 !?) 11...♕xe7 12 d3 e4! 13 ♘f4 exd3 14 e4 ♗e6 15 b3 ♖ab8, with approximate equality (Taimanov).

10 d3 ♖b8 11 ♗d2 ♗f5?!

The plan of exchanging the light-squared bishops will only serve to emphasise Black's weakness on those squares as well as leave him with a permanently inferior dark-squared bishop. Correct is central development via 11...♗e6, with White retaining a slight edge after 12 ♘d5, e.g. 12...b5 13 cxb5! ♖xb5 14 ♘ec3 (Radulov).

12 ♕c2 ♕d7 13 ♘d5 b6 14 ♘ec3 ♘xd5 15 cxd5! ♘e7 16 e4! ♗h3 17 b4! ♗xg2 18 ♔xg2

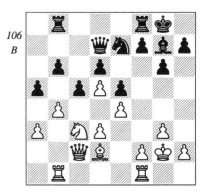

106 B

White's strategy has been far more successful than Black's: White's bishop has more scope and so does his knight, White's d5-pawn controls important central space, whereas Black's d-pawn is a fundamental weakness. Black has no compensation whatsoever for his problems.

18...axb4 19 axb4 f5 20 bxc5! bxc5?

After this normal recapture, White will get at Black's d-pawn. Unattractive, but a better chance, is 20...dxc5 21 ♘b5 f4. White retains a clear advantage after 22 f3, but the closed nature of the position makes a break-in difficult to achieve.

21 ♖xb8! ♖xb8 22 ♖b1! ♕c7 23 ♖xb8+ ♕xb8 24 ♕a4 ♕d8 25 ♘b5

White's three pieces co-ordinate beautifully, with the immediate plan being 26 ♕a7 followed by 27 ♗a5. Black is lost.

25...♕d7 26 ♕a8+ ♔f7

Or 26...♗f8 27 ♗h6 ♕c8 28 ♕a7! ♗xh6 29 ♕xe7 ♗f8 30 ♘xd6, winning.

27 ♕b8 1-0

The fall of the d-pawn is the end of the game: 27...♘c8 28 ♕xc8! ♕xb5 29 ♕e6+ ♔f8 30 ♕xd6+ etc.

(3) **5...♗xc3!?**

Here we follow the game E.Mednis-B.Larsen, New York (WFW) International 1990.

Only a very strong player or a rank amateur would dare this capture. Black voluntarily exchanges off his recently developed bishop, weakening his kingside, strengthening White's centre, and leaving White with the potential of the bishop pair. Apart from the

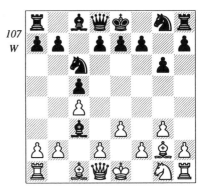

107
W

practical aspect of bringing about a very unbalanced position, Black expects that White's central pawn mass will be an unwieldy one and that White's dark-squared bishop will have little scope. In our specific position, the text appears to be a theoretical novelty. In the post-mortem, Larsen showed me some examples where he had played the same idea for both White and Black in similar positions. He added that the idea is only viable if the opponent has played e3/e6 since then there are problems developing the queen's bishop. It is worth adding that in Y.Seirawan-U.Andersson,Tilburg 1990, played almost simultaneously with this game, after White's 5 a3 d6 6 e3 Andersson also continued with 6...♗xc3. Black in that case is even a bit better off than in our game as Black's ...d6 is more useful than White's a3.

6 bxc3

Capturing towards the centre is thematic, yet I was not quite at ease doing so, because now it will be more difficult to liberate the c1-bishop and the a-pawn becomes isolated. Seirawan also recaptured thus. In any case, the next time I will have to face Black's capture, I will respond with 6 dxc3. If then 6...f5, White plays 7 e4! because opening the position should be in the interest of his bishops.

6...f5 7 f4?!
I realised that the dark-squared bishop is thereby blocked in some more, but I wanted to prevent ...e5. Larsen considers 7 e4!? as correct here too.

7...♘f6 8 ♘f3 b6 9 0-0 ♗b7 10 d3 ♘a5 11 ♕e2 ♕c7 12 ♗b2?!
Because of the closed nature of the position a black knight has more potential than White's dark-squared bishop and Black has a sound pawn formation. All of this means that Black stands well. The text is a waste of time; better is 12 ♗d2.

12...0-0 13 ♖ae1 ♖ae8 14 ♗c1?!
More time wasted. Either 14 ♘d2 followed by e4 or the immediate 14 h3 make more sense.

14...e6 15 h3 d6 16 ♘h2 ♗xg2 17 ♕xg2 ♕c6!
With White ready to get something going on the kingside starting with 18 g4, Larsen takes the wind out of White's sails by exchanging queens. In an endgame Black can unhurriedly work to capitalise on the strategic assets of the better pawn formation and superior minor piece.

18 g4 ♕xg2+ 19 ♔xg2 ♖f7 20 e4?!

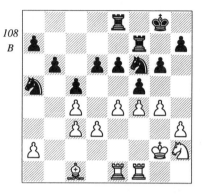

This optimistic advance leaves holes in its wake and the access to g4 by the knight provides insufficient compensation. Correct is 20 ♔g3, followed by 21 ♘f3. Black still has the advantage, but White has many fewer weaknesses to worry about. After the text Larsen continues his masterful demonstration of the theme(s) behind 5...♗xc3!? and never gives me a chance to recover. The instructive game course was:

20...fxe4! 21 g5 ♘h5 22 ♖xe4 ♔f8! 23 ♖fe1 ♖fe7! 24 ♔f3 d5! 25 cxd5 exd5 26 ♖xe7 ♖xe7 27 ♗d2?! ♖xe1! 28 ♗xe1 ♘c6 29 ♘g4 ♔e7 30 ♘e3 ♔e6 31 ♔g4 ♘g7 32 ♘c2 ♘e7! 33 ♗d2 ♘gf5 34 ♔f3 ♘c6 35 ♔g4 a6 36 ♔f3 ♔d6 37 ♗e1 b5! 38 ♗d2 a5 39 a3 ♘ce7 40 ♗e1 ♘c8! 41 ♗d2 ♘b6 42 ♗e1 ♘a4 43 ♗d2 ♔e6 44 ♔e2 ♘b6 45 ♔f3 c4 46 dxc4 ♘xc4 47 ♗e1 ♘cd6 48 ♗f2 ♔d7 49 ♗b6 ♘c4 50 ♗f2 ♘d2+ 51

♔e2 ♘e4 52 ♗e1 ♔c6 53 ♘a1 ♘c5 54 ♘c2 ♘e6 55 ♗d2 ♘d6 56 ♔d3 ♘c4 57 ♗c1 ♘c5+ 58 ♔e2 ♘b3!! 59 ♗e3 ♘d6 60 ♔d3 ♔d7 61 ♗a7 ♘c4 62 f5!? gxf5 63 ♗b8 ♔e6 64 h4 ♘c1+ 65 ♔d4 f4 66 ♔c5 ♘e2 67 ♔xb5 ♔f5 68 ♔c6 ♘xc3 69 ♘d4+ ♔g4 70 h5 ♔xg5 71 ♘e6+ ♔xh5 72 ♘xf4+ ♔g4 73 a4 h5 74 ♘xd5 ♘xd5 75 ♔xd5 ♘b6+ 76 ♔c6 ♘xa4 77 ♔b5 ♘c3+ 78 ♔xa5 ♘e2 79 ♗h2 h4 80 ♔b4 ♔h3 81 ♗e5 ♔g2 82 ♔c4 h3 83 ♔d3 ♘g3 0-1

18 The "automatic" move: 1...g6

Want to be able to play your move without having to bother to look at what White has opened with? Do I have a move for you! It is 1...g6. Of course, it does not guarantee victory or anything else. Yet you will have the confidence of having played a correct move. The inherent playability of 1...g6 became understood in the 1960s and its reputation was solidified by Raymond Keene and George Botterill's outstanding treatise *The Modern Defence*, published in 1972. It was not always thus. A typical evaluation was that of Alexander Alekhine in the tournament book of the 1924 New York International. In his review of the openings played, he characterised the 1 e4 g6(?) seen in Edward Lasker-J.R.Capablanca as the "Joke Opening". In the comments to the actual game he was, however, more restrained and accurate: "From the present-day theoretical standpoint this move cannot be regarded as wholly valid, because Black commits himself to a certain position without being able to influence in any way his adversary's development in the centre."

Why is 1...g6 a sound move? Because – when followed by the obvious 2...♗g7 – it has no particular deficiencies and furthers

the objectives of good opening play by developing the dark-squared bishop towards the centre and preparing castling. Nevertheless, it needs to be stressed that Black must understand the nuances of this defence very well, as otherwise White's centre will smother him. This is particularly true where White opens with 1 e4 and 2 d4 (or 1 d4 and 2 e4).

The main characteristics of the "kingside fianchetto defence" are:

(1) Maximum flexibility, i.e. the kingside fianchetto can be used against any White opening.

(2) It is a counterplay defence: since the g7-bishop points at d4, Black expects to undermine that point. The usual method is via the ...e5 or ...c5 advance.

(3) Black delays the development of his king's knight so as to enhance the power of the bishop.

In regard to the last point, it should be added that if White uses a very aggressive build-up, e.g. one with f4, many Black players prefer to transpose into the Pirc Defence (1 e4 d6 2 d4 ♘f6) or the King's Indian Defence (1 d4 ♘f6 2 c4 g6 3 ♘c3 ♗g7 4 e4 d6) by playing ...♘f6 early on. In using systems with ...c5, knowledge of Accelerated Dragon variations in the Sicilian Defence (1 e4 c5 2 ♘f3 ♘c6 3 d4 cxd4 4 ♘xd4 g6 or 1 e4 c5 2 ♘f3 g6 3 d4 ♗g7) is helpful.

I shall take a brief look at a thematically important variation after each of White's sound opening moves: 1 e4, 1 d4, 1 c4, 1 ♘f3 and 1 g3. Since 1...g6 is sensible against the "normal moves", it is so against the others also. For instance, after 1 b3 g6 2 ♗b2 ♘f6 Black doesn't have to be concerned with 3 ♗xf6 exf6 because after 4...♗g7, 5...0-0 and 6...f5 the chances are already equal.

(1) **1 e4 g6 2 d4 ♗g7 3 ♘c3**

The usual initiation to sharp variations. Quieter play results after 3 ♘f3 d6. If Black wants more unbalanced situations he can select 3...c5. However, he has to be ready for Sicilian variations after 4 ♘c3 or 4 c4 and Benoni positions after 4 d5.

3...d6 4 f4 c6

If Black wants to stay in the "kingside fianchetto" the text is the soundest plan. Andy Soltis has played it with considerable success. Black frees his queen for queenside play, gets ready for an eventual ...b5 and protects d5. However, this does ignore White's rather strong kingside build-up. Therefore many Black players prefer to switch into the Pirc Defence with 4...♘f6. (1 e4 d6 2 d4 ♘f6 3 ♘c3 g6 4 f4 ♗g7 is the Pirc move-order.)

5 ♘f3 ♗g4

Applying pressure on the thematic point d4. The immediate 5...♕b6 leaves the queen misplaced after 6 h3!.

6 ♗e3 ♕b6 7 ♕d2

White does not have to worry about the b-pawn now or a move later, e.g. 7...♕xb2?! 8 ♖b1 ♕a3 9 ♖xb7 ♘d7 10 ♖b3 when the opening of the position favours the side with better development and more of the centre, i.e. White.

7...♗xf3 8 gxf3 ♘d7 9 0-0-0 ♕a5

Since d4 is secure, Black must aim for other targets. The text attacks a2 and prepares a storming of the queenside with b5. Therefore White's next is forced.

10 ♔b1

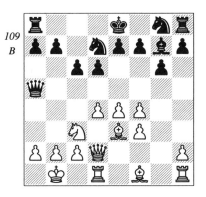

*109
B*

Black's "automatic" move now has been 10...b5. However, White gets a very strong attack after 11 e5, 11 f5 or 11 h4 and 12 h5. Therefore, I am now following J.Polgar-C.Crouch, Hastings 1992/93.

10...0-0-0!?

Black brings his king to relative safety by castling on the same side as White.

11 Rg1 ⌾b8 12 Rg5 ⌾c7 13 d5!? ⌾b6?!

A poor place for the knight. According to Crouch the critical continuation is to complete Black's kingside development by means of 13...⌾gf6!. Then after 14 e5 (14 dxc6 bxc6 should be fine for Black) 14...⌾xd5 15 ⌾xd5 cxd5 16 exd6 exd6 17 Rxd5 ⌾b6! 18 Rxd6 Rxd6 19 ⌾xd6 ⌾xd6 20 Rxd6 Re8 Black has good compensation for the slight material deficiency.

14 dxc6 bxc6 15 ⌾d3?!

Feeble. As subsequently demonstrated by Polgar, White has a strong initiative after 15 a4! ⌾f6 16 a5 ⌾c8 17 ⌾a2.

15...⌾f6 16 Ra5 ⌾fd7 17 ⌾a4?

Overeager. It was time for 17 Ra3 with unclear play. Now Black can exploit White's clumsy piece placement to gain the advantage.

17...⌾c5! 18 ⌾a3

The only move. Capturing any way is worse, e.g. 18 ⌾xc5? dxc5 19 ⌾e2 Rxd1+ 20 ⌾xd1 ⌾c4!. For the rest of the game I shall use abbreviated notes from Crouch's analysis in *Chess Informant* 58, game 133.

18...⌾cxa4 19 Rxa4 ⌾xa4 20 ⌾xa4 ⌾a8 21 ⌾c4 Rb8? (correct is 21...e6) **22 b3! ⌾c3 23 ⌾xf7 ⌾a5 24 f5 gxf5 25 exf5 Rb4 26 ⌾a3 Rh4 27 ⌾b2 Rb8!? 28 c4! d5! 29 cxd5 Rxh2 30 ⌾c1 ⌾e5 31 ⌾e6?** (correct is 31 ⌾xc6+ with a draw) **31...⌾c3??** (Black has the advantage after 31...⌾c7) **32 ⌾f4**

⌾xa2 **33 ⌾xe5 Ra1+ 34 ⌾c2 Rxc1+ 35 ⌾xc1 ⌾xe5 36 dxc6 Re8 37 Rd7 h5 38 ⌾d5 1-0.**

(2) **1 d4 g6 2 c4**

Of course, with 2 e4 White can transpose into the 1 e4 variations discussed earlier. Most d4 players, understandably, prefer to stay in a more closed opening.

2...⌾g7 3 ⌾c3 c5

The sharpest way to exploit the early kingside fianchetto. Black's main alternative is 3...d6 4 e4 when he has the following choices:

(a) 4...⌾f6 transposes into the King's Indian Defence (1 d4 ⌾f6 2 c4 g6 3 ⌾c3 ⌾g7 4 e4 d6) and is Black's most solid continuation.

(b) 4...e5 leads to an unpleasant endgame after 5 dxe5! dxe5 6 ⌾xd8+ ⌾xd8 7 f4! – see *From The Opening Into The Endgame* by E.Mednis, Cadogan Books, Revised Edition, 1991.

(c) 4...⌾d7 and 4...⌾c6 are risky but keep the promise of the kingside fianchetto defence going.

4 d5 ⌾xc3+!? 5 bxc3 f5!

Roman Dzindzichashvili is the ideological father of Black's plan: creating a weakened and unwieldy pawn structure on White's queenside, though at the cost of the bishop pair and some kingside weakening. Black hopes to keep the position sufficiently closed so as to be able to work on White's pawn weaknesses.

We will follow the game L.Alburt-D.Vigorito, New York Open 1993.

6 h3!?

With the idea of opening up the kingside with 7 g4. The immediate 6 g4 can be met by 6...fxg4 7 h3 g3!. Other known moves are 6 ♘f3, 6 ♕a4, 6 h4 – all with as yet unclear consequences.

6...d6 7 ♘f3 ♕a5 8 ♕c2 ♘f6 9 ♗h6! ♘bd7 10 e3 ♘b6 11 ♗d3 ♗d7 12 0-0 ♕a4 13 ♕b3!

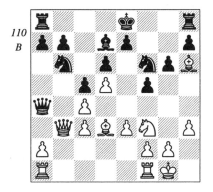

*110
B*

Black has applied the thematic pressure on c4, yet White is covering it expertly. Black should now bring his king into safety with 13...0-0-0 followed by 14...♔b8 and awaiting developments. As played, he allows White to favourably open up the kingside.

13...♘e4?! 14 ♗xe4! fxe4 15 ♘d2 0-0-0 16 f3! exf3 17 ♖xf3 ♕a6 18 ♖f7!?

White could safeguard c4 by 18 ♖f4 but with justification he goes for more.

18...♗a4 19 ♕b2 ♘xc4?!

The defensive 19...♖d7 is in order with White having some pull after 20 ♖f4 followed by 21 ♖af1.

20 ♘xc4 ♕xc4 21 ♖b1! ♕xd5 22 ♖xe7 ♗c6?

The incursion on b7 will be deadly. Yet Black is also in trouble after the better 22...♗d7 23 c4 ♕c6 24 ♗f4 b6 25 ♖d1.

23 c4 ♕d3 24 ♕xb7+!! ♗xb7 25 ♖bxb7 ♖d7 26 ♖exd7 ♕f5 27 ♖dc7+ ♔d8 28 ♖f7 1-0

(3) **1 c4 g6 2 ♘c3 ♗g7 3 g3 d6**

The "automatic" move now is 4 ♗g2, giving Black a wide choice of plans: 4...c5, 4...e5 and 4...♘f6.

We will follow the game L.Ljubojević-G.Kasparov, Thessaloniki Olympiad 1988.

4 d4!?

White is ready to switch over to a King's Indian after 4...♘f6. However, the World Champion is determined to handle the opening as the King's Fianchetto defence.

4...c5!? 5 ♗e3?!

This clumsy defence of d4 cannot lead to an advantage. Kasparov considers the alternatives as follows: (1) 5 ♘f3 ♘c6 6 d5 ♘a5; (2) 5 d5 ♗xc3+ 6 bxc3 ♕a5; (3) 5 dxc5 ♗xc3+ 6 bxc3 dxc5 7 ♕xd8+ ♔xd8 8 ♗e3 ♘d7. In all cases he evaluates the resulting positions as "unclear".

5...cxd4! 6 ♗xd4 ♘f6 7 ♘d5?!

Black will soon wind up with more central influence. Kasparov considers White's best to be 7 ♗g2 ♘c6 8 ♘f3 0-0 9 0-0 with equality.

7...♘bd7 8 ♘f3 0-0 9 ♗g2 e5! 10 ♗c3

Black also has a clear advantage after 10 ♘xf6+ ♘xf6 11 ♗c3 ♘e4! 12 ♕b3 ♗e6 (Kasparov).

10...♘xd5! 11 cxd5 ♘c5 12 0-0

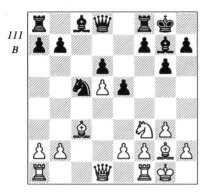

111 B

Black has an unmistakable advantage because he has a clear road to kingside play via ...f5, whereas White's prospects for an attack against Black's only weakness are stillborn. Moreover, the poor location of White's c3-bishop even gives Black chances for the initiative on the queenside. Kasparov now suggests as strongest 12...b5! 13 b3 a5 14 ♘d2 f5! with an advantage on both flanks. I will give the rest of the game just with the always objective markings by the World Champion. Full analysis appears in *Chess Informant* 46, game 8.

12...♗d7?! 13 ♘d2 ♖c8?! 14 ♖c1 f5 15 ♘c4 ♗b5?! 16 ♘a3 ♗e8 17 ♕d2 ♖f7 18 ♗b4 ♖fc7 19 ♖c2 ♘a6 20 ♗c3 e4 21 ♗xg7 ♔xg7 22 ♖fc1 ♗f7 23 g4 fxg4 24 ♗xe4 ♕f6 25 ♘b5 ♖xc2 26
♖xc2 ♖xc2 27 ♕xc2 ♘c5 28 b4?! ♘xe4 29 ♕xe4 h5 30 a3 g5 31 ♘d4 a6 32 ♘e6+? ♔h6 33 ♔g2? ♗g6 34 ♕e3 ♕f5 35 ♕d4 ♕e4+ 36 ♔g1 ♕xd4 37 ♘xd4 ♗e4? 38 f3 gxf3 39 exf3 ♗b1 40 ♔f2 ♔g6 41 b5? ♗a2 42 bxa6 bxa6 43 ♘c6 ♔f5 44 ♘b4 ♗c4 45 ♔e3 a5 46 ♘c6 ♗xd5 47 ♘d4+ ♔e5 48 ♘e2 ♗f7 49 ♘g1? ♗c4 50 ♘h3 ♔f5 51 ♘f2 d5 0-1

(4) **1 ♘f3 g6 2 g3**

Here 2 e4 is a common alternative. Many GMs who normally prefer closed openings like the safe, sound Classical Variation of the Pirc Defence which results after 2...♗g7 3 d4 d6 4 ♘c3 ♘f6 5 ♗e2 0-0 6 0-0.

2...♗g7 3 ♗g2 c5

Of course, 3...♘f6 is playable, imitating White's flexible kingside fianchetto development. Black can also advance the primary central pawns: 3...d6, 3...d5 or 3...e5.

4 e4 ♘c6 5 d3 d6 6 0-0 e5 7 c3 ♘ge7

A Réti Opening has arisen in which Black's flexible kingside fianchetto and delayed king's knight development have given him good central influence.

We continue following A.Chernin-Av.Byhovsky, USSR 1983.

8 a3

Since the d4 advance is difficult to execute, White prepares to advance on the queenside.

8...0-0 9 b4 cxb4

Black enhances White's centre in order to prepare some queenside counterplay. A solid alternative is 9...b6.

10 axb4 b5! 11 ♘a3 ♖b8 12 ♗e3

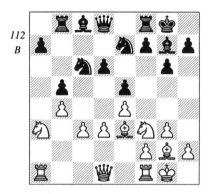

*112
B*

A key position. Black should either play on the kingside with 12...f5 or establish approximate queenside parity with 12...a5! – in either case with equal chances.

12...a6?!

By doing neither Black allows White to start dictating matters. Chernin exploits his opportunities very well. I have made use of Chernin's analysis in *Chess Informant* 36, game 1 in providing the brief comments that follow.

13 d4! exd4 14 ♘xd4 ♗b7 15 ♖c1 ♖e8 16 ♘b3!? ♗a8 17 ♕d2 ♘c8 18 ♖fd1 ♕e7 19 ♘c2 ♘e5 20 ♘a5 ♗f8 21 ♗f4 ♕c7 22 ♘e3 ♘b6 23 ♕a2 ♖bc8 24 ♘d5 ♕d8 25 h4 ♘a4!? 26 c4 ♗xd5 27 exd5 ♕f6 28 ♖c2! ♘d7 (28...♕f5!) 29 ♕b3 ♘db6 30 cxb5 ♘c3 31 ♗g5! ♕h8 32 ♖f1 ♘e2+? 33 ♖xe2 ♖xe2 34 bxa6 ♖c3 35 ♕d1 ♖a2

36 a7 ♖c8 37 ♘c6 ♕c3 38 ♕f3 ♕xf3 39 ♗xf3 ♖e8 40 ♖c1 ♗g7 41 ♗e3 ♘a8 42 ♘e7+ ♔f8 43 ♘c8 ♖xe3 44 fxe3 ♗h6 45 ♖c3 ♗g7 46 ♖b3 1-0

(5) **1 g3 g6 2 ♗g2 ♗g7 3 e4**

Of course, White has a lot of high-quality alternatives, e.g. 3 c4, 3 d4 or 3 ♘f3.

3...e5

Black can aim for the Pirc Defence with 3...d6 and 4...♘f6 or for Sicilian formations with 3...c5.

4 ♘e2

More ambitious is 4 ♘f3 – but we have already seen that deployment in the previous section.

4...♘e7!? 5 0-0 0-0 6 d4

Black can cope with this early advance quite well. Something slower like 6 c3 probably gives better chances for a slight edge.

6...exd4 7 ♘xd4 d5! 8 ♘c3 dxe4 9 ♘db5 ♘a6 10 ♘xe4 ♗d7

The centre pawns have disappeared and apart from the a6-knight all Black's pieces stand well. He is on the verge of full equality.

11 ♘d4 h6!

To be able to continue with ...♘c6 without being bothered by ♗g5, e.g. 11...♘c6?! 12 ♗g5!.

12 c3 ♘c6 13 ♘xc6 ♗xc6 14 ♗e3 ♕e7

I have been following G.Forintos-L.Lengyel, Kecskemet 1972. Black has equalised and can look forward to middlegame developments.

19 Sister Openings

Sister openings are those where there are sufficient strategic similarities so that if a player likes and understands one opening, then it is likely that he/she will both like and be successful in employing the other one. In this chapter I will consider two pairs of sister openings.

(1) *Caro-Kann Defence vs. 1 e4 and Slav Defence vs. 1 d4*

If you are successfully playing the Caro-Kann Defence against 1 e4 (1 e4 c6 2 d4 d5), the chances are excellent that you will be happy and successful in playing the Slav Defence against 1 d4 (1 d4 d5 2 c4 c6). Of course, the reverse applies equally well. Let us briefly discuss the strategic similarities:

- If White exchanges pawns in the centre, then after ...cxd5 Black's central pawn formation is the same in both defences.
- If White does not exchange in the centre, then in the main line variations Black himself will have to exchange by playing ...dxe4/...dxc4. This again will lead to the same central formation for Black in both defences.
- Because Black's e-pawn is not moved early on, he is able to develop the c8-bishop via its original diagonal.

- In the main variations Black will have somewhat less central space.

However, Black's position is always inherently sound and solid. Any precipitous attacks by White will give Black excellent prospects for successful counterplay.

Of course, the specific variations of the Caro-Kann and the Slav are quite different. However, Black's central pawn structure is often the same, the light-squared bishop can be developed similarly and the overall strategic approach is the same. I will now illustrate the "sisterhood" by selecting a main line variation for each defence, with Black playing an early ...♗f5.

(A) Caro-Kann Defence B19
1 e4 c6 2 d4 d5 3 ♘c3 dxe4 4 ♘xe4 ♗f5 5 ♘g3 ♗g6 6 h4

The light-squared bishop – Black's problem bishop in e.g. the French Defence – has not only been successfully developed, but even has more scope than the corresponding white light-squared bishop. White's chances for retaining a normal opening advantage depend on his slight central superiority in having the only primary central pawn on the fourth rank and his one tempo edge in development.

Because of the power of Black's light-squared bishop, it has become recognised that White should exchange it off. Since White plans to castle on the queenside, the text-move is a safe way of gaining a spatial advantage on the kingside, prior to an exchange of bishops.

6...h6 7 ♘f3 ♘d7 8 h5 ♗h7 9 ♗d3 ♗xd3 10 ♕xd3 e6 11 ♗d2 ♕c7 12 0-0-0 ♘gf6 13 ♘e4 0-0-0 14 g3

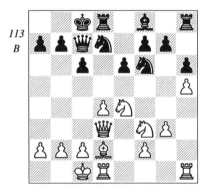

113
B

Diagram 113 shows a characteristic main-line position in the Caro-Kann. White continues to be a bit better, yet Black has no weaknesses. With his last move White prepares ♗f4 and Black takes the opportunity to lighten his load by an exchange of knights.

14...♘c5 15 ♘xc5 ♗xc5 16 c4 ♗d6 17 ♗c3 ♔b8 18 ♕e2

In G.Sax-A.Karpov, Haninge 1990, the former World Champion now played 18...♔a8. The immediate 18...c5 seems more thematic to me, challenging the d4-pawn.

Karpov then provides the following analysis: 19 dxc5 ♗xc5 20 ♗e5 ♗d6 21 ♖xd6 ♖xd6 22 ♗xd6 ♕xd6 23 ♘e5 with a slight edge to White, because of the more active knight and the central influence due to the c4-pawn. Black does remain sound and solid, but, as can be seen from this variation, if White also plays like a rock, Black's prospects for a win are scant.

(B) Slav Defence D18
1 d4 d5 2 c4 c6 3 ♘c3 ♘f6 4 ♘f3 dxc4

Here is an opportune moment for this capture, since the active 5 e4 leads after 5...b5 to an unclear gambit, while after the "normal" 5 e3 b5 6 a4 b4, the queen's knight gets misplaced, affording Black fairly ready equality.

5 a4

Only thus can White expect some opening advantage: the pawn gets recovered comfortably, but at the cost of a weakened queenside and a non-developing move (5 a4).

5...♗f5 6 e3 e6 7 ♗xc4 ♗b4 8 0-0 0-0 9 ♘h4 (D)

One of the many new ideas within the historical main line. Formerly most common was 9 ♕e2 ♘bd7 10 e4 ♗g6 11 ♗d3 ♗h5 12 ♗f4 (Black was threatening to play 12...e5) 12...♖e8 (again planning 13...e5). Though White has a central superiority, Black's position is solid, his development is complete and the potential for

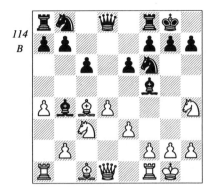

central counterplay via the ...e5 or ...c5 advance is bright. Current opinion is that White should prevent such counterplay by playing 13 e5 ♘d5 14 ♘xd5.

The point of the text-move is to exchange off Black's light-squared bishop, thereby giving White the bishop pair and prospects for controlling e4. Black can temporarily leave the bishop where it is, retreat to g6 immediately or cause White to weaken his kingside prior to the retreat to g6. I believe that the last approach gives the best chances for counterplay.

9...♗g4 10 f3 ♗h5 11 g4 ♗g6 12 ♘g2

Black's light-squared bishop will apparently be boxed out after the coming e4, so it is tempting to retain the h4-knight. Yet the retreat costs time and the knight on g2 is hardly well placed itself. Consistent and leading to a slight plus for White is 12 e4 ♘bd7 13 g5 ♘e8 14 ♘xg6 hxg6 15 ♗e3 ♘d6 16 ♗e2!, L.Polugayevsky-E.Torre, Biel 1989.

Of course, White is not worse after the text, but Black's chances for counterplay are brighter. To illustrate this point, I am giving the course of H.Olafsson-E.Mednis, Reykjavik 1982, where the over-optimistic play of the Icelandic GM ran into the solidity of the Slav: 12...♘d5! 13 ♕b3 a5! 14 e4 ♘b6 15 ♗e3 ♘xc4 16 ♕xc4 ♕e7! 17 h4?! f6! 18 h5 ♗f7 19 h6 e5 20 ♕e2?! exd4! 21 ♗xd4 ♖d8 22 ♗e3 g6 23 ♗f4 ♘d7 24 ♘e3 ♘e5 25 ♗g3 ♕c5 26 ♗f2? ♖d2! 27 ♘ed5 ♕d6! 28 ♗h4 ♗xc3 29 ♘xf6+ ♔h8 0-1.

(2) *Pirc Defence vs. 1 e4 and King's Indian Defence vs. 1 d4*

The strategic themes of the Pirc and King's Indian Defence are quite similar: to fianchetto the king's bishop, establish an initial central presence via ...d6 and plan to challenge White's superior centre by attacking d4. This last step is usually accompanied by the ...c5 or ...e5 advance. The similarities and differences inherent in these openings can be best illustrated by comparing the positions resulting from the respective "Classical Variations":

(A) Pirc Defence B08
1 e4 d6 2 d4 ♘f6 3 ♘c3 g6 4 ♘f3 ♗g7 5 ♗e2 0-0 6 0-0 (see diagram 115)

(B) King's Indian Defence E95
1 d4 ♘f6 2 c4 g6 3 ♘c3 ♗g7 4 e4 d6 5 ♘f3 0-0 6 ♗e2 (see diagram 116)

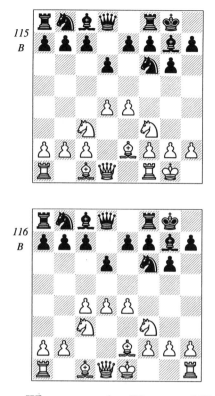

When comparing Diagrams 115 and 116 we can clearly see the following features:

(1) Black's position is exactly the same in both.

(2) In Diagram 116:
- White's c-pawn helps with central control, whereas in Diagram 115 the c-pawn is still on c2.
- White is a tempo behind in developing his kingside compared to Diagram 115.

The above differences allow us to reach the following conclusions:

(1) In the Pirc Defence Black has less risk of being smothered by White's superior centre, as compared to the King's Indian.

(2) In the Pirc Defence Black has less chances for establishing early effective counterplay because White is one development tempo ahead of the corresponding King's Indian position and, moreover, since White's centre is less extended, there is less to attack.

These concepts will be well illustrated by considering a characteristic main line variation from each opening:

Pirc Defence – from Diagram 115:

6...c6

Because Black is a tempo behind the King's Indian, it is not so easy to get in ...e5. The immediate 6...e5?! leads to a very unpleasant ending after 7 dxe5 dxe5 8 ♕xd8 ♖xd8 9 ♗g5; the preparatory move 6...♘bd7 allows Black to be pushed back after 7 e5 ♘e8 8 ♗g5, with initiative for White. The 6...c5 advance also leads to a lifeless position for Black after 7 dxc5 dxc5 8 ♗e3!.

The text guards d5, thereby taking the sting out of an early 7 e5 because of 7...♘d5!. A valid alternative to 6...c6 is 6...♗g4, with the follow-up 7 ♗e3 ♘c6, aiming for ...e5.

7 h3 ♕c7

White's last prevented both ....♗g4 and ...♘g4; therefore Black uses his queen to prepare ...e5.

8 ♗f4 ♘h5

Again 8...♘bd7 9 e5 is good for White. The text chases the dark-squared bishop off the h2-b8 diagonal, although at the cost of decentralising the knight.

9 ♗e3 e5 10 ♕d2 ♘d7 11 a4 ♖e8 12 ♖ad1 exd4

Black is behind in development and must rush to complete it. After the immediate 12...♘hf6, White plays 13 d5 with strong pressure against the d6-pawn.

13 ♘xd4 ♘hf6 14 f3 ♘c5 15 ♗c4 a6 16 b4 a6 17 b4 ♘e6 18 a5!

White's characteristic spatial superiority gives him a normal opening advantage, V.Tukmakov-W.Uhlmann, Děčin 1977.

King's Indian Defence – from Diagram 116:

6...e5

Here this move is playable as the endgame after 7 dxe5 dxe5 8 ♕xd8 ♖xd8 9 ♗g5 ♖e8 is only slightly superior for White.

7 0-0 ♘bd7

Sharper is 7...♘c6 8 d5 ♘e7, as favoured by the World Champion Garry Kasparov. The text is the "sister" plan to the Pirc Defence's 6...c6.

8 ♖e1 c6 9 ♗f1

White must anticipate ...exd4 followed by ...♖e8, applying pressure on e4. By getting the light-squared bishop out of the way, the e1-rook can now smoothly protect that pawn.

9...exd4

The sister plan of the Pirc variation above: Black enhances somewhat White's central superiority in order to create counterplay. The alternatives are not better:

(a) 9...♖e8 10 d5! leads to spatial advantage for White, while Black's e8-rook is misplaced for the thematic ...f5 break.

(b) 9...a5 is Black's most common plan, but with 10 dxe5! dxe5 11 ♘a4 White can start exploiting the dark-squared weaknesses (b6, c5, d6) on Black's queenside.

10 ♘xd4 ♘g4 11 h3 ♕b6 12 ♕xg4 ♗xd4 13 ♕e2 ♖e8 14 ♗h6 ♘c5 15 ♕d2 ♗e5 16 ♔h1 f5 17 ♖ad1 ♘xe4 18 ♘xe4 fxe4 19 ♖xe4 ♗f5 20 ♖e2

I am following the game K.Lerner-L.Vogt, Berlin 1989. White has a slight advantage due to: (1) the central influence provided by the c4-pawn, and (2) the permanent weakness of Black's kingside. (White won quickly – on move 30 – after some inaccuracies by Black.)

20 Long-range sacrifices by Black

At the beginning of the game the player with the black pieces starts off with a handicap. The pre-requisite for successful play with Black is not only to realise this but also to act accordingly. The acknowledged all-time openings expert is Robert J. Fischer. Note his wisdom, as told by Robert Byrne in the introduction to my book *How to beat Bobby Fischer*:

'Some years ago, in going over my games, he looked up in surprise whenever he noticed that I was jumping the gun in playing for an attack with the black pieces. Disapprovingly, he advised, "You've got to equalise first with Black before looking for something."'

Because at the start Black can't afford what White can, it follows that Black also has to be much more careful about sacrificing material. Sure, go ahead and sacrifice if it wins, but be exceedingly wary of doing it on "general principles". Otherwise you will just find yourself, time and time again, material down with nothing to show for it.

Not surprisingly, it is in open games (i.e. those starting with 1 e4) where the chances are best than a pawn sacrifice by Black "for development" will turn out to be worthwhile. As a typical example, consider the following variation of the Two Knights Defence (C59):

1 e4 e5 2 ♘f3 ♘c6 3 ♗c4 ♘f6 4 ♘g5 d5 5 exd5 ♘a5 6 ♗b5+ c6 7 dxc6 bxc6 8 ♗e2 h6 9 ♘f3 h6 10 ♘e5 ♗d6 11 f4 exf4 12 ♘xf3 0-0 13 d4 c5 14 0-0 ♖e8

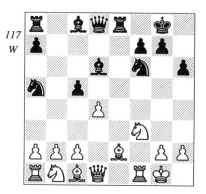

Here Black has full compensation for the sacrificed pawn because of the following factors:
- Black is ahead in overall development and his e8-rook controls the only open file.
- because of the missing f-pawn White's kingside has been weakened, as has the e3-square.
- Black's pieces are well placed to line up against White's king, with ...♗b7 and ...♕c7 coming up.

Yet in the domain of closed games (1 d4, 1 c4, 1 ♘f3, 1 g3),

Black's opportunities for early long-range sacrifices are limited. In my opinion, one of the great developments in opening theory over the past 30 years is the Benko Gambit, where Black sacrifices a pawn for apparently "nothing" on move three and lives to tell about it. The thematic justification for the gambit can be seen from the following main line variation (A58):

1 d4 ♞f6 2 c4 c5 3 d5 b5 4 cxb5 a6 5 bxa6 g6 6 ♞c3 ♝xa6 7 ♞f3 ♝g7 8 g3 d6 9 ♝g2 ♞bd7 10 0-0 0-0 11 ♝f4 ♛b6 12 ♜b1 ♛b7 13 ♜e1 ♜fb8

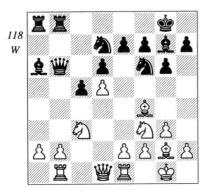

118
W

Black's compensation derives from the strong pressure that his rooks exert on White's queenside, with Black's g7-bishop standing by to do the same. Moreover, because of these factors, it is very difficult for White to work on realising his extra pawn, the a-pawn. Yet I want to emphasise to Black players that one must truly understand Benko Gambit positions

in great depth – otherwise you will wind up a pawn down for nothing.

Of course, long-range strategic pawn sacrifices are a well-known concept. What I will be presenting in greater detail is a much less frequent type of material sacrifice. It occurs in an important modern variation and leads to most interesting and unusual positions:

Catalan Opening E04

1 d4 ♞f6 2 c4 e6 3 g3 d5 4 ♝g2 dxc4 5 ♞f3 c5 6 0-0 ♞c6

The above move-order is a standard sequence from the Catalan Opening, where White's 5 ♞f3 risks a pawn sacrifice. Quite often the above position results from an English/Réti Opening, e.g. 1 c4 e6 2 ♞f3 ♞f6 3 g3 d5 4 ♝g2 c5 5 0-0 ♞c6 6 d4 dxc4.

7 ♛a4 cxd4

The most challenging response. Safer, of course, is 7...♝d7, with White keeping a normal opening advantage after 8 ♛xc4.

8 ♞xd4 ♛xd4

Now it's too late for safety with 8...♝d7?! since White obtains a clear advantage after 9 ♞xc6 ♛b6 10 ♞d2 ♝xc6 11 ♝xc6+ bxc6 12 ♞xc4 ♛b5 13 ♛c2 ♝e7 14 b3, E.Cobo-Vasquez, Skopje Olympiad 1972, as Black has no compensation for the split queenside pawns.

9 ♝xc6+ ♝d7

Black does not get enough for the exchange after 9...bxc6?! 10 ♛xc6+ ♛d7 11 ♛xa8 ♝c5 12 ♞c3

0-0 13 ♖d1 ♕c7 14 ♕f3 ♗b7 15 ♗f4!, L.Christiansen-Lhagva, Lucerne Olympiad 1982.

10 ♖d1 ♕xd1+!?

It hardly makes sense to voluntarily enter an inferior ending with split pawns after 10...♗xc6?! 11 ♕xc6+ bxc6 12 ♖xd4 c5 (no better is 12...♖d8 13 ♖xc4 ♖d1+ 14 ♔g2 ♔d7 15 ♘c3, A.Pomar-Palacios, Malaga 1965) 13 ♖xc4 ♗d6 14 ♘d2! ♔d7 15 b3, L.Kavalek-I.Radulov, Montilla 1974.

11 ♕xd1 ♗xc6

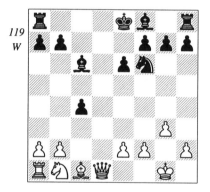

119 W

On an arithmetic count of material Black, with a rook, bishop and pawn for the queen is OK However, because of the power of the queen, in situations where she can effectively co-ordinate with other piece(s), the queen's side generally has the advantage. Moreover, here the c-pawn is quite vulnerable so that most likely Black will wind up with a material inferiority.

Therefore, Black must look for compensation in strategic terms,

i.e. in terms of the contours of the position. These show the following:

- White's kingside has been fundamentally weakened since the light-squared bishop is missing.
- Black's light-squared bishop in particular and the bishop pair in general can be effective in the attack against White's king.
- White is behind in developing his queenside forces.
- Apart from the protruding c-pawn, Black's position contains no weaknesses.

After considering the above factors, Black's objective must be to attack White's king! The success of that endeavour will determine the correct evaluation of Diagram 119. I will now consider two thematic variations for White: 12 ♗g5?! and 12 ♘d2.

(I) **12 ♗g5?!**

White develops the queen's bishop with what he thinks is a gain of time and looks forward to 12...♗e7?! 13 ♘d2 b5 14 a4 0-0 15 axb5 ♗xb5 16 ♘e4!, keeping a slight advantage, V.Tukmakov-L.Alburt, Odessa 1976. However, Black has prepared an improvement in the spirit of the variation, i.e. kingside attack.

12...♘e4! 13 ♗e3 h5! 14 f3

This is an additional unwelcome weakening, but 14 ♘d2 is met by 14...♖d8.

14...♘f6 15 ♘d2 ♖d8 16 ♕c1 h4! 17 ♘xc4 hxg3 18 hxg3 ♖d5!

The threatened 19...Rdh5 forces another kingside weakening. Black now has the slightly superior chances.

19 g4 &e7 20 &xa7?!

20 g5 looks like the best defence.

20...@xg4!! 21 fxg4

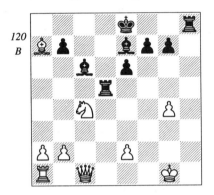

120
B

The critical position. Black has three logical choices, according to T.Georgadze:

(1) **21...Rg5?** fails to 22 Wf4! Rh1+ 23 &f2 Rxa1 24 Wb8+ &d8 25 @d6+ &d7 26 Wc8+ &e7 27 @xb7! and White wins.

(2) **21...Rh1+** is the game continuation, E.Mochalov-Z.Sturua, USSR 1979: 22 &xh1 Rh5+ 23 &g1 Rh1+ 24 &f2 &h4+ 25 &e3 &g5+ 26 &d3 Rxc1 27 Rxc1 &xc1, with a slight edge for Black but drawn on move 34.

(3) **21...&g5!** is Georgadze's "simple" suggestion: (a) 22 &e3? Rd1+ ! 23 Wxd1 Rh1+ 24 &f2 &h4#, (b) 22 @e3? Rc5!! and Black wins, (c) 22 Wf1 Rd8 23 &f2 &f4!, and after the forced 24 Wg1 Rh2+

25 Wxh2 &xh2 Black's active pieces give him a clear advantage.

(II) **12 @d2** (from diagram 119)

Best: White goes about developing the queenside while also attacking the c-pawn. Now "normal" moves by Black are unattractive since, at best, they lead to positions where he has to grovel for a draw:

(1) **12...b5** 13 a4! &e7 (alternatively, 13...a6 14 axb5 &xb5 – note that 14...axb5? fails after 15 Rxa8 &xa8 16 @xc4! bxc4 17 Wa4+ – 15 Wc2 Rc8 16 b3! c3 17 @c4! &b4 18 &a3!) 14 axb5 &xb5 15 @xc4! 0-0 16 b3 Rfc8 17 &a3! &xa3 18 @xa3 &a6 19 @c2, J.Hjartarson-H.Olafsson, Reykjavik 1986 and now, according to Hjartarson, the best way for Black to keep his disadvantage to a minimum is 19...Rd8 20 We1 &b5.

(2) **12...c3?!** 13 bxc3 0-0-0 14 Wb3 &c5 15 @f3! @e4 16 @d4! Rxd4!? 17 cxd4 &xd4 18 Rb1 &xf2+ 19 &f1 h5 20 &f4, H.Olafsson-J.Hjartarson, Reykjavik 1984 when Black does not have enough compensation.

(3) **12...&e7?!** 13 @xc4 0-0 14 b3 Rfd8 15 We1 Rac8 16 &a3, Gorelov-Salov, USSR 1982. Black is down some material and has nothing to show for it.

Therefore, again the only correct approach is the kingside attack.

12...h5! 13 @xc4

The text is the start of a suggested improvement by the Soviet theoretician Y.Neishtadt. The alternatives have to do with the attempt to prevent the opening of the h-file by advancing White's h-pawn:

(1) **13 h4 ♖d8 14 ♕c2 ♗c5 15 ♘xc4 ♘g4 16 e3 0-0.** Neishstadt calls this position unclear. What is clear is that Black's minor pieces are well trained against White's weakened kingside, with the weakness of f3 most obvious.

(2) **13 h3 ♖d8** (13...h4?! 14 g4) **14 ♕c2 ♗c5 15 ♘xc4 ♘e4 16 ♘e3 ♗b6 17 b4 h4!? 18 b5 ♗d5 19 g4 0-0 20 ♘d1 ♖c8 21 ♕b2,** when in the game Jokel-J.Wolf, Correspondence 1988/89, Black now decided to go for broke with the sacrifice 21...♘xf2!? 22 ♘xf2 f5 leading to a position which J. Wolf accurately evaluates as "unclear".

13...♖d8 14 ♕c2 h4 15 ♗f4!

The point of Neishtadt's move-order: not only is the queen's bishop quickly developed, but it can also help protect the vulnerable white king.

15...hxg3 16 ♗xg3

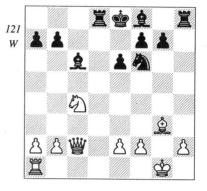

Neishstadt evaluates this position as slightly better for White and A.Sokolov in *ECO E* Revised concurs with this evaluation. My impression is that Black has real attacking chances which come close to compensating the small – approximately half-a-pawn – material disadvantage.

What then is the correct evaluation of Diagram 119? I feel that Black is theoretically no worse off than in more conventional variations (i.e. those after 7...♗d7). Therefore those players who as Black strive for an early initiative should be satisfied.